The Restoration Comedy of Wit

The Restoration Comedy of Wit

BY

Thomas H. Fujimura

BARNES & NOBLE, Inc.
NEW YORK

Printed in the United States of America

CONTENTS

PREFACE

Restoration comedy, which has long been relegated to a position beneath its merit, appears to be coming into its own; for in recent years, there have been several noteworthy studies of the comic writers and of the period. These have been significant not only for their contribution to our body of knowledge but for their implicit assumption that we need no longer apologize for Restoration comedy.

Yet, it is not clear that anyone has offered a satisfactory explanation of the grounds on which we can accept the plays with complete assurance of their worth, nor is it evident that anyone has succeeded in dispelling the common belief that this comedy deals with immoral characters and situations. The result of this critical silence on a crucial point is that the plays still exist in a region of twilight approbation, and remain much in need of an adequate apologia.

With every work of art there is a core of intrinsic "meaning," which historical research can do much to bring to light where the work is of any antiquity; and there is also a peripheral "meaning" which every new age sees, or finds, in the work. The critical studies of Restoration comedy published during the present century—and the most recent as well as the earliest—have never been quite able to distinguish between these two, largely because our intellectual milieu has heretofore been hostile to a clear appraisal of the views expressed in the plays. But now, with the emergence of naturalism as a major philosophical position, it is possible, I think, to approach these plays more sympathetically—and hence, perhaps more objectively.

No doubt the point of view in this study—that this comedy is a witty presentation of a naturalistic outlook on life—is li-

Preface

able to some suspicion of contemporary bias; but it has the virtue, I hope, of being firmly grounded on historical evidence. The comedies of the Restoration represent a body of dramatic writing second only to that of the Elizabethan period in interest and significance, and it would be regrettable if we continued to neglect them, or minimized their importance, through failure to appreciate their essential integrity and worth.

In the preparation of this study, which has extended not unpleasantly over a period of several years, I owe much to my many friends—and most to my sister—whose interest in the work has been the greatest source of encouragement. I am especially indebted to Professors Joseph Wood Krutch, Marjorie Hope Nicolson, and Oscar James Campbell for patiently reading several early versions in manuscript. I am also grateful to Miss Harriet Anderson of the Princeton University Press and to Professor A. Grove Day for assistance in seeing this book through the press.

Finally, I wish to express my gratitude to those who have kindly given permission to quote copyrighted materials: to Basil Blackwell & Mott for quotations from *The Dramatic Works of Sir George Etherege*, ed. H. F. Brett-Smith (1927); to the Clarendon Press, for quotations from *Critical Essays of the Seventeenth Century*, ed. Joel E. Spingarn (1908), *Brief Lives, chiefly of Contemporaries, set down by John Aubrey, between the Years 1669 & 1696*, ed. Andrew Clark (1898), *The Correspondence of Richard Steele*, ed. Rae Blanchard (1941), *The Complete Works of George Savile, First Marquess of Halifax*, ed. Walter Raleigh (1912), *Restoration Comedy 1660-1720* by Bonamy Dobrée (1924); to the Oxford University Press, for quotations from *Comedies by William Congreve*, ed. Bonamy Dobrée (in the World's Classics series, 1944), and *The Letterbook of Sir George Etherege*, ed. Sybil Rosenfeld (1918); to A. A. Wyn, Inc., for quotations from *William Wycherley* (Mermaid edi-

Preface

tion); to G. Bell & Sons, for quotations from *The Comedy of Manners* by John Palmer (1913), and *The Diary of Samuel Pepys*, ed. Henry B. Wheatley (1946); to the Yale University Press, for quotations from *The Comic Spirit in Restoration Drama* by Henry Ten Eyck Perry (1925); to the Macmillan Company, for quotations from *In Praise of Comedy* by James Feibleman (1939), *A History of English Poetry* by W. J. Courthope (1895-1910), and *English Comedy* by Ashley H. Thorndike (1929); to the Johns Hopkins Press, for quotations from *The Critical Works* by John Dennis, ed. Edward Niles Hooker (1939, 1943); to Dodd, Mead & Company, for quotations from *The Old Drama and the New* by William Archer (1923); and to Mrs. Helen Green Baldwin, for a quotation from the *Dictionary of Philosophy and Psychology*, ed. James Mark Baldwin (1928).

University of Hawaii   T.H.F.
May, 1952

PART ONE

I

INTRODUCTION

RESTORATION COMEDY has at last achieved some measure of respectability: it is now studied in many American colleges and universities. But it wears the cloak of respectability uneasily, and it is still not entirely immune from moralistic charges of lubricity and immorality.[1]

This moralistic attack has had a serious consequence insofar as it has obscured the literary merit of Restoration comedy, and it has taxed the ingenuity of critics to find an adequate apologia for the plays on purely literary grounds. But following the publication of Palmer's *Comedy of Manners* in 1913, there developed a fairly consistent position which is now the mainstay of apologists for Restoration comedy. The salient features of this approach are familiar from reiteration by able critics like Dobrée, Perry, and Miss Lynch. The chief point of the "manners" interpretation is that Restoration comedy is artificial, and that critical consideration should be directed to the treatment rather than to the content.[2] Restoration comedy is said to be amoral because it deals with fashionable manners rather than with morals, and it is said to be significant because of its polished style, its satire on social follies, and its veracious depiction of seventeenth century high life.

[1] For a comprehensive review of critical opinion on Restoration comedy, see W. Heldt, "A Chronological and Critical Review of the Appreciation and Condemnation of the Comic Dramatists of the Restoration and Orange Periods," *Neophilologus*, VIII, 39-59, 109-128, 197-204 (Oct., 1922; Jan. and Apr., 1923). For more recent strictures, cf. *Representative English Plays*, eds. J. S. P. Tatlock and R. G. Martin, New York, 1938, p. 503; George Sherburn, in *A Literary History of England*, ed. Albert C. Baugh, New York, 1948, p. 763.

[2] Cf. Bonamy Dobrée, intro. to *Comedies by William Congreve*, London, 1944, p. vii.

[3]

Introduction

The adequacy of this interpretation is open to serious question however. Too much has been sacrificed, I think, in the attempt to salvage a few crumbs of literary merit; for the "manners" critics have removed the odium of immorality only by denying that the plays have any serious content. It is a great disparagement of Restoration comedy (or of any other literary work) to say that the moral consideration does not enter at all because the dramatists were never disturbed by the moral problem.[3] If one accepts this premise, he must conclude, as Perry does, that Restoration comedy "could not but be a superficial literature."[4] Actually most literary works are committed morally, for good or for evil, because they are inextricably bound up with human decisions and actions—though that is not to say that they must be committed to Christian morality. It is my belief that the morality of Restoration comedy is naturalistic, and that the dramatists dealt with moral issues, though wittily rather than soberly. The "manners" interpretation, which is really a variation on the theory of art for art's sake, disregards the place of morality in art, and consequently emasculates the literary work that it is intended to justify.

The "manners" interpretation also suffers from several other limitations. When content is discussed, the "manners" critics limit it principally to the social satire, with a consequent disregard of the dramatists' naturalistic views and antisocial wit.[5] Furthermore, the social satire is interpreted superficially as a matter of ribands and lace and fine manners, with the laughter directed mainly at affected fops and clumsy country bumpkins; little is said about the attacks on marriages of convenience, on unnatural conduct, hypocrisy, and "enthusiasm." The comic spirit is seen in the light of Bergson's social laugh-

[3] Henry Ten Eyck Perry, *The Comic Spirit in Restoration Drama*, New Haven, 1925, p. 11.
[4] *Ibid.*, p. 131.
[5] Cf. Kathleen M. Lynch, *The Social Mode of Restoration Comedy*, New York, 1926, pp. 214-217.

Introduction

ter or Meredith's thoughtful laughter, rather than as the egoistic, non-utilitarian laughter of Hobbes' theory which is embodied in the plays. Perhaps to compensate for this superficiality, the "manners" critics usually stress the historical significance of the comedies, as in Dobrée's estimate: "If we were to try to sum up what the comedy of this period as a whole achieved, it would be to say that it gave a brilliant picture of its time rather than a new insight into man."[6] No doubt Restoration comedy does faithfully reflect certain phases of contemporary life,[7] but this historical significance has little to do with the aesthetic merit of the plays. The "manners" critics run into another difficulty in their distinction between content and treatment (which is basic for their interpretation, since they insist that a work of art must be judged by the treatment and not the content). Such a distinction, though valid for purposes of analysis, does violence to the unity of the aesthetic experience.

The final weakness of the "manners" interpretation is that it is a modern rather than a seventeenth century view, and without historical justification. The term *manners*, as used by critics like Palmer and Dobrée, is a sophisticated, modern conception: it implies the whole contexture of fine society, with its mores, affectations, conventions; all the outward form, and even more, the style, of fashionable life by which the individual is bound. The *comedy* of manners, then, is the laughable born of the inability of men to conform to an artificial social standard (as in the country bumpkins), or of excessive attempts at conformity (as in the fops), or of conformity so successful that the individual loses his human elasticity (in a Bergsonian sense). *Manners*, in this sense, is extensive and ubiquitous; it is the faint gossamer thread of fashionable and artificial convention on which the characters

---

[6] Bonamy Dobrée, *Restoration Comedy 1660-1720*, Oxford, 1924, p. 171.
[7] Cf. Gellert Spencer Alleman, *Matrimonial Law and the Materials of Restoration Comedy*, Wallingford, Pa., 1942.

cross the Niagara of this life. Indeed, so important is it that the very needs of man on his instinctive side are ephemeralized into a part of that broader pattern of social life. This is the modern conception of "manners" comedy.

In the seventeenth century, the term *manners* was used in a much simpler and narrower sense, especially in literary criticism. One of the few approximations to the modern sense is to be found in a remark on Southerne in *A Comparison between the Two Stages*: "I think very few exceed him in the Dialogue; his Gallantry is natural, and after the real manner of the Town."[8] But this is hardly the equivalent of the modern conception. In the literary criticism of the Restoration, *manners* was about equivalent to *ethos*, or character.[9] Dryden defined *manners* as follows: "The manners, in a poem, are understood to be those inclinations, whether natural or acquired, which move and carry us to actions, good, bad, or indifferent, in a play; or which incline the persons to such or such actions. . . . From the manners, the characters of persons are derived; for, indeed, the characters are no other than the inclinations, as they appear in the several persons of the poem; a character being thus defined,—that which dis-

[8] *A Comparison between the Two Stages*, ed. Staring B. Wells, Princeton, 1942, p. 19. A poorer example, but one more frequently quoted, in support of the modern use, is from Congreve's *Double-Dealer*:

L. FROTH: I vow Mellefont's a pretty Gentleman, but methinks he wants a Manner.
CYNT.: A Manner! What's that, Madam?
L. FROTH: Some distinguishing Quality, as for Example, the *bel air* or *Brillant* of Mr. *Brisk*; the Solemnity, yet Complaisance of my Lord, or something of his own that should look a little *Je-ne-scay-quoysh* (II, i)—In *Comedies by William Congreve*, ed. Dobrée.

This passage is cited in *A New English Dictionary on Historical Principles*, ed. Sir James A. H. Murray. It is also quoted by Allardyce Nicoll in *A History of Restoration Drama*, London, 1923, p. 184, and *The Theory of Drama*, New York, 1931, pp. 222-223, where it is used as the basis for his definition of the comedy of manners. Nicoll treats it too seriously, I think, in view of the fact that the ridiculous Lady Froth uses the term "Manner."
[9] "Manners," *A New English Dictionary*.

tinguishes one man from another."[10] *Manners* here represents
the basic, underlying motives and causes of human action;
and *character* is the outward mark of distinction which is the
product of manners. The term *manners* is used in a psychological rather than in a social sense. Collier likewise tells us
that in dramatic usage, "The *Manners* . . . have a signification
somewhat particular," and that "*Aristotle* and *Rapin* call
them the Causes and Principles of Action."[11]

The difference between the Restoration use of *manners*
and the modern use is brought out most clearly by contrasting
the foregoing passages with one from Hazlitt: "We find . . .
[in novels] . . . a close imitation of men and manners; we
see the very web and texture of society as it really exists, and
as we meet with it when we come into the world."[12] By
manners, Hazlitt meant, as do critics of the "manners" school,
the social matrix of customs and modes into which the individual fits and to which his outward deportment conforms.

The whole conception of "manners" comedy must be regarded as a modern interpretation which is sound neither
critically nor historically. Yet an examination of the most
important critical works now available on Restoration comedy
reveals the extent to which the "manners" interpretation
dominates modern opinion.

John Palmer's *Comedy of Manners* (1913) shows the
typical artificialization of Restoration comedy in a comment
like the following: "It is a first law of the cloud-cuckoo-land
of *The Country Wife* that the act of sex has no more suggestion of the indecently amorous than tumbling upstairs or losing

[10] John Dryden, "The Grounds of Criticism in Tragedy," *The Works of
John Dryden*, ed. Sir Walter Scott and George Saintsbury, Edinburgh, 1882-
1893, VI, 266-269.
[11] Jeremy Collier, *A Short View of the Immorality and Profaneness of
the English Stage*, in *Critical Essays of the Seventeenth Century*, ed. Joel
E. Spingarn, Oxford, 1908, III, 282.
[12] William Hazlitt, *Lectures on the English Comic Writers*, in *The Collected Works of William Hazlitt*, ed. A. R. Waller and Arnold Glover,
London, 1903, VIII, 106.

one's hat in a gale."[13] The same view is presented more explicitly in a short work entitled *Comedy* published not long after the longer book: "In the comedy of manners men and women are seen holding the reality of life away, or letting it appear only as an unruffled thing of attitudes. . . . Artificial comedy is our holiday from the sublime and beautiful, from the coarse and real. It is sublimation of the trivial, turning to fine art the accidents and trappings of life. . . . The comedy of manners is life in terms of a muffin."[14] This is the tenor of the longer work also; and it represents an attempt to create a purely fanciful picture of Restoration comedy as artificial comedy, by neglecting entirely such elements as the malice of the raillery passages, the sexual wit, the skepticism, and the coarsely realistic scenes involving people like Gripe, Dufoy, and the Widow Blackacre.

Bonamy Dobrée's *Restoration Comedy 1660-1720* (1924) has the same weakness of treating the plays as artificial comedy divorced from reality: "Here we feel that no values count, that there are no rules of conduct, hardly laws of nature. Certainly no appeal, however indirect, is made to our critical or moral faculties. . . . We are permitted to play with life, which becomes a charming harlequinade without being farce. It is all spontaneous and free, rapid and exhilarating; the least emotion, an appeal to common sense, and the joyous illusion is gone."[15] Such an idealized interpretation neglects completely the malice of spirited young ladies like Harriet, the brilliant cynicism of rakes like Dorimant, the opportunism of the servants, the crudeness of Ben, the treachery of Olivia, and the misanthropy of Manly. Pulsating beneath the brilliant surface of Restoration high life, with its perukes and lace and fine talk, is a substratum of human lust, malice, and cynicism, which gives to Restoration comedy its vitality and

[13] John Palmer, *The Comedy of Manners*, London, 1913, p. 294.
[14] John Palmer, *Comedy*, New York, 1914, pp. 33-35.
[15] Dobrée, *Comedies of William Congreve*, pp. 13-14.

Introduction

force. Such an interpretation is also quite false to the spirit of this comedy, in which an ideal like decorum does indeed demand the use of our critical faculty.

Henry Ten Eyck Perry's *Comic Spirit in Restoration Drama* (1925), a much more impressionistic piece of criticism than the first two, offers an interpretation of Restoration comedy based on Meredith's conception of the Comic Spirit as a philosophical spirit, with "sage's brows, and the sunny malice of a faun." But the Meredithian conception hardly seems in accord with the harsh laughter in the comedies over such misfortunes as venereal disease, mistaken matches, and lost maidenheads; and the antisocial attacks on marriage, the clergy, and the parent-child relationship. The theory of laughter accepted by dramatists like Etherege and Wycherley was, after all, the egoistic one expounded by Hobbes, according to which men laughed from a sudden realization of their superiority over someone else.

Kathleen M. Lynch's *Social Mode of Restoration Comedy* (1926) proceeds along the lines of Bergson's rather than of Meredith's theory of laughter. Her interpretation is briefly this: there are two levels of comedy in Restoration drama, with a double standard of the comic, one for the fools and Witwouds, and another for the Truewits.[16] We laugh, with the Truewits, at the first group because it fails to come up to an artificial social standard; then, by a curious mental readjustment, we laugh at the Truewits because they conform too well to the same artificial standard, and hence cannot express their whole nature. According to this Bergsonian view, Truewits like Mrs. Millamant and Dorimant are laughable insofar as their self-imposed rigidity prevents the full expression of their personality.[17] There are several questions raised by such an interpretation: would Congreve have desired a fuller expression of Mrs. Millamant's personality in view of his own

[16] Lynch, *The Social Mode of Restoration Comedy*, p. 7.
[17] *Ibid.*, p. 8, p. 181.

[9]

Introduction

belief in decorum (true wit); is the double standard of the comic valid; and would Congreve have understood such a double standard? I think the answers must all be in the negative.

These studies by Palmer, Dobrée, Perry, and Miss Lynch offer the best exposition of the "manners" interpretation; and they share pretty equally the merits and weaknesses of this point of view. The chief flaw in this approach is that though it removes the burden of the moralistic censure, it does so only by making the comedies superficial and effete as literary works. These critics argue that Restoration comedy cannot be immoral because it is artificial and has nothing to do with morality or with serious human problems: it is concerned only with manners, or style, both social and literary.

Restoration comedy is better described, I believe, as naturalistic and witty, and a far more suitable nomenclature would be *the comedy of wit.*

After 1660, Restoration critics recognized a new type of comedy which was quite distinct from the old Jonsonian comedy of humors. And the outstanding characteristic of this new comedy produced by dramatists like Dryden and Etherege was *wit* rather than *manners.* In 1668, in the preface to *The Sullen Lovers,* Shadwell, who admired Jonson, attacked the new comedy of wit that Dryden advocated:

Though I have known some of late so Insolent to say that *Ben Johnson* wrote his best *Playes* without Wit; imagining, that all the Wit in *Playes* consisted in bringing two persons upon the Stage to break Jests, and to bob one another, which they call Repartie, not considering that there is more wit and invention requir'd in the finding out good Humor, and Matter proper for it, then in all their smart reparties. For, in the Writing of a Humor, a Man is confin'd not to swerve from the Character, and oblig'd to say nothing but what is proper to it: but in the *Playes* which have been wrote of late, there is no such thing as perfect Character, but the two chief persons are most commonly a Swearing, Drinking, Whoring, Ruffian for a Lover, and an impudent ill-bred *tomrig* for a Mistress, and these are the fine People of the *Play*; and there is that Latitude in this, that almost any thing is proper for them to say; but their chief Subject is bawdy, and profaneness, which they call *brisk writing*, when the most dissolute of Men, that rellish those things well enough in private, are *chok'd* at 'em in publick: and methinks, if there was nothing but the ill Manners of it, it should make Poets avoid that Indecent way of writing.[18]

This anticipates the strictures of both Collier and Sir Richard Blackmore. According to this description, the new comedy is characterized by witty dialogue, repartee, brisk writing, sexual and skeptical wit, and libertine characters.

In the following year, Shadwell renewed the attack on the new comedy in both the prologue and the preface to *The Royal Shepherdess*, and he contrasted his own writing with the new type of play:

> It is a Vertuous Play, you will confess,
> Where Vicious men meet their deserv'd success.
> Not like our Modern ones, where still we find,
> Poets are onely to the Ruffians kind;
> And give them still the Ladies in the Play,
> But 'faith their Ladies are as bad as they.
> They call 'em Ayery, Witty, Brisk, and Wild,
> But, with their Favours, those are terms too mild.[19]

To these attacks, Dryden replied, in the preface to *An Evening's Love* (1671), that comedy is hedonic in purpose; and he also implied that there were two distinct types of comedy —one based on wit and the other on humor—which were equally valid: "the business of the poet is to make you laugh: when he writes humour, he makes folly ridiculous; when wit, he moves you, if not always to laughter, yet to a pleasure that is more noble."[20]

Toward the end of the century, when the comedy of wit

---

[18] Thomas Shadwell, Preface to *The Sullen Lovers*, in *The Complete Works of Thomas Shadwell*, ed. Montague Summers, London, 1927, I, 11.

[19] Shadwell, Prologue to *The Royal Shepherdess*, in *The Complete Works*, I, 101.

[20] Dryden, *Works*, III, 248.

Introduction

had run its course, Sir Richard Blackmore attacked it for its "confident Discourses, immodest Repartees, and prophane Raillery,"[21] and Collier fulminated against its immorality and profaneness also. As late as 1701 and 1702, John Dennis argued in favour of humors comedy over wit comedy. In "The Advancement and Reformation of Modern Poetry," he declared that comedy ought to instruct by the *Ridiculum*, and the next year, in "A Large Account of the Taste in Poetry," he argued that humors comedy was superior to wit comedy because it had much more of the *Ridiculum*. These remarks indicate that critics recognized a new type of comedy characterized by wit (repartee, raillery, brisk writing, sheer wit), and by principles that were libertine and naturalistic. There is some justification, I think, for substituting the term *comedy of wit* for the present *comedy of manners* to describe the plays of Etherege, Wycherley, and Congreve.

The supreme importance of wit in the Restoration and in this type of comedy is evident from contemporary remarks. In the epilogue to *The Wild Gallant* revived (1667), Dryden wrote:

> Of all dramatic writing, comic wit,
> As 'tis the best, so 'tis most hard to hit,
> For it lies all in level to the eye,
> Where all may judge, and each defect may spy.

Etherege, Wycherley, and Congreve were extolled for their wit, and Dryden was acclaimed as "Prince of Witts."[22] Steele also observed that, "The seat of wit, when one speaks as a man of the town and the world, is the playhouse."[23] In fact, wit is one of the key words in late seventeenth and early eighteenth century aesthetics, and many of the important critical docu-

---

[21] Sir Richard Blackmore, Preface to *Prince Arthur* (1695), in Spingarn, *Critical Essays*, III, 230.

[22] Earl of Rochester, "A Trial of the Poets for the Bays"; Dryden, "To My Dear Friend Mr. Congreve on his Comedy call'd *The Double-Dealer*"; Bevil Higgons, "To Mr. Congreve, on his Play called *The Old Batchelor*"; Milbourne, On Dryden's *Amphitryon*, in Dryden, *Works*, VIII, 3.

[23] Sir Richard Steele, *Spectator* #65, May 15, 1711.

Introduction

ments of this period deal with it: the speculations of Hobbes as to the nature of wit, the controversial prefaces and verses of Shadwell and Dryden as to the relative merits of humors comedy and wit comedy, Blackmore's "Satyr against Wit" and his preface to *Prince Arthur*, Collier's *Short View* attacking wit comedy, Dennis' essays advocating humors as against wit comedy, Addison's *Spectator* papers (#58-62) on true and false wit, and innumerable pieces of critical writing of lesser note. In fact, the very bulk of the criticism devoted to wit indicates its importance in the period.

Wit is the very quintessence of Restoration comedy. Yet its role in the plays has never been thoroughly studied, perhaps because it is so elusive an element. Where it has received some attention, notably in the criticism of the "manners" school, it has usually been identified with verbal pyrotechnics in epigrams and repartee.[24] But wit is far broader and more nebulous in its meaning than this, and also more significant. Restoration writers seldom gave the same definition for the term, but they would have agreed with Richard Flecknoe that wit is very important and that "it is the spirit and quintessence of speech."[25] It is evident that modern critics have, first, neglected the role of wit in Restoration comedy, and, second, failed to recognize the full significance of the concept in the Restoration.

That dramatic wit should not have received more attention from modern critics of Restoration comedy is especially surprising in view of the fact that *The Way of the World* is based on the distinction between true wit and false wit. Congreve's remarks in the dedicatory epistle on this point are quite explicit:

[24] Dobrée, *op. cit.*, pp. 36-37. Also, Dane Farnsworth Smith, *Plays about the Theatre in England from 'The Rehearsal' in 1671 to the Licensing Act in 1737*, London and New York, 1936, p. ix.

[25] Richard Flecknoe, "Short Discourse of the English Stage," in Spingarn, *Critical Essays*, II, 94.

Introduction

Those Characters which are meant to be ridicul'd in most of our Comedies, are of Fools so gross, that in my humble Opinion, they shou'd rather disturb than divert the well-natur'd and reflecting Part of an Audience; they are rather Objects of Charity than Contempt; and instead of moving our Mirth, they ought very often to excite our Compassion.

This Reflection mov'd me to design some Characters, which shou'd appear ridiculous not so much thro' a natural Folly (which is incorrigible, and therefore not proper for the Stage) as thro' an affected Wit; a Wit, which at the same time that it is affected, is also false. As there is some Difficulty in the Formation of a Character of this Nature, so there is some Hazard which attends the Progress of its Success, upon the Stage: For many come to a Play, so over-charg'd with Criticism, that they very often let fly their Censure, when thro' their Rashness they have mistaken their Aim. This I had Occasion lately to observe: For this Play had been acted two or three Days, before some of these hasty Judges cou'd find the leisure to distinguish betwixt the Character of a *Witwoud* and a *Truewit*.

Truewit and Witwoud, along with Witless, constitute the most common figures in wit comedy; and since these characters are differentiated on the basis of wit, we must know what wit meant in the seventeenth century before we can fully appreciate the comedies. It is not uncommon for a modern critic to remark that "Brisk, Witwood, and Tattle, who are meant to be contemptible characters, are as lively and amusing, and say as many good things, as Mirabell and Mellefont."[26] The confusion betrayed in such a comment stems from a failure to distinguish between true wit and false wit. From the point of view of wit, Witwoud and Brisk *are* contemptible and ridiculous creatures: they are livelier and more amusing figures than Mirabell only from a *comic* point of view. The Truewits are, after all, *witty*, rather than comic figures.

There remains the important task, then, of determining what the Restoration meant by wit and what its role is in the comedies. Further, one must examine the intellectual back-

[26] W. J. Courthope, *A History of English Poetry*, New York, 1895-1910, IV, 449.

ground of the comedies, in order to determine why the content of the witticisms is so often skeptical and libertine. I think we shall discover that Etherege, Wycherley, and Congreve were not filthy-minded, immoral dramatists dabbling with sexual ideas, as the moralistic critics assert. We shall find, too, that they were not superficial gallants trifling with life and playing a graceful game of make-believe, as the "manners" critics seem to believe; but that they were sensible, cultivated gentlemen with a naturalistic attitude toward life and a profound interest in the intellectual and aesthetic ideal which their age epitomized in the concept of wit. Most important, a study of these men and their works will show how greatly we have erred in our estimate of them, and how significant they still are for us today.

II

THE NATURE OF WIT

Basic to an appreciation of Restoration comedy is an understanding of the seventeenth century notion of wit. But an investigation of wit is rendered difficult by its mercurial quality, for it is about as difficult to pin down as the equally nebulous concept of nature in the same period. The discussions of wit range from Cowley's definition by elimination, in his ode "Of Wit," to more systematic analyses like those of Thomas Hobbes, and the *Spectator* papers of 1711. But there is no clear and consistent view accepted by all writers, and even Hobbes, from whom one might expect more precision in view of his philosophical calling, used the term wit in several different senses in the same work.

Another difficulty, though a minor one, is the fact that the concept of wit changed during the course of the century. As the age of enlightenment approached, there was a growing emphasis upon judgment and truth to nature, at the expense of fancy and "sheer wit." Furthermore, with the emergence of middle-class taste in literature, the antisocial wit of the Restoration gradually fell into disrepute, and there was a movement to temper wit with morality, notably in Addison's *Spectator* papers of the next century.

These changes, however, did little more than shift the emphasis; they did not alter the basic meanings of wit. Thus, Addison, in analyzing wit in the *Spectator* papers, in 1711, restated Locke's ideas on wit as expressed in *An Essay Concerning Human Understanding* in 1690; in condemning punning, he echoed the sentiments of Dryden in "The Defence of the Epilogue" of 1672; and in censuring emblems and "bouts rimez" as examples of false wit, he was in accord

The Nature of Wit

with earlier Restoration ideals.[1] Likewise, when Dennis noted in 1692 that Cowley had fallen into disrepute because of his farfetched conceits,[2] he was in agreement with Dryden, who had censured Cleveland's unnatural style in 1668, in "An Essay of Dramatic Poesy." The various notions of wit are sufficiently stable, then, to make an analytical study feasible; a historical study is hardly possible here.

The Restoration interest in wit represents the last phase of a continental movement which appeared as Marinism in Italy, Gongorism in Spain, and *la préciosité* in France. In England, this movement had earlier affected the work not only of John Lyly but of the metaphysical poets, and its influence continued to be felt as late as the Restoration.[3] The movement also contributed a body of critical opinion which is of considerable interest. Baltasar Gracián, for example, discussed the literary theory of this school in his *Agudeza y Arte de Ingenio* (1648), and in his *El Discreto* (1646) he set forth his conception of the well-bred man, which sheds an illuminating light on the ideal of the Truewit.[4] But for our purpose, the views of Thomas Hobbes on wit, though often indebted to continental sources, are most significant, because he not only gave the most comprehensive account of wit in seventeenth century England, but he greatly influenced more important literary figures like Davenant, Dryden, Dennis, and

[1] As a sign of changing standards, it is illuminating to see how, in its earlier stages, the interest in wit was characterized by a taste for forms of wit condemned by Restoration critics and by Addison. See Mario Praz's *Studies in Seventeenth-Century Imagery*, I (London, 1939), which discusses the popular taste for emblems.

[2] John Dennis, Preface to *The Passion of Byblis*, in *The Critical Works*, ed. Edward Niles Hooker, Baltimore, 1938, I, 2.

[3] The effect of *la préciosité* on Restoration drama has been examined by Kathleen M. Lynch in her *Social Mode of Restoration Comedy*. However, this study is limited pretty much to the social aspect of *la préciosité*, and the intellectual concern with wit, it seems to me, has not been given adequate consideration.

[4] For other significant European writers on wit, like Pallavicino and Pellegrini, see Benedetto Croce, *Aesthetic As Science of Expression and General Linguistic*, London, 1929.

The Nature of Wit

Addison.[5] Consequently, Hobbes' ideas are useful as a point of reference in any analysis of seventeenth century views of wit in England.

In expounding his political ideas, Hobbes began by analyzing the nature of man; and in his psychological analysis, he divided the rational faculties into two—the fancy and the judgment—both of which he treated as chiefly cognitive in function. The fancy he also regarded as the creative faculty, capable of synthesis in discovering similitudes in things unlike; the judgment he regarded as a more purely analytical faculty that discovered dissimilitudes in things apparently alike. "And both *Fancie* and *Judgement*," he wrote, "are commonly comprehended under the name of *Wit*."[6] At other times, Hobbes identified wit separately with either fancy or with judgment. On this basis, we can distinguish among three very broad conceptions of wit: (1) wit as comprehending both fancy and judgment; (2) wit as judgment; and (3) wit as fancy. Of these, the second conception (wit as judgment) needs most emphasis; for being least familiar, it has often been neglected by modern scholars in their analysis of neoclassical wit.[7]

In its most general sense, wit included both fancy and judgment, and was equivalent to *ingenium* and *l'esprit*. It might mean a man's natural aptitude, in the sense suggested by Huarte in his *Examen de Ingenios*,[8] or more precisely, wit could be identified with mental acumen (the *agudeza* of Gracián). Some of its characteristics, according to David

[5] For a thorough discussion of Hobbes' views on wit, see Clarence DeWitt Thorpe, *The Aesthetic Theory of Thomas Hobbes*, Ann Arbor, 1940. Thorpe also discusses Hobbes' influence on his contemporaries.

[6] Thomas Hobbes, *Human Nature, or the Fundamental Elements of Policy*, x, 4, in *The English Works of Thomas Hobbes*, London, 1839, IV, 56.

[7] Cf. Edward N. Hooker's definition of wit: 1. wit as combining judgment and imagination, in the general sense of *ingenium* or *l'esprit*, and 2. wit as fancy. Introduction to The Augustan Reprint Society, *Series One: Essays on Wit*, No. 2, Ann Arbor, 1946, pp. 1-2.

[8] Translated into English in 1698 as *The Tryal of Wits*.

The Nature of Wit

Abercromby in his *Discourse of Wit*, were "Vivacity, sharpness, penitrancy."[9] Wit also suggested sophistication, as in Gerrard's comment on Hippolita, in *The Gentleman Dancing-Master*, "So much wit and innocency were never together before" (1, i)—as though wit and innocence were incompatible.[10] Wit, in this general sense, implied intellectual superiority in perception and knowledge, and consequently, acumen, penetration, and sophistication.

Wit was often identified with the product of such general mental activity, as in Davenant's remark, "*Wit* is the laborious and the lucky resultances of thought, having toward its excellence, as we say of the strokes of Painting, as well a happinesse as care."[11] In such "lucky resultances of thought" there was evident the inventive activity of the fancy, which, in an unaccountable way, hit upon a happy thought, and there was also the activity of the judgment, which exercised a supervisory labor. In a more limited sense, wit was sometimes identified with the spirit of the product, as in Abercromby's remark that wit is "the Life of Discourse, as Salt, without which nothing is relished, a Celestial Fire, a Spiritual Light."[12]

Here we have the most comprehensive meaning of wit, in the general sense of *ingenium*. The term was used loosely to designate any of the following—a faculty of the mind, its activity, a special quality of either the faculty or its activity, a product of the faculty or of its activity, or the quintessence of such a product. Wit was described as acute, sharp, agile, penetrating, spiritual, and lively; it was associated with the fortuitous discovery of ideas and images, and with a careful arrangement of these; it was regarded as both assimilative

[9] David Abercromby, *A Discourse of Wit*, London, 1686, p. 17.

[10] See also, Bishop Burnet's association of wit and cunning in his account of the second Duchess of York, in *History of His Own Time*, London, 1818, I, 411.

[11] Davenant, Preface to *Gondibert*, in Spingarn, II, 20.

[12] Abercromby, *A Discourse of Wit*, p. 7. See also, Motteux, Prologue to Farquhar's *The Inconstant* (1702), in *The Complete Works of George Farquhar*, ed. Charles Stonehill, Bloomsbury, 1930, I, 223.

and discriminatory; and it was considered the quintessence of any work. This notion of wit is so comprehensive, however, that it is less illuminating than some of the narrower conceptions.

In the second sense, wit was equated with the judgment, the analytical faculty that dissected and discriminated, that governed the unbridled fancy, organized the work of art, and acted as a normative force in thought and creation. Perhaps it would be more accurate to say that in the general conception of wit as a combination of judgment and fancy, the first was sometimes emphasized so much that it became equivalent to wit. Thus, Thomas Hobbes observed, "And in any discourse whatsoever, if the defect of discretion be apparent, how extravagant soever the fancy be, the whole discourse will be taken for a sign of want of wit; and so will it never when the discretion is manifest, though the fancy be never so ordinary."[13] This identification of wit and judgment is not in accord with modern conceptions of wit, but is to be expected from an age which regarded reason as important in aesthetics.

In the literary criticism of the Restoration, wit (judgment) was regarded as a normative element and was frequently identified with the very comprehensive ideal of decorum. This conception of wit as decorum was probably one of the most popular, especially in the rhetorical form in which Dryden defined it: "If wit has truly been defined, 'a propriety of thoughts and words,' then that definition will extend to all sorts of poetry. . . . Propriety of thought is that fancy which arises naturally from the subject, or which the poet adapts to it. Propriety of words is the clothing of those thoughts with such expressions as are naturally proper to them; and from both these, if they are judiciously performed, the delight of

[13] Hobbes, *Leviathan*, I, viii, in *The English Works*, III, 59. See also, Dennis, "A Defence of Mr. *Wycherley*'s Characters in the *Plain-dealer*" (1721), in *The Critical Works*, II, Baltimore, 1943, p. 234; Dennis, Preface to *Miscellanies in Verse and Prose*, London, 1693.

The Nature of Wit

poetry results."[14] Expressed more simply, decorum meant natural thoughts naturally expressed; and decorum (true wit) in art meant the exercise of judgment in creative activity. The forces of rationalism and science were at work to shape the notion of wit into such a conception; and wit, as manifested in style, was pushed toward naturalness and simplicity. The salutary effect on the style of preaching and on the speeches by members of the Royal Society has been commented on by Burnet and Sprat.[15] The ideal of decorum also had a beneficial effect on Restoration comic dialogue, for it led to a reaction against metaphysical conceits, and toward the end of the century, it tended to restrain even "sheer wit."

The rhetorical definition of wit, like many another neoclassical element in seventeenth century writing, owed much to Roman criticism. In his controversy with Shadwell, Dryden criticized Jonson for being deficient in true wit, and he enumerated the qualities of wit mentioned in the sixth book of the *Institutio Oratoria*.[16] Quintilian had taken up the analysis of wit in connection with his discussion of laughter; but like Dryden in his rhetorical definition of wit, Quintilian stressed the qualities in wit related to style. *Urbanitas* ("language with a smack of the city in its words, accent and idiom . . . the opposite of rusticity"), *venustus* ("that which is said with grace and charm"), *salsus* (the seasoning of writing, in moderation), *facetus* ("a certain grace and polished elegance"), *iocus* ("the opposite of seriousness"), and *dicacitas* ("the language of banter")[17]—these were a few of the facets of wit suggested by Quintilian, and some of these were embodied in the seventeenth century conception of decorum.

In the Restoration, the rhetorical interest in elegance and

---

[14] Dryden, Preface to *Albion and Albanius* (1685), *Works*, VII, 228.
[15] Burnet, *History of His Own Time*, I, 211; Thomas Sprat, *The History of the Royal Society of London*, London, 1722, p. 113.
[16] Dryden, Preface to *An Evening's Love*, in *Works*, III, 244-245.
[17] Quintilian, *Institutio Oratoria*, tr. H. E. Butler, London and New York, 1921-2, Book VI, Chapt. iii in Vol. II, 447-449.

The Nature of Wit

decorum was epitomized in the notion of the "turn," which the period substituted for the "conceit" of the metaphysical school. According to the account in Boileau's "Art of Poetry," reason finally asserted itself against the earlier taste for quibbling and permitted "conceits" only in the epigram, "Provided that by art, and in due time, /They turned upon the thought, and not the rhyme." This restriction led to a cultivation of the heroic couplet, and also of epigrammatical expression in both prose and verse; and it resulted in such famous lines as Dryden's on Shadwell in "MacFlecknoe"—"The rest to some faint meaning make pretense, /But Shadwell never deviates into sense." The same "propriety of thought and words" is to be found in the "turns" that crop up in Restoration comedy. In Congreve's *Love for Love*, when Tattle is reproached for his "secresie" when he chatters about a supposed love affair, he expresses himself with the same neat balancing of ideas: "Gad so, the Heat of my Story carry'd me beyond my Discretion, as the Heat of the Lady's Passion hurry'd her beyond her Reputation" (III, iii). The "turn" appears even in prose works like the *Memoirs of Count Gramont*, in which the quarrel between Lady Castlemaine, the old mistress of Charles, and Miss Stewart, the new and untried one, is described in the following manner: "Lady Castlemaine was with child, and threatened to miscarry if her rival was preferred. Miss Stewart threatened that she never would be with child, if her request was not granted."[18] Dryden was particularly impressed by the beautiful "turns" in poetry, but said he was unacquainted with them till a Scottish wit pointed them out to him in Waller and Denham. "Some sprinklings of this kind I had also formerly in my plays," he admitted, "but they were casual, and not designed. But this hint, thus seasonably given me, first made me sensible of my own wants, and brought me afterwards to seek for a supply of them in

[18] Anthony Hamilton, *Memoirs of Count Gramont*, ed. Allan Fea, London, 1906, p. 158.

other English authors."[19] Dryden and other dramatists seem to have applied this lesson to comedy, for the "turn" is an important element in Restoration comedy, where it contributes much to the pointedness and consummate elegance of the dialogue.

This rhetorical view represents only one aspect of wit as decorum, for this conception extended beyond propriety of style to propriety of conduct. This notion of wit as decorum of conduct appears to be the basis for the "manners" conception of an artificial code of manners in Restoration comedy. Wit, in this sense, was indeed the possession only of a man who had frequented the best society; for, as Richard Flecknoe observed, it could be learned only from nature and conversation and not by art and precept.[20] However, decorum of conduct was based upon intelligence as well as upon familiarity with the most cultivated society, and it was never embodied in any artificial code of manners. Decorum represented an ideal of conduct and speech to which a cultivated gentleman aspired; and though it was learned through social intercourse, it was based on judgment and not on mere convention. Dryden used this notion of wit as a criterion in his criticism of wit; and on this score he was very severe on his predecessors (particularly Jonson), of whom he said, "I have always acknowledged the wit of our predecessors, with all the veneration which becomes me; but I am sure, their wit was not that of gentlemen; there was ever somewhat that was ill-bred and clownish in it, and which confessed the conversation of the authors."[21]

This emphasis on gentlemanly wit might be expected in view of the author's social position and taste. There was also classical precedent for it familiar to the aristocratic writers of

[19] Dryden, "Essay on Satire," *Works*, XIII, 116.
[20] Flecknoe, "A Short Discourse of the English Stage," in Spingarn, II, 94.
[21] Dryden, "Defence of the Epilogue," *Works*, IV, 239. For a favorable comment on Jonson's wit, see "An Essay of Dramatic Poesy," *Works*, XV, 351.

The Nature of Wit

the period. One of the best statements of this point of view is to be found in Aristotle's description of the witty person, in his *Nicomachean Ethics*, as the mean between the buffoon and the boor:

People whose fun is in good taste are called witty, a name which implies the happy turns of their art. . . . But as it is never necessary to look far for subjects of ridicule and as an excessive fondness for fun and mockery is pretty universal, it happens that not only true wits but buffoons are described as witty, because they are amusing. But it is clear from what has been said that there is a difference, and indeed a wide difference, between the two.

The characteristic of the mean state is tact. A person of tact is one who will use and listen to such language only as is suitable to an honorable gentleman; for there is such language as an honorable gentleman may fitly use and listen to in the way of fun and the fun of a gentleman is different from that of a slavish person, and again, the fun of a cultivated person from that of one who is uncultivated. We may see this to be so at once by a comparison of the old and the new comedy; in the former it was obscenity of language which raised a laugh, but in the latter it is rather innuendo, and this makes a great difference from the point of view of decorum.

* * * * *

But the buffoon is the slave of his own sense of humor; he will spare neither himself nor anybody else, if he can raise a laugh, and he will use such language as no person of refinement would use or sometimes even listen to.

The boor is one who is useless for such social purposes; he contributes nothing, and takes offense at everything. (iv, 14)

Aristotle's distinction among these three figures corresponds to that in Restoration comedy among Truewit, Witwoud (the buffoon), and Witless (the fool or country bumpkin): the chief point of difference among them is in their regard for decorum. Like Congreve, Aristotle also pointed out how Witwoud is frequently confused with Truewit, because he is amusing—but Witwoud is "the slave of his own sense of humour." And like Dryden in his criticism of Jonson, Aristotle distinguished between the old comedy and the new, and he preferred the new because it used innuendo (*double-entendre*) rather than obscenity in its jests. The same distinction between gentlemanly wit and coarse wit was made by both Cicero and Quintilian.[22]

English writers followed such classical precedents. The Earl of Shaftesbury observed, "In a Gentleman we allow of Pleasantry and Raillery, as being manag'd always with good Breeding, and never gross or clownish."[23] In his translation of Aristotle's *Rhetoric*, Hobbes identified the polite jest with *irony*, and the vulgar with *scurrility*: "The latter of these has in it a kind of baseness: the former may become a man of good breeding."[24] Then he identified irony with "the mocking speech," or raillery[25]; and the love of raillery he attributed to man's egoism, for "men laugh at *jests*, the *wit* whereof always consisteth in the elegant *discovering* and conveying to our minds some *absurdity* of *another*."[26] Such "witty contumely," he thought, is especially popular with young men.[27]

This polite jesting, or raillery (Quintilian's *dicacitas*), seems to have been extremely popular in the Restoration, though there were some, like Evelyn[28] and the anonymous

[22] "There are, generally speaking, two sorts of jests: the one, coarse, rude, vicious, indecent; the other, refined, polite, clever, witty"—Cicero, *De Officiis*, I, xxix, tr. Walter Miller, London and New York, 1913, p. 107. Quintilian cited Cicero in his discussion of the ridiculous, and he suggested a similar distinction in his remark that "if these [the ridiculous] are made to appear in others the result is called raillery, while if they recoil upon the speakers it is called folly"—Quintilian, *op. cit.*, VI, iii, tr. Lane Cooper, in *An Aristotelian Theory of Comedy*, New York, 1922, p. 93. H. E. Butler does not use the term *raillery* in his translation.
[23] Earl of Shaftesbury, "Sensus Communis: An Essay on the Freedom of Wit and Humour" (1709), in *Characteristicks of Men, Manners, Opinions, Times*, London, 1737, I, 67.
[24] Hobbes, *The Whole Art of Rhetoric*, III, 17, in *The English Works*, VI, 510.
[25] Hobbes, *The Art of Rhetoric*, I, in *The English Works*, VI, 515. This section is appended to *The Whole Art of Rhetoric*.
[26] Hobbes, *Human Nature*, IX, 13, in *The English Works*, IV, 46.
[27] Hobbes, *The Whole Art of Rhetoric*, II, 14, in *The English Works*, VI, 467.
[28] *Diary*, July 10, 1669.

author of *Raillerie a la Mode* (1673), who protested against the excessive taste for it. The witty Count de Gramont was described as one "who on all occasions started agreeable raillery."[29] How it colored the social intercourse of the Wits can be gathered from a letter that Etherege wrote to Buckingham, rallying the Duke upon his retirement to Yorkshire: "Who could ever have prophecy'd (though he had a double Gift of Nostradamus's Spirit) that the Duke of Buckingham who never vouchsafed his Embraces to any ordinary Beauty, wou'd ever condescend to sigh and languish for the Heiress apparent of a thatch'd Cottage, in a straw Hat, flannen Petticoat, Stockings of as gross a thrum as the Blew-Coat Boy's Caps at the Hospital, and a Smock (the Lord defend me from the wicked Idea of it!) of as course a Canvas as ever serv'd Apprenticeship to a Mackarel Boat?"[30] The same air of irony and banter permeates the literature of the period; and in wit comedy, raillery appears in isolated exchanges or in extended passages of repartee, as in the first encounter of Dorimant and Harriet.

Such raillery sprang from the satirical temper of an urbane, sophisticated group, and it can be found in such diverse forms as the raillery passages in wit comedy, the letter of Etherege, Buckingham's *Rehearsal*, and Dryden's satirical verse.[31] Personal raillery could easily degenerate into lampoon and libel; and in fact, Rochester is said to have employed a footman to collect scandalous material so that he might circulate lampoons,[32] and a notorious person who called himself "Julian, Secretary to the Muses," distributed the anonymous lampoons of malicious authors. But such direct abuse was not considered

[29] Hamilton, *Memoirs of Count Gramont*, p. 284.
[30] Etherege, *The Letterbook of Sir George Etherege*, ed. Sybil Rosenfeld, London, 1928, pp. 411-412.
[31] Cf. the raillery scenes in Molière's *Le Misanthrope*, which are almost identical with those in Restoration comedy. Of particular interest are the satiric portraits of acquaintances.
[32] Burnet, *History of His Own Time*, I, 295.

The Nature of Wit

true wit because it was ill-mannered and gross. The ideal of fine raillery is best explained by Dryden's laudatory remarks on Lucian:

His wit, says Ablancourt, was full of urbanity, that Attick salt, which the French call—fine raillery; not obscene, not gross, not rude, but facetious, well mannered, and well bred. . . .
. . . If the pleasure arising from comedy and satire be either laughter, or some nobler sort of delight, which is above it, no man is so great a master of irony as our author. That figure is not only a keen, but a shining weapon in his hand; it glitters in the eyes of those it kills; his own gods, his greatest enemies, are not butchered by him, but fairly slain.[33]

This stress on the social side of wit seems to validate the "manners" interpretation. But this is in appearance only. The conception of decorum (and of raillery as gentlemanly wit) was more than a social ideal: it was, first of all, an intellectual and aesthetic ideal. Whereas the "manners" critics think of conformity to a conventional *social* code, the men of the Restoration were thinking of an acceptable level of *intellectual* refinement. Furthermore, decorum was never an artificial code of manners, nor a mere matter of ribands and fine talk and elegant manners. It was a vital ideal, a standard of thought and conduct to which the intelligent and cultivated person aspired, and it implied not only intellectual discrimination, elegance, and sound judgment, but naturalness. Decorum (true wit) might be defined simply as a natural elegance of thought and conduct, based on respect for sound judgment, fidelity to nature, and a due regard for beauty. Intelligence, elegance, and taste are obviously manifested in social intercourse; but these virtues are intellectual and aesthetic, and not principally social.

[33] Dryden, *Works*, XVIII, 75-76. See also, Dryden's familiar remark on Horace's fine satire, and the "vast difference betwixt the slovenly butchering of a man, and the fineness of a stroke that separates the head from the body, and leaves it standing in its place"—Dryden, "Essay on Satire," *Works*, XIII, 98.

The Nature of Wit

The third conception of wit is to be found in Hobbes' identification of wit with fancy, the faculty which discovered similitudes in things unlike, as distinguished from the judgment, which discovered dissimilitudes in things seemingly alike.[34] This distinction between wit and judgment often discriminated against fancy (wit); for although fancy was the creative faculty, it was regarded as wild, unbridled, and irrational. Sir William Temple expressed the consensus of critics when he remarked, "Without the Forces of Wit all Poetry is flat and languishing; without the succors of Judgment 'tis wild and extravagant."[35] Such suspicion of fancy was natural, of course, in a rationalistic age.

In rhetorical discussions, fancy was often identified with *inventio*, the first division of classical rhetoric (as in Shadwell's definition of wit as "the invention of remote and pleasant thoughts of what kind soever"[36]); and it was associated with the poetic act of inventing, or discovering, similitudes. Hobbes attributed to the fancy "those grateful similes, metaphors, and other tropes" of poets and orators,[37] and his disciple Walter Charleton also described the fancy as "the inventive and adorning" faculty, to which he attributed "the similitudes and the rare incidents which give pleasure through vivid imagery and novelty."[38] Here the rhetorical and psy-

[34] Hobbes, *Leviathan*, I, 8, in *The English Works*, III, 57. Cf. Addison's definition, in his *Spectator* #62, which is a restatement of Locke's description of wit as "lying most in the assemblage of ideas, and putting them together with quickness and variety, wherein can be found any resemblance or congruity."

[35] Temple, "Of Poetry," in Spingarn, III, 81. Cf. Thomas Shadwell, Preface to *The Humorists*, in *The Complete Works*, I, 187-188. Locke thought that the product of fancy is irrational, and that "it is a kind of affront to go about to examine it, by the severe rules of truth and good reason; whereby it appears that it consists in something that is not perfectly conformable to them"—John Locke, *An Essay Concerning Human Understanding*, ed. Alexander C. Fraser, Oxford, 1894, II, 204. For intimations that there were laws of association to explain the workings of the fancy, see Hobbes, *Leviathan*, I, 3, in *The English Works*, III, 12.

[36] Shadwell, Preface to *The Humorists*, in *The Complete Works*, I, 188.

[37] Hobbes, *Human Nature*, X, 4, in *The English Works*, IV, 56.

[38] Quoted by Thorpe, *Aesthetic Theory of Thomas Hobbes*, p. 180.

chological definitions of wit overlap. The fancy, as the creative faculty, is concerned, then, with the invention of figures and with the adorning of a work of art, for the purpose of giving pleasure through the vividness and novelty of whatever is conceived.

The stress on the invention of similitudes is particularly important, because this is what makes Restoration comic dialogue so graphic and striking. The similitude is a familiar literary device, and its use in *verse* dialogue is not uncommon, but its use in comic *prose* dialogue distinguishes wit comedy from most English prose drama. The familiar accent of witty prose dialogue is to be found in a passage like the following from Wilde's *Lady Windermere's Fan*:

> LORD DARLINGTON: Oh, nowadays so many conceited people go about society pretending to be good, that I think it shows rather a sweet and modest disposition to pretend to be bad. Besides, there is this to be said, if you pretend to be good the world takes you very seriously, if you pretend to be bad they don't. Such is the stupidity of optimism.
>
> LADY WINDERMERE: Don't you *want* the world to take you seriously then, Lord Darlington?
>
> LORD DARLINGTON: No, not the world. Who are the people the world takes seriously? All the dull people one can think of. (Act I)

In contrast to Wilde's, here is a typical passage of Restoration dialogue from *The Country Wife*—and one which is not especially striking or novel:

> ALITHEA: Sister, what ails you? you are grown melancholy.
>
> MRS. PINCH: Would it not make any one melancholy to see you go every day fluttering about abroad, whilst I must stay at home like a poor lonely sullen bird in a cage?
>
> ALITHEA: Ay, sister; but you came young, and just from the nest to the cage: so that I thought you liked it, and could be as cheerful in't as others that took their flight themselves early, and are hopping abroad in the open air. (III, i)

The Nature of Wit

This is good Restoration comic dialogue: graphic, lively, and figurative. In the elaboration of the simile, it is more consciously artistic than Wilde's passage; yet its sentiments are more natural than those affected by Lord Darlington. Restoration dialogue, at its best, possesses this virtue of clarity, naturalness, and figurativeness, for it stands midway between poetry and prose. The generous use of similitudes lends color, liveliness, and force to wit comedy, and the figures cease to be pleasant only when they become excessive or are labored.[39]

The similitude is not in itself witty, of course, since it is merely the outward form in which the wit appears; a figurative expression becomes witty only when the thought is novel and surprising. The vividness of the figure, however, contributes to the shorthand communication of wit, by facilitating our grasp of what is said; and consequently, the similitude, though not witty in itself, enhances the brilliance of a witty remark. Aristotle prized metaphor above all else for giving "clearness, charm, and distinction to the style"[40]; and in translating the *Rhetoric*, Hobbes likewise considered figures of speech so important that he appended a small section on tropes and figures. Following Aristotle, who regarded the learning process as one of the essential elements in aesthetic pleasure and the metaphor as a contributing factor in learning,[41] Hobbes also pointed out how the similitude gives us pleasure:

But *metaphors* please; for they beget in us, by the *genus*, or by some *common* thing to that with another a kind of *science*. As when an *old man* is called *stubble*; a man suddenly learns that he grows up, flourisheth, and withers like grass, being put in mind of it by the qualities common to *stubble* and to *old men*.

[39] Cf. the remarks by Heartwell, Sharper, and Bellmour on Vainlove's pursuit of Araminta, in Congreve's *Old Batchelor*, i, iv.
[40] Aristotle, *The Rhetoric of Aristotle*, tr. Lane Cooper, 3.2, New York, 1932, p. 187.
[41] Aristotle, *Poetics*, iv, tr. S. H. Butcher, in *The Great Critics*, ed. Smith and Parks, p. 31. Aristotle, *Rhetoric*, tr. Cooper, 3.10, pp. 206-207.

The Nature of Wit

That which a *metaphor* does, a *similitude* does the same.[42]

This, I think, is a partial explanation of the peculiar intellectual pleasure that wit comedy affords us. The similitude brings us a sudden realization of a new relationship: it is not the laborious grasping of a scientific theory or of a mathematical problem; rather it is a sense of fresh knowledge that flashes upon us suddenly.

On the psychological side, as distinguished from the rhetorical, the conception of wit as fancy embraces three main points: the faculty, the product, and the effect. These are all suggested in Dryden's commendation of Davenant's wit: "I found him then of so quick a fancy, that nothing was proposed to him, on which he could not suddenly produce a thought extremely pleasant and surprising; and those first thoughts of his, contrary to the old Latin proverb, were not always the least happy; and as his fancy was quick, so likewise were the products of it remote and new. He borrowed not of any other; and his imaginations were such as could not easily enter into any other man."[43] For true wit (fancy), the faculty must be quick and original, the product must be remote and new, and the effect must be pleasant and surprising.

Being most familiar, this conception has received more attention from modern students of wit than any other. Yet the role of fancy (wit) in Restoration comedy needs to be stressed, because there has been a tendency among "manners" critics to minimize its importance. The plays of Etherege, Wycherley, and Congreve have been described by Palmer as "pure comedies of intellect" or "of pure reason."[44] This is quite misleading. When the intellect appears in the plays, it is often in its fanciful sports, but seldom as discursive reason. Restora-

[42] Hobbes, *The Whole Art of Rhetoric*, III, 9, in *The English Works*, VI, 496.
[43] Dryden, Preface to *The Tempest*, in *Works*, III, 107.
[44] Palmer, *Comedy*, p. 17.

[31]

tion comedy has a superficial appearance of intellectuality, and one may consequently conclude, with the "manners" critics, that its appeal is purely intellectual. But some of the wit is as fanciful and sophistical as the following passage from *The Old Batchelor*, in which Bellmour says that though he enjoyed Silvia, she was still true to Vainlove:

VAIN: So was true as Turtle—in imagination—*Ned*, ha? Preach this Doctrine to Husbands, and the married Women will adore thee.
BELL: Why faith I think it will do well enough—If the Husband be out of the way, for the Wife to show her Fondness and Impatience of his Absence, by chusing a Lover as like him as she can, and what is unlike, she may help out with her own Fancy.
VAIN: But is it not an Abuse to the Lover to be made a Blind of?
BELL: As you say the Abuse is to the Lover, not the Husband: For 'tis an Argument of her great Zeal towards him, that she will enjoy him in Effigie. (i, i)

Somewhat superior to this is such paradoxical wit as we find in the "proviso" scene in *The Way of the World*:

MILLA: And d'ye hear, I won't be call'd Names after I'm Marry'd; positively I won't be call'd Names.
MIRA: Names!
MILLA: Ay, as Wife, Spouse, my Dear, Joy, Jewel, Love, Sweet-heart, and the rest of that nauseous Cant, in which Men and their Wives are so fulsomly familiar. (iv, v)

Such wit was employed for the purpose of securing novelty and surprise; and it lends a delightfully playful quality to Restoration comedy.

Critics were generally in agreement over the importance of novelty and surprise in wit, and following Hobbes, many regarded the excitation of the mind as pleasurable in itself and consequently desirable.[45] According to this point of view,

[45] See Clarence DeWitt Thorpe, "Addison and Some of His Predecessors on 'Novelty,'" *PMLA*, LII, 1114-1129 (1937).

the experience of wit is a titillation of the mind arising from the novelty of the idea (a similitude, paradox, antithesis, etc.); and the aesthetic pleasure is due as much to the excitation of the mind as to the intuition of new knowledge. Contrary to popular opinion, the gallant in Restoration comedy is a pursuer of wit, and is interested in this form of intellectual pleasure and excitement; hence his concern is more intellectual and aesthetic than sensual.

This brief analysis of wit as fancy points up certain features of wit comedy that do not always receive adequate attention. In the rhetorical definition, the connection between wit and the discovery of striking similitudes is of special interest, for it is the conception of the poetic act as the finding of metaphors and similes that helps to nourish the vogue for a highly figurative prose dialogue. In the psychological definition, we have a partial explanation of certain other qualities of wit comedy: its fanciful and superficially intellectual character, its paradoxical and sophistical wit, and its effect of novelty and pleasant surprise.

No discussion of wit would be complete without some consideration of the distinction between true wit and false wit, since there is a large body of writing devoted to this subject. Of these, the most familiar are the series of *Spectator* papers (#58-62) on true wit, false wit, and mixed wit. This subject seems to have been of considerable interest to cultivated people in the Restoration, and Miss Hamilton, whom the witty Count de Gramont married, is described as having "an admirable discernment in distinguishing between solid and false wit."[46] She would probably have made a good critic of wit comedy, since this distinction between true and false wit is extremely important in these plays.

Perhaps the best introduction to this subject is Abraham Cowley's ode "Of Wit," which is an attempt to define true

[46] Hamilton, *Memoirs of Count Gramont*, p. 128.

wit by describing what it is not. Cowley declared that wit is
"not a Tale, 'tis not a Jest/Admir'd with Laughter at a feast";
" 'Tis not to force some lifeless Verses meet"; " 'tis not to
adorn, and gild each part"; " 'Tis not when two like words
made up one noise"; it is not bawdry; " 'Tis not such Lines
as almost crack the Stage"; "Nor upon all things to ob-
trude/And force some odd Similitude." The whole poem is
dominated by the ideal of decorum; and one might object, as
Addison did to Dryden's rhetorical definition of wit, that the
ode presents only a general notion of what good writing is
rather than of what true wit is. The poem is principally a
warning against literary excess, against what is glittering on
the surface but dross beneath, and also against puns, bawdry,
and forced similitudes. But these are all examples of false
wit; and it is apparent that wit must be judged by the criterion of decorum. Furthermore, the poem suggests that
false wit is also anything that is lifeless.

These suggested criteria explain the criticism of wit in the
Restoration. Most commonly, critics treated as false wit any
sort of quibbling—a play on words, whether on the sound or
sense (the play on sense appearing usually as a "conceit,"
paradox, or antithesis; the play on sound as a pun). "The
jingle of a . . . poor paronomasia" was a special abomination
to Dryden, and he was very severe on Jonson for resorting
to puns in his play.[47] In fact, the belief was prevalent that
the Elizabethan age was particularly addicted to quibbling,
and Critick, in *A Comparison between the Two Stages*, censured Sidney, Donne, Overbury, and Jonson for what he
considered an "old fashion'd Custom." To which Ramble
retorted, "your Quibble does well now a Days, your best
Comedies tast of 'em; the *Old Batchelor* is rank."[48] Contemporary evidence seems to substantiate Ramble's assertion: Addison's *Spectator* #61 on punning, the notoriety of the pun-

---

[47] Dryden, "An Account of the Poem *Annus Mirabilis*," in *Works*, IX,
96. Dryden, "Defence of the Epilogue," *Works*, IV, 237-238.
[48] *Op. cit.*, p. 44.

The Nature of Wit

ster Captain Swan, the story of Dennis being confounded by a pun, and numerous references to quibbling would seem to indicate that this form of false wit maintained its perennial popularity in the Restoration.

As a special form of quibbling, the *double-entendre* deserves some notice because it is the principal form that sexual wit assumes in wit comedy. The notorious "china" scene in *The Country Wife* is an extended passage of *double-entendre*, and it has contributed perhaps as much as anything else to the common belief that Restoration comedy is marred by lubricity. In the seventeenth century, writers were generally agreed that bawdry is false wit,[49] and the author of the prologue to Farquhar's *Constant Couple* assured the audience: "The Ladies safe may smile: for here's no Slander, /No Smut, no lewd-tongu'd Beau, no double Entendre."[50] They had classical precedent for this attitude; for example, in Quintilian's warning to abstain from "*double entendre* and obscenity."[51] Yet a sound critic like Dryden demurred against the censure of all sexual wit, though he admitted that "barefaced" ribaldry is not wit[52]; Wolseley undertook to defend sexual wit on the basis of an abortive theory of naturalistic art in his preface to Rochester's *Valentinian*; and Congreve introduced *double-entendres* into his plays while censuring the "senseless ribaldry" of a Petulant. There is a distinction to be made, obviously, between gross and senseless obscenity, on the one hand, and sexual ideas expressed wittily and gracefully—as suggested by Aristotle in the *Ethics* in distinguishing between the old comedy and the new.

A second type of false wit is excess of any sort, particularly

[49] Sir Robert Howard, Preface to *Four New Plays*, in Spingarn, II, 100-101. Shadwell, Prologue to *The Royal Shepherdess*, in *The Complete Works*, I, 101. Sir Samuel Tuke, *The Adventures of Five Hours*, ed. A. E. H. Swaen, Amsterdam, 1927, pp. 240-241. Blackmore, Preface to *Prince Arthur*, in Spingarn, III.
[50] Farquhar, *The Complete Works*, I, 87.
[51] Quintilian, *Institutio Oratoria*, VI, iii, tr. Butler, II, 463.
[52] Dryden, Preface to *The Second Miscellany*, in *Works*, XII, 294-295.

in the use of similitudes. Many a Witwoud falls into this error, and this excess is made doubly obnoxious by the copious flow of flat and stale comparisons. Wycherley's Dapperwit is a great coiner of such flat similitudes; while Congreve's Witwoud is clever, but is deficient in decorum because he spouts comparisons on all occasions. Dryden censured the excessive and injudicious display of wit in Fletcher and Shakespeare,[53] and he found fault with Ovid for being "witty out of season."[54] He even criticized one writer of wit comedy (generally believed to be Congreve, though Dennis asserts that Dryden meant Wycherley): "I knew a poet . . . who being too witty himself, could draw nothing but wits in a comedy of his; even his fools were infected with the disease of their author."[55]

A more purely dramatic type of false wit is the noise and bustle on the stage, associated in the main with farce. "The little Poetasters of the fourth rate," Shadwell remarked, "hold, that Wit signifies nothing in a Comedy; but the putting out of Candles, kicking down of Tables, falling over Joynt-stools, impossible accidents, and unnatural mistakes."[56] In *The Plain Dealer*, Novel mistakes noise and breaking windows for true wit, and he exclaims, "Don't we esteem the monkey a wit amongst beasts, only because he's mischievous?" (v, ii).[57]

The importance of false wit in wit comedy is seen in the fact that the chief *comic* figure is Witwoud, a person who has the faults enumerated above. By nature he is related to Witless; but he aspires to be a Wit, and since he lacks judgment and taste, he falls between Witless and Truewit—"Not quite

[53] Dryden, Preface to *An Evening's Love*, in *Works*, III, 245.
[54] Dryden, Preface to *Ovid's Epistles*, in *Works*, XII, 12.
[55] Dryden, "A Parallel of Poetry and Painting," *Works*, XVII, 320.
[56] Shadwell, Dedication of *A True Widow*, in *The Complete Works*, III, 284.
[57] See also, the censure of Mockmode for thinking there is wit in breaking glasses, in Farquhar's *Love and a Bottle*, II, ii, *The Complete Works*, I, 31-32.

so low as Fool, nor quite a Top, / But hangs between 'em both, and is a Fop."[58] The comedy in the plays is sometimes provided by Witlesses like Etherege's Sir Nicholas Cully and Congreve's Sir Joseph Wittol; but the better comic figure, as Shadwell pointed out, is "your witty, brisk, airy Fopps that are *Entreprennants*."[59] An examination of wit comedy bears this out; for the most striking comic figures are to be found in the gallery of Witwouds—Sir Fopling Flutter, Dapperwit, Sparkish, Novel, Brisk, Tattle, Witwoud, Sir Novelty Fashion, Lord Foppington, and Sir Courtly Nice. The weakness they share in common is a lack of judgment and decorum, rather than a social defect as is suggested by the "manners" critics; and this is true even of a fop like Sir Fopling Flutter. Dennis observed that the most troublesome fools are those with wit (fancy) but no judgment: "For he who has Wit without Judgment is but a half Wit, and therefore has but imperfect Views."[60] Witwouds like Sir Fopling and Dapperwit are brisk but insipid, and pass for wits only with the undiscriminating, since their ideas are superficial and without judgment.

In contrast to them, the Truewit shows judgment and observes decorum. Wycherley's Manly put the case concisely when he said, "I ever thought the man of most wit had been like him of most money, who has no vanity in showing it everywhere, whilst the beggarly pusher of his fortune has all he has about him still only to show" (v, ii). The Truewit unites all the good qualities of judgment and fancy that have been discussed earlier, and his composite nature is suggested by Burnet's description of several notable Wits: "Sidley had a more sudden and copious wit, which furnished a perpetual

[58] "A Familiar Epistle to Mr. Julian, Secretary to the Muses," in *The Works of His Grace, George Villiers, Late Duke of Buckingham*, London, 1715, II, 225.
[59] Shadwell, Preface to *The Humorists*, in *The Complete Works*, I, 188.
[60] Dennis, "A Defence of Mr. *Wycherley*'s Characters in the *Plain-dealer*," in *The Critical Works*, II, 233-234.

run of discourse: but he was not so correct as Lord Dorset, nor so sparkling as Lord Rochester."[61] Suddenness, copiousness, and sparkle are characteristic of the fanciful side of wit, while correctness represents the judicious side: the Truewit possesses these intellectual virtues in a superlative degree. Wit also implies a high degree of mental cultivation. Mirabell and Valentine are educated gentlemen who possess an easy familiarity with the best authors both ancient and modern. Valentine has been reading Epictetus when the play opens, and Mirabell and Mrs. Millamant have Suckling and Waller on their lips. To this cultivation and taste, they add a rich fancy and an original mind. But their understanding has been cultivated more than their reason, and hence they possess perceptive and acute rather than deeply speculative minds. These are also the qualities that one finds in the witty authors of Restoration comedy.

In the present chapter I have tried to clarify the notion of wit and to show how it is a better key to Restoration comedy than the conception of "manners." Wit is a very comprehensive and ambiguous term, and it is sometimes contradictory in its implications: as judgment, it implies restraint, good taste, common sense, and naturalness; as fancy, on the other hand, it implies whatever is novel and striking and remote. The conception of wit as judgment (decorum) emphasizes the neoclassical side of wit comedy. The conception of wit as fancy emphasizes the whimsical, novel, and striking qualities of the comedy which we generally designate by the term *witty*; on this side, wit comedy is anticlassical and reveals its kinship with metaphysical poetry. The ambiguity of the term detracts somewhat from the usefulness of wit as a key. Yet the very scope and nebulousness of wit indicate, I think, the complexity of the comedy which embodies this aesthetic and intellectual ideal, and the inadequacy, therefore, of any attempt to sum it up as artificial comedy of manners.

[61] Burnet, *History of His Own Time*, I, 295.

III

THE INTELLECTUAL BACKGROUND
OF WIT COMEDY

THE NEXT POINT that needs examination is the "immorality"
and "profaneness" of Restoration comedy, since this subject
has been somewhat obfuscated by the "manners" critics.
Though insisting on the amorality of the plays (insofar as
effect is concerned), they have agreed generally with the
moralistic critics that the content is immoral,[1] and at best
they have by-passed this subject by emphasizing "manners."
The consequence has been to leave us with several misconceptions about Restoration comedy: first, that it depicts an
immoral society; and second, that it reflects only the superficial side of high society (its "manners"), and not much
of the serious concerns of the day. It is time, I think, that we
determined how accurate this belief is; and this is best done
by examining the intellectual background of the plays, to
see to what extent contemporary ideas influenced the content
of Restoration comedy. The key words in such an examination are naturalism, libertinism, and skepticism.

The most important of these, and the least susceptible of
definition, is naturalism. This is a term that we usually as-
sociate with Zola and the biological sciences of the nineteenth
century, when it also became an important philosophical position. But naturalism has always been a tendency of human
thinking. The seventeenth century produced at least two very
important naturalistic thinkers in Hobbes and Spinoza, and
Restoration comedy was strongly naturalistic, too, despite
the absence of literary manifestoes. In England there were
many forces at work to foster such a temper, not the least of

[1] Cf. Palmer, *Comedy of Manners*, pp. 191-192.

which was the Royal Society, with members prominent not only in science but in literature and politics. The Royal Society encouraged naturalism by excluding the investigation of divine and spiritual matters as too "hard to be reduc'd to any certain Observation of the Senses," and limiting itself, therefore, to what was empirically verifiable.[2] This reliance on empiricism, at the expense of the transcendental, was also to be found in the writings of an influential philosopher like Locke.

Naturalism might be defined briefly as a point of view which excludes the supernatural and accepts the empirical method.[3] This view can be traced back to the Greeks, who saw man as a rational animal in a logical and natural cosmos, and in the ancient world it found most explicit statement in the philosophy of Epicurus, as set forth by Lucretius. Christianity, on the other hand, set up a transcendental realm inaccessible to reason, from which man dangled by the thread of Grace; man then had his being in two worlds, the natural realm where he exercised his reason, and the supernatural realm where he depended on faith—a dichotomy expressed most beautifully in the Middle Ages by Dante. The Renaissance and the seventeenth century marked a return to the naturalistic point of view, with a revival of classical naturalism (Democritus, Epicurus, Lucretius), and interest in the "new philosophy" as set forth by Galileo, Newton, Gassendi, Copernicus, and Harvey.

[2] Sprat, *History of the Royal Society*, p. 345ff.
[3] Cf. James Bissett Pratt, *Naturalism*, New Haven, 1939, p. 5. The following definition of *naturalism* appears in the *Dictionary of Philosophy and Psychology*, ed. James Mark Baldwin, New York, 1928, II, 137-138: "The theory that the whole of the universe or of experience may be accounted for by a method like that of the physical sciences, and with recourse only to the current conception of physical and natural science; more specifically, that mental and moral processes may be reduced to the terms and categories of the natural sciences. It is best defined negatively as that which excludes everything distinctly spiritual or transcendental." For a modern symposium on naturalism, see *Naturalism and the Human Spirit*, ed. Yervant H. Krikorian, New York, 1944.

Intellectual Background of Wit Comedy

The conflict of the "new philosophy" with Christian super-naturalism produced an attitude of skepticism among men of rationalistic bent, who were left "wandering between two worlds." The demoralizing impact of the new scientific discoveries is vividly described in John Donne's "An Anatomy of the World," in which the poet declared that the "new philosophy calls all in doubt." Montaigne also gave eloquent expression to his skepticism in the "Apology for Raimond de Sebonde" and the familiar phrase "Que scay-je." There was a breakdown in the medieval pattern of thought, for where the intellectual foundations had once stood firm against time and change, there were only the shifting sands of opinion. The Marquess of Halifax commented on the loss of absolutes:

The Fundamentals in Divinity have been changed in several Ages of the World.

Philosophy, Astronomy, etc. have changed their Fundamentals as the Men of Art no doubt called them at the time. Motion of the Earth, etc.

Even in Morality one may more properly say, There *should be* Fundamentals allowed, than that there *are* any which in Strictness can be maintained.[4]

The witty and skeptical St. Evremond, an intimate of the Wits at Whitehall, noted also: "We have other notions of Nature, than the Antients had. . . . In short, every thing is changed, Gods, Nature, Politicks, Manners, Humours, and Customs."[5] To the impact of the "new philosophy" as a disintegrating force were added the schisms within the Church and, in England, the political disorders of the mid-century. Clarendon observed that the Civil Wars had the unsettling effect of breaking down moral and social standards and of

[4] Halifax, "Political Thoughts and Reflections," in *The Complete Works of George Savile, First Marquess of Halifax*, ed. Walter Raleigh, Oxford, 1912, pp. 209-210.

[5] St. Evremond, "Of the Poems of the Antients," in *The Works of Monsieur de St. Evremond*, London, 1728, II, 350.

fostering individualism, for "every one did that which was good in his own Eyes."[6]

Among thinking men, there was a general suspicion of dogmatism in any form. Abercromby prefaced his *Discourse of Wit* with the remark, "I pretend not to impose on any Mans Understanding, my own irregular Fancies, as inclining more to Scepticism in disputable matters, than to that Bold, and Magisterial air of Dogmatical Philosophers." It was the same skeptical temper that led Rochester to reject inspiration in religion as incredible, and to accept only what seemed reasonable.[7] St. Evremond likewise was skeptical of knowledge transcending sense or reason,[8] and also of religion and immortality.[9] Among scientific men, Joseph Glanvill warned "Against Confidence in Philosophy, and Matters of Speculation,"[10] and he wrote a book entitled *Scepsis Scientifica: Or, Confest Ignorance, the Way of Science; In An Essay of The Vanity of Dogmatizing, and Confident Opinion* (1665).

It is a short step from this skeptical temper to the disillusionment of Cowley's poem, "The Tree of Knowledge. That there is no Knowledge. Against the Dogmatists," in which he concluded that by eating of the Tree of Knowledge, man obtained nothing, for "the onely *Science* Man by this did get, / Was but to *know* he nothing *Knew*." St. Evremond questioned his friend's wisdom in pursuing philosophical speculation at all, because there was no certain knowledge in such matters;[11] and he declared that he had given up philosophy as an idle and futile pursuit, after a conversation with

---

[6] Edward Hyde Clarendon, *The Life of Edward Earl of Clarendon*, Oxford, 1759, II, 39.

[7] Gilbert Burnet, *Some Passages of the Life and Death of the Right Honourable John Earl of Rochester*, London, 1680, p. 72, p. 45.

[8] St. Evremond, "A Letter to the Dutchess of Mazarin, with a Discourse upon Religion," *Works*, II, 249.

[9] St. Evremond, "To Monsieur . . . ," *Works*, I, 27.

[10] Joseph Glanvill, *Essays on Several Important Subjects in Philosophy and Religion*, London, 1676, p. 1.

[11] St. Evremond, "To Monsieur . . . ," *Works*, I, 27.

Intellectual Background of Wit Comedy

Gassendi.[12] Rochester rejected the human reason in "A Satyr Against Mankind," and expressed complete nihilism in his poem "On Nothing." This distrust of dogmatism and "enthusiasm," the skepticism of established beliefs, and, at times, the disillusionment that follows on skepticism, explain, in large part, the skeptical and cynical wit in Restoration comedy which has been labelled "profane" and "immoral."

In fostering such a skeptical and naturalistic temper in seventeenth century England, no one was more influential than Thomas Hobbes. By challenging orthodox thinking, he no doubt unsettled the convictions of many intelligent men; at the same time, as a firm believer in naturalism, he was undoubtedly a persuasive advocate for his own beliefs. It would be an exaggerated estimate to assume that he single-handedly converted the court of Charles and made naturalistic thinkers of the King and of dramatists like Etherege and Wycherley. At any rate, Burnet blamed Buckingham for introducing Hobbes to Charles and thus contributing to "the King's ill principles and bad morals."[13] The Earl of Clarendon also admitted Hobbes' great influence at court: "After the Kings return, he came frequently to the Court, where he had too many disciples."[14] And Aubrey records that "while he was at London, he was much sought after and courted: taught and directed those that sought after him."[15] This period of his stay in the metropolis extended from 1660 to 1675, the years during which Etherege and Wycherley were most productive. The influence of Hobbes was pervasive and widespread, and Aubrey noted: "Mr. John Dreyden, Poet

[12] St. Evremond, "A Judgment on the Sciences to which a Gentleman may apply himself," *Works*, I, 51-52.
[13] Burnet, *History of His Own Time*, I, 108.
[14] Edward Hyde Clarendon, *A Brief View and Survey of the Dangerous and Pernicious Errors to Church and State, in Mr. Hobbes's Book, Entitled Leviathan* (1676), p. 9.
[15] John Aubrey, *Brief Lives, chiefly of Contemporaries, set down by John Aubrey, between the Years 1669 & 1696*, ed. Andrew Clark, Oxford, 1898, I, 341, marginal note.

Laureat, is his great admirer, and oftentimes makes use of his doctrine in his playes—from Mr. Dreyden himselfe."[16]

An important reason for Hobbes' popularity with the Wits was his attractive personality. According to Aubrey, Hobbes had "a sharpe Witt"; also "being naturally of a cheerful and pleasant humour, he affected not at all austerity and gravity and to looke severe," and he was well loved "for his pleasant facetiousness and good-nature."[17] Aubrey likewise gives a pleasant account of Hobbes' relations with Charles, and his wit combats with the courtiers:

> About a weeke after he had orall conference with his majesty at Mr. S. Cowper's, where, as he sate for his picture, he was diverted by Mr. Hobbes's pleasant discourse. Here his majestie's favours were redintegrated to him, and order was given that he should have free accesse to his majesty, who was always much delighted in his witt and smart repartees.
>
> The wits at Court were wont to bayte him. But he feared none of them, and would make his part good. The king would call him the *beare*: "Here comes the beare to be bayted!"[18]

Among his many friends he numbered Wits like Cowley, Dryden, Davenant, and Waller, and he may have known Etherege, Sedley, and Wycherley, since he moved in the same circles as they. Aside from his dogmatic temper, Hobbes had much in common with these men—in his wit, his cheerful personality, his interest in music and literature, and in his rationalistic approach to life. The "pernicious" doctrines of Hobbes were listened to eagerly, not only because they were presented wittily, but because they harmonized with the predilections of the Wits. Hobbes gave the most articulate expression to the intellectual tendencies of the age that affected wit comedy, and for that reason, a brief analysis of his doctrines contributes much to our understanding of the content of Restoration comedy.

The views that created the greatest stir were his religious

[16] *Ibid.*, I, 372.   [17] *Ibid.*, I, 347-349.   [18] *Ibid.*, I, 340.

ideas, expressed in the *Leviathan* (1651), the general opinion
of which is summed up in Anthony à Wood's note: "Hobs his
Leviathan hath corrupted the gentry of the nation, hath in-
fused ill principles into them, atheisme."[19] In this book
Hobbes expressed his anticlerical bias by subordinating the
church to the king, and he also expounded a mechanistic philosophy which was hostile to the Christian position. His friend
Waller praised him for having singlehandedly "pulled-downe
all the churches, dispelled the mists of ignorance, and layd-
open their priest-craft."[20] But there were many unfriendly
critics who were severe in their censure. Burnet considered
the *Leviathan* "a very wicked book," containing ill principles
in religion and ethics, and he commented on their harmful
effects: "this set of notions came to spread much: the novelty
and boldness of them set many on reading them; the impiety
of them was acceptable to men of corrupt minds, which were
but too much prepared to receive them, by the extravagancies
of the late times."[21] The Earl of Clarendon wrote *A Brief
View and Survey of the Dangerous and Pernicious Errors
to Church and State, in Mr. Hobbes's Book, Entitled Leviathan*, in which he warned the reader against the seductive
charms of the author's style and personality, and charged
Hobbes with bringing Christianity and the clergy into low
esteem and with encouraging levity and raillery in religious
matters.[22]

Though there is danger of exaggerating the extent of
Hobbes' influence, there is no doubt of the direction in which
he influenced people. The Town Gallant is described as
"Hobbian" in his religion, and "he Swears the *Leviathan* may
supply all the lost Leaves of *Solomon*."[23] The gallant in wit

[19] Anthony à Wood, *The Life and Times of Anthony à Wood*, ed.
Llewelyn Powys, London, 1932, p. 208. See also, p. 142.
[20] Aubrey, *Brief Lives*, p. 358. See also, p. 372.
[21] Burnet, *History of His Own Time*, I, 207-208.
[22] Clarendon, *A Brief View*, pp. 203-207, p. 231.
[23] *The Character of a Town-Gallant*, London, 1675, p. 7.

comedy is similarly biased, and is, according to Blackmore, "a great Admirer of Lucretius" and a derider of religion.[24] The indifference of the court and of Charles to religion is commented on by Pepys on several occasions. On October 2, 1660, he found but a thin congregation at the Abbey for vespers, and he reflected, "So I see that religion, be it what it will, is but a humour, and so the esteem of it passeth as other things do." In his conversation with his influential relative, the Earl of Montagu, on July 15, 1660, Pepys discovered the Earl to be "a sceptic in all things of religion"—like most of the courtiers at Whitehall. The King was probably a deist;[25] and according to Burnet, Buckingham "had no principles of religion," and Rochester conceived of God as "a vast power, that had none of the Attributes of Goodness or Justice."[26] These lax religious views were shared by the witty dramatists, and as early as October 18, 1666, Evelyn remarked that he went seldom to the public theatres "as they were abused to an atheistical liberty."

The term atheism was bandied about rather loosely in the seventeenth century, and the Wits who were suspected of it were actually deists rather than atheists. At the same time, there is little doubt that the witty dramatists did "expose Religion" insofar as they were skeptical and applied their wit to religious matters. Nevertheless, their wit was directed toward the exposure of the clergy rather than of religion itself. The most familiar type of "profane" wit is an anticlerical hit like the following from Farquhar's *Love and a Bottle*:

> ROEBUCK: What, are the Soldiers more charitable than the Clergy?
> CRIPPLE: Ay, Sir, A Captain will say Dam'me, and give me

[24] Blackmore, Preface to *Prince Arthur*, in Spingarn, III, 230.
[25] Buckingham, "A Short Character of King Charles II of England," *The Works of . . . Buckingham*, II, 238.
[26] Burnet, *History of His Own Time*, I, 107. Burnet, *Some Passages of the Life and Death of . . . Rochester*, p. 22.

Six-pence; and a Parson shall whine out God bless me, and give me not a farthing: Now I think the Officers' Blessing much the best. (I, i)

Or Bellmour's remark in Congreve's *Old Batchelor*: "If I had gone a whoring with the *Practice of Piety* [instead of *The Innocent Adultery*] in my Pocket, I had never been discover'd" (IV, xxi). These are hits at the clergy rather than at religion; and much "profane" wit of this sort is covert criticism of certain clerical failings, such as avarice, ambition, hypocrisy, lechery, and lack of charity and true faith.

The same criticism is to be found in more explicit form in the writings of other Wits. Halifax, a Wit and probably a deist, objected to clergymen who wore their livery for the sake of receiving wages,[27] and to people who wore their religion ostentatiously on the outside.[28] Dryden was even more sharp in his criticism of the clergy:

> For authors, such as our new authors are,
> Have not much learning, nor much wit to spare;
> And as for grace, to tell the truth, there's scarce one,
> But has as little as the very parson:
> Both say, they preach and write for your instruction;
> But 'tis for a third day, and for your induction.
> The difference is, that though you like the play,
> The poet's gain is ne'er beyond his day;
> But with the parson 'tis another case,
> He, without holiness, may rise to grace;
> The poet has one disadvantage more,
> That if his play be dull, he's damned all o'er,
> Not only a damn'd blockhead, but damn'd poor.
> But dulness well becomes the sable garment;
> I warrant that ne'er spoiled a priest's preferment.[29]

Seen in this light, the anticlerical wit, as well as the more explicit criticism of the clergy, hardly seems profane today.

[27] Halifax, "The Character of a Trimmer," *The Complete Works*, p. 73.
[28] Halifax, "The Lady's New-Year's Gift," *The Complete Works*, p. 3.
[29] Dryden, Epilogue to *The Husband His Own Cuckold*, a play by his son, *Works*, X, 424-425.

Intellectual Background of Wit Comedy

From the point of view of religion, what is more serious than such criticism is the naturalistic position embodied in the comedies.

Hobbes' naturalistic ideas were influential not only in religion but in psychology and ethics. In his analysis of human nature, Hobbes included only what could be described physiologically and psychologically, and he excluded anything as transcendental as the soul or the conscience: "Man's nature is the *sum of his natural faculties and powers*, as the faculties of *nutrition, motion, generation, sense, reason*, etc. These powers we do unanimously call *natural*, and are contained in the definition of man, under these words, *animal* and *rational*."[30] Hobbes' views on man's rational nature I have discussed to some extent in the preceding chapter. On the animal side, Hobbes believed that man is motivated by two basic passions—aversion and desire. And on this psychological basis, he erected a relativistic and hedonic ethics.[31]

Pleasure, both intellectual and sensual, is especially important in Hobbes' psychology and ethics. Happiness is a feeling of well-being due to the satisfaction of one's appetites, and it is possible only through constant activity and constant satisfaction.[32] Hence even the carnal pleasure of sex is good, though less permanent than intellectual pleasure; for it, too, contributes to man's happiness.[33] Hobbes' disciple Walter Charleton was of the opinion that the passions are natural

[30] Hobbes, *Human Nature*, I, 4, in *The English Works*, IV, 2.

[31] "Every man, for his own part, calleth that which *pleaseth*, and is delightful to himself, *good*; and that *evil* which *displeaseth* him: insomuch that while every man *differeth* from another in *constitution*, they differ also from one another concerning the common distinction of good and evil. Nor is there any such thing as absolute goodness, considered without relation"—Hobbes, *Human Nature*, VII, 3, in *The English Works*, IV, 32. See also, *Leviathan*, I, 6, in *The English Works*, III, 41. Cf. Spinoza, *The Philosophy of Spinoza* (Modern Library), p. 216.

[32] Hobbes, *Human Nature*, VII, 5, in *The English Works*, IV, 33.

[33] Hobbes, *Leviathan*, I, 6, in *The English Works*, III, 45.

and are therefore good.[34] This is in marked contrast to the puritan condemnation of pleasure.

These hedonic views of Hobbes were further reenforced by the general libertinism of the age and by the revival of Epicureanism. On May 12, 1656, Evelyn wrote in his diary, "Little of the Epicurean philosophy was then known amongst us"; but by 1676, Epicureanism was so familiar to the educated public that in Shadwell's *Virtuoso* the opening scene presented a young gallant exclaiming over Lucretius: "Thou great *Lucretius*! Thou profound Oracle of Wit and Sense! thou art no Trifling-Landskip-Poet, no Fantastick Heroick Dreamer, with empty Descriptions of Impossibilities, and mighty sounding Nothings." St. Evremond was a confessed admirer of Epicurus,[35] and he believed it natural for men to pursue sensual pleasures.[36] The libertinism of the Wits is summed up in Rochester's views as set forth by Burnet: "And he thought that all pleasure, when it did not interfere with these [not to hurt others or prejudice his own health], was to be indulged as the gratification of our natural Appetites. It seemed unreasonable to imagine these were put into a man only to be restrained, or curbed to such a narrowness: This he applied to the free use of Wine and Women."[37] These are the views of a Wit who was an intimate friend of Wycherley and Etherege and who ostensibly served as a model for the latter's Dorimant.

Libertine principles like these and naturalistic psychology served as the basis for the characterization in Restoration comedy. The Truewits are egoistic and libertine, and they conform to Hobbes' description of young men as "violent in their desires. Prompt to execute their desires. Incontinent. Inconstant,

[34] Walter Charleton, *Natural History of the Passions*, London, 1674, p. 187, p. 170.
[35] St. Evremond, "On the Morals of Epicurus," *Works*, II, 364.
[36] St. Evremond, "Of Pleasures," *Works*, I, 46.
[37] Burnet, *Some Passages of the Life and Death of* . . . *Rochester*, pp. 38-39.

easily forsaking what they desired before. Longing mightily, and soon satisfied." They are also "lovers of mirth, and by consequence such as love to jest at others."[38] This description is truer to the character of Dorimant, Bellmour, Horner, and Courtall than the "manners" description of them as butterflies posturing before the social mirror. These young men are drawn as egoists and libertines, concerned principally with the objects of their desire or aversion: they pursue the pleasures of wine, women, and wit, and they ridicule Witless, Witwoud, and unnatural creatures. It was precisely on these grounds that Dennis defended the character of Dorimant against Steele's moralistic censure: Dorimant is portrayed as malicious, egoistic, and libertine because that is the true nature of young men.[39] More idealistic men like Shaftesbury and John Eachard might object to such an egoistic conception of man as Hobbes advanced,[40] but the witty dramatists seem to have turned to him for the psychology and principles of their characters.

The stress on pleasure is also to be found in Hobbes' aesthetics. For him, the aesthetic experience is principally an experience of pleasure due to the stimulation of the mind, which, in turn, produces a salutary motion within the body.[41] This stimulation is achieved through the satisfaction of curiosity, or "lust of the mind," which is an appetite for new knowledge.[42] This hedonic aesthetics, with its psychological (and even physiological) approach, was in direct opposition to the conventional didactic theory of men like Collier; and it was the hedonic theory that was accepted by the Wits.

[38] Hobbes, *The Whole Art of Rhetoric*, II, 14, in *The English Works*, VI, 466-467.
[39] Dennis, "A Defence of Sir *Fopling Flutter*," *The Critical Works*, II, 246-247.
[40] Shaftesbury, "Sensus Communis: An Essay on the Freedom of Wit and Humor," *Characteristicks*, I, 91-93. John Eachard, *Mr. Hobbs's State of Nature Considered*, London, 1672, p. 7.
[41] Hobbes, *Human Nature*, VII, 1, in *The English Works*, IV, 31.
[42] Hobbes, *The Whole Art of Rhetoric*, I, 11, in *The English Works*, VI, 441-442. See also, *Leviathan*, I, 6, in *The English Works*, III, 43.

Intellectual Background of Wit Comedy

In the preface to *An Evening's Love*, Dryden argued that though tragedy is didactic, comedy is intended for "divertisement and delight." He distinguished further between wit comedy and humors comedy, and observed that while the latter renders folly ridiculous, wit comedy "moves you, if not always to laughter, yet to a pleasure that is more noble."[43] This "nobler" pleasure is the titillation of the mind that wit affords. This hedonic view of comedy was also endorsed by Congreve and Farquhar[44] and by the anonymous author of *A Vindication of the Stage*.[45] Perhaps the best expression of this hedonic view of art is the remark of St. Evremond's editor on that witty writer: "He is a Gentleman, who having much leisure, seeks how to pass away the time agreeably; who writes sometimes on one subject, sometimes on another, only for his own amusement; he is a man of wit who proposes to divert himself, as well as a certain number of Gentlemen, with whom he converses."[46] This is the urbane and hedonic temper of amateur writers like Etherege, Wycherley, and Congreve.

Closely related to this point is the role of laughter in wit comedy. In humors comedy, laughter is necessary for didactic purposes; but in wit comedy, laughter is less important, as Dryden pointed out. This is evident if we turn to the witty passages in Congreve or Etherege where the Truewits engage in verbal play; for there is titillation of the mind rather than laughter. The most risible situations usually involve the minor figures, Witwoud and Witless, who are ridiculed because they are deficient in wit. Such laughter gives malicious pleasure to the audience as well as to the Truewits, and is best explained by Hobbes' theory of of egoistic laughter. In fact, such a theory alone can explain adequately the prominence

[43] Dryden, Preface to *An Evening's Love*, in *Works*, III, 247-248.
[44] Prologue to *The Way of the World*; Prologue to *Sir Harry Wildair*.
[45] *A Vindication of the Stage*, London, 1698, p. 4.
[46] St. Evremond, *Works*, III, xvii.

in the plays of raillery and of malicious laughter at Witwoud
and Witless which is intended to be a source of pleasure rather
than of social correction.

In addition to the stress on hedonism, naturalistic aesthetics
may often embody the doctrine that the poet must "follow
nature" and avoid the "Gothic," a point of view that leads
to realism in technique and to rejection of the fanciful and
extravagant in content.[47] In the seventeenth century, the
important idea of imitation, and the related notion of verisi-
militude, often implied photographic realism. Thus Cowley,
in his ode "To the Royal Society," warned the artist "Who
to the life an exact copy would make" not to copy Rubens or
Van Dyke:

> Much less content himself to make it like
> Th' Idaeas and the Images which lie
> In his own Fancy, or his Memory.
>   No, he before his sight must place
>   The Natural and Living Face;
>   The real object must command
> Each Judgment of his Eye, and Motion of his Hand.

This close copying of life is also suggested in the prologue to
Wycherley's *Plain Dealer* when the speaker says, "But the
coarse dauber of the coming scenes / To follow life and
nature only means." The dictum "to follow nature" is ambiguous, of course, because of the ambiguity of the term
nature, but there is little doubt that much speculation on the
writer's subject and technique in the Restoration is naturalistic

[47] For criticism of "Gothic" literature, see Temple, "Of Poetry," in
Spingarn, III, 96. Dryden (like Addison somewhat later) took the minority
view in defending poetical fictions like "hippocentaurs and chimeras," but
so strong was the popular distrust of the fanciful that he resorted to a
naturalistic argument in his defense—that these imaginary creatures are
actually "conjunctions of two natures, which have a real separate being"—
Dryden, "The Author's Apology for Heroic Poetry and Poetic License,"
Works, V, 120-121. For attribution to Hobbes of this popular rejection
of the fanciful, see "On Mr. Hobbs" by the Earl of Mulgrave, in Dryden's
Miscellany Poems, London, 1716, III, 441.

in emphasis.[48] In actual practice, realism is a striking feature of Restoration comedy: here the fashionable life of the gallants and ladies is presented realistically, and the low-life of London is mirrored in the meetings at ordinaries, the adventures with whores and bawds, and the encounters with bailiffs and the watch. Realistic effects were also sought for in the theatre, and on June 11, 1668, Pepys saw even horses brought on the stage.

So pervasive was naturalistic thinking in aesthetics that even the doctrine of decorum in style and characterization must be reviewed in this light; for decorum is naturalistic insofar as it stands for the reasonable (the empirically verifiable and knowable), the normal, and the probable. Decorum of style meant natural thoughts naturally expressed, and it led to the "close, naked, natural way of Speaking" of the Royal Society. Decorum of characterization required that young men be portrayed naturalistically as amorous, mercurial, and easily aroused, while old men should be feeble, avaricious, and uxorious. In actual practice, the ideal of decorum usually led to idealization and to type characters, but critical discussions of decorum often reveal a naturalistic substratum. After stressing the importance of decorum, Collier added: "To manage otherwise is to desert *Nature*, and makes the *Play* appear monstrous and Chimerical. So that instead of an *Image of Life*, 'tis rather an Image of Impossibility."[49] In accordance with such naturalistic ideals, Restoration writers followed nature (whatever the conception of nature might be), they eschewed unnatural subjects (ghosts, chimeras, fairies, etc.), and they were realistic in their technique.

---

[48] See Arthur O. Lovejoy's article, " 'Nature' as Aesthetic Norm," *Modern Language Notes* #42, 444-450, November, 1927. Lovejoy lists the following categories of "Nature" as objects to be imitated in art: 1. "Nature" as empirical reality. 2. "Nature" as the essence or Platonic Idea of a kind. 3. "Nature" as the generic type. 4. "Nature" as the average type. 5. "Nature" as antithetical to man and his works. Section II of the article, on "Nature" as the implied desiderata in works of art, points up realism of technique.

[49] Collier, *Short View*, in Spingarn, III, 282.

Because of this naturalistic bias, the writers of wit comedy presented the Truewit realistically as a young man true to his own libertine and egoistic nature. On the other hand, they ridiculed those who deviated from nature: the affected coxcomb, the superannuated coquette, the pretender to wit, the lecherous old man, and the lustful woman who affects virtue. The Truewits in the plays often express the dramatists' detestation of unnatural creatures. In Wycherley's *Country Wife*, Horner says of a Witwoud like Sparkish: "A pox on 'em, and all that force nature, and would be still what she forbids 'em! Affectation is her greatest monster" (I, i). The Marquess of Halifax warned his daughter that to depart from decorum is unnatural and monstrous: "Unnatural things carry a *Deformity* in them never to be *Disguised*; the *Liveliness* of *Youth* in a riper Age, looketh like a *new patch* upon an *old Gown*; so that a *Gay Matron*, a cheerful *old Fool* may be reasonably put into the List of the *Tamer* kind of *Monsters*."[50] Hand in hand with this hatred of the unnatural went a love of sincerity and truth to nature, a temper quite familiar to us today from the works of naturalistic writers like Dreiser and Farrell.

In the Restoration, there was no adequate manifesto of naturalistic aesthetics, though now and then a writer offered a naturalistic argument in defense of what was condemned as immoral. D'Urfey, for example, defended the licentious passages in *The Comical History of Don Quixote* on the ground that if the characters did and said reprehensible things, he was simply giving a true copy of life.[51] Perhaps the most adequate statement of naturalistic aesthetics is Robert Wolseley's preface to Rochester's *Valentinian*, intended as a defense of that

[50] Halifax, "The Lady's New-Year's Gift," in *The Complete Works*, pp. 32-33.
[51] Thomas D'Urfey, *The Comical History of Don Quixote*, Part III, London, 1729, p. 206.

author's "obscene wit."[52] Wolseley began with a partial concession to the didactic school; then he suggested a theory of art for art's sake, for he said a work of art should be judged, not by its content, but its style (fundamentally the "manners" point of view). The defense of Rochester's "obscene wit" was concluded, however, with this naturalistic argument:

I take Wit then in Poetry, or poetical Wit (for that is the Wit here in Question), to be nothing else but *a true and lively expression of Nature*. . . . *true* this expression of Nature must be that it may gain our Reason, and *lively* that it may affect our Passions: upon the whole matter, to draw and describe things that either are not in Nature or things that are otherwise than they are, or to represent 'em heavily (as the *Essayer* does) and colour 'em dully, this is the only false Wit and the vicious Poetry; on the other hand, to make a very like Picture of any thing that really exists is the perfection as well of Poetry as painting.[53]

The content of a literary work is to be confined to Nature (what actually exists), and the technique must be an undistorted copying of what "really exists." The defense of Rochester's art is based on the ground that though the subject dealt with is sexual, it is a faithful copy of nature.

Naturalistic thinking of this sort was congenial to the Wits and to the authors of wit comedy, for they conceived of man as a part of nature—a rational animal who is egoistic and libertine. Art they regarded as a realm in which man finds expression and satisfaction of his desires; and wit comedy was a hedonic enterprise undertaken by the Wit for his diversion, and for the expression and satisfaction of his malicious, sexual, and aesthetic desires.

Wit comedy was also an artistic expression of the Wit's naturalistic views; and as such, it was a product, not merely

[52] This essay presents a curious medley of critical viewpoints, and as a consequence, its value as a statement of naturalism in art has been neglected, and it has received credit only as a somewhat inadequate statement of art for art's sake. Cf. Spingarn, *Critical Essays of the Seventeenth Century*, I, lxxxv.

[53] Spingarn, III, 21-22.

of a libertine court, but of the intellectual climate to which Hobbes, Charleton, Dryden, and Locke contributed. To understand wit comedy, therefore, we must determine the connection between its content and the intellectual background. In examining the diaries, memoirs, and letters of the period, we should look for clues to the intellectual temper of the period rather than search for stories of Sedley's indecent behavior, Buckingham's relations with the Countess of Shrewsbury, or scandal about Charles' mistresses. In fact, for an understanding of wit comedy, the King's interest in science, his deism, his cynical view of man, and his friendly relations with Hobbes are far more worth examining than his loose life. It is true that the seductions, amorous escapades, assignations, and betrayals of the comedies can be duplicated by actual episodes at the court of Charles; but this is less significant than the fact that the naturalism, libertinism, and skepticism of wit comedy spring from the naturalistic and skeptical temper of the age.

Some readers of Restoration comedy may be content with the bright, shimmering image of aristocratic manners. But to stop here is to miss the most significant element in the plays—the wit, and the naturalistic and skeptical temper that underlie it. It is clear that the writers of wit comedy were not immoral and profane, as the casual reader unfamiliar with the intellectual temper of the age would assume. The charge of immorality, cynicism, and profaneness must be reviewed against the intellectual background. The picture that is sometimes painted of a dissipated circle, idle, drunken, and debauched, is hardly true; for the Wits were usually gifted men, who offended more orthodox contemporaries by subscribing, often unwittingly, to a naturalistic philosophy. There were excesses in the lives of Etherege and Wycherley and Sedley, to be sure, but they were also cultivated men of acute minds who had a keen interest in the intellectual currents of the day. An examination of their plays reveals the fact that

Intellectual Background of Wit Comedy

Restoration comedy is not a shallow reflection of a shallow society intent upon manners. On the contrary, it reflects the troubled intellectual life of the times, and as a successful aesthetic expression of a perennially popular attitude toward life, it is far more significant than is commonly supposed.

THE AESTHETICS OF
WIT COMEDY

IT NOW REMAINS to consider the aesthetics of wit comedy: first, its effect, and second, its structure. Some readers may feel that the "manners" critics have dealt adequately with the aesthetic problem, in rejecting the moral test and in setting up "manners" as the criterion. Critics like Dobrée, Palmer, and Perry have ably presented the view that the plays are dispassionate in treatment and intellectual in their appeal, and consequently amoral, and that style, both literary and social, is the chief concern. They have also stressed the sincerity of the writers to vindicate the comedies morally.

However, this whole point of view, though no doubt aesthetic by comparison with the moralistic approach, is not adequate. To describe the plays as wholly intellectual in appeal is really to deny their aesthetic nature, for, as Kant pointed out, there is considerable difference between "a judgement of cognition" and "a judgement of taste." In reading wit comedy, we are also never quite dispassionate, since we are involved in the action insofar as we side with the Truewits against the Witwouds and Witlesses. There is always a judgment of value involved which, though basically aesthetic, embraces other values. Thus, the circumscription of interest to the style represents a serious neglect of these other values. There is little doubt that moral valuations are often involved in the aesthetic experience, and this is true of wit comedy. Finally, to use the sincerity of the writer as a moral argument in defense of wit comedy is to confuse an ethical with an aesthetic argument.[1] What is apparent from these facts is

[1] Cf. Croce, *Aesthetic As Science of Expression and General Linguistic*, pp. 53-54.

The Aesthetics of Wit Comedy

that the "manners" critics have taken too narrow a view of Restoration comedy, and that consequently they have not only devitalized it but have failed to show how other valuations enrich the "judgement of taste."

"The live question with regard to Restoration comedy is still . . . whether the code which it expresses can be brought into accord with any reasonably respectable modern one."[2] This is the ethical question recently raised by John Harrington Smith, and the fact that it still rises in the mind of a modern critic seems to indicate that the "manners" interpretation has never been quite convincing or adequate. I am therefore suggesting a naturalistic and hedonic theory of art as the proper approach, to do away with the moral obstacle and also to get to the heart of wit comedy. Particularly important in such an approach is the role of wit, for wit is playful and hedonic in character, and hence serves to palliate the naturalism and the freedom of speech and conduct. Wit comedy necessarily deals with morality insofar as it touches on human relations, but since it is witty, it approaches morality from an aesthetic rather than a practical point of view. This whole problem can be clarified, I think, if we consider the nature of aesthetic experience, with particular regard to wit.

The aesthetic experience, according to Stephen C. Pepper, must be vivid in quality, highly organized, and pleasurable.[3] Of particular importance is the high degree of organization, or unity (of the work as well as of the experience), for this alone makes possible the exclusion of practical considerations.[4] The work of art is like a house within whose walls we are content to remain, because we are, at the moment, fully engrossed in the pleasurable activity within. From this point of view, Horace's familiar juxtaposition of *utile* and *dulce* is not valid (though it is understandable in view of the practical

[2] John Harrington Smith, *The Gay Couple in Restoration Comedy*, Cambridge, Mass., 1948, p. 100.

[3] Stephen C. Pepper, *The Basis of Criticism in the Arts*, Cambridge, Mass., 1946, p. 141.

[4] Cf. John Dewey, *Art as Experience*, New York, 1934, p. 254.

The Aesthetics of Wit Comedy

orientation of the Roman mind), and the stress on *utile* by critics like Collier is questionable. The function of a work of art is not to teach, but to facilitate an experience that is at once vivid, complete, and pleasant. For this reason, the choice of subject matter is not of such primary importance as Collier believed: the artist may deal with devils and libertines as well as with saints. On the other hand, it is not sound to assert, with the "manners" critics, that content is completely unimportant. The sounder position, I think, is to reject content (and morality) as the primary criterion of the aesthetic experience, but, at the same time, to recognize the fact that we cannot disregard it completely and be satisfied with a simple theory of art for art's sake.

First of all, moral judgments may enter negatively and make an aesthetic experience impossible because the content is morally displeasing. For readers to whom the content of wit comedy is distasteful, I have suggested the importance of seeing the comedies in the light of philosophical naturalism; and this should not be difficult today, since most readers are already familiar with the naturalistic writings of Dreiser, Farrell, Faulkner, Cain, and Caldwell. The characters in naturalistic works are presented as egoistic, malicious, and libertine, in accordance with the writers' conception of human nature; and if this fact is recognized, the moral obstacle will become less formidable.

Second, the moral sense is undoubtedly aroused by most literary works, because they deal with human character and action. But our moral faculty is exercised within the aesthetic framework, and is subordinated to the aesthetic experience. For example, our hatred of Iago's villainy must be a contemplative one: the moment that a person is impelled to clamber on the stage to punish Iago, the aesthetic experience is nullified. The moral standard in the work of art may be puritanical, prudential, or libertine; it does not constitute a separate part to be judged by itself. In wit comedy, the moral standard is naturalistic; but the realistic depiction of libertine and egoistic conduct is assimilated into the aesthetic experience by the witty treatment and the beauty of the language, and our moral judgment is necessarily affected by the aesthetic framework in which it is exercised.

Third, when a work of art is said to satisfy our moral faculty, it is only in a very general sense. The work of art introduces us to an orderly and meaningful world, and a world which is meaningful because the values in it (both *utile* and *dulce*) are the values that we ourselves prize. There is no need for a point for point correspondence between the mores of the society portrayed and our own mores; all that is required, from the negative point of view, is that there be no serious endorsement of practices that would be abhorrent to a normal civilized person, such as cannibalism or incest. In wit comedy, the diffused sense of a meaningful world is not destroyed by the sexual irregularity of some of the characters, particularly since the libertine conduct is confined to the masculine Truewits and to the less reputable figures. We are also satisfied that the hypocritical, the stupid and boorish, and the affected are punished, and that the Truewit, with whom we identify ourselves, is rewarded. We agree with the dramatist's valuation, in the degradation of Witless and Witwoud, and in the elevation of Truewit, who represents taste, common sense, decorum, wit, and youth. The values in *The Way of the World* differ from those in *Oedipus Rex*, but they both create in us the impression of a meaningful world in which there are values that we cherish.

Finally, in the aesthetic experience, there is a willing suspension of our moral judgment to a considerable degree, so that we momentarily accept the values of the author, even though they are not in complete accord with our own. If a reader could enjoy only the writer whose standards he accepted completely, none but a reader who was morally anesthetized could find pleasure in such disparate authors as

The Aesthetics of Wit Comedy

Bunyan, Dante, Ovid, and Petronius. Obviously, there is considerable flexibility in our moral sense, as long as our primary concern is not the morality of the work. In the aesthetic experience, there is no conversion to a particular doctrine; and whatever dogmas or creeds are presented, we view them contemplatively. Thus, in reading Dante, we need not become Catholics; but, for the sake of the aesthetic experience, we must accept imaginatively the assumptions of the Catholic faith. Similarly, in reading wit comedy, we are not called upon to become libertines, skeptics, or egoists. But during the reading, we must willingly suspend our disbelief so far as not to reject the naturalistic assumptions of the play.

The primary purpose of aesthetic activity is hedonic, and not practical; and the idea of persuasion, which is so important in neoclassical criticism (principally because of rhetorical influences), must be relegated to a very minor position. The authors of wit comedy were interested principally in the pleasure to be derived from aesthetic activity; and in the evaluation of their work, the standard one must use is the quality and degree of pleasure they afford. The importance of pleasure in the aesthetic experience and the nature of that pleasure cannot be overemphasized, since this is the crucial point in the disagreement over the merits of wit comedy. If one begins with the assumptions of a Collier, that pleasure is evil, one cannot appreciate wit comedy.

In the plays, there is the pleasure arising from the vicarious satisfaction of our malice, egoism, sexuality, and cynicism, when we identify ourselves with the Truewits. Our pleasure is aroused also by the beauty of the language, in the fine balance of ideas, the rhythm of the speech, and the pointedness of the expression. There is pleasure, too, in perceiving the fine sense of proportion, of moderation, good taste, and naturalness implicit in the ideal of decorum. There is the pleasure to be derived from the cleverness of the Truewits,

The Aesthetics of Wit Comedy

their intellectual superiority, vivacity, acuteness, and originality, and the fine felicity of their similitudes.

Finally, fusing all this is the satisfaction one feels in the successful synthesis achieved through the witty apprehension of life. The witty muse dances gaily over the surface of life, thrusting a sharp lance now and then at the heavy torso of mundane existence; its eyes sparkle with gaiety, and there is a radiance in its features at once intellectual and malicious and playful. We are carried away by it, and we join in the dance of the witty muse, content for the moment with its gay whirling. We do not forget the larger issues of life, nor do we flee them, as Lamb suggested; rather we are so affected by the magic touch of the witty muse that we see such issues in a shimmer of beauty, as when the first sun-drenched day of spring sets the dewdrops glistening on the flower tips. Our vision is transformed—and perhaps constricted—but such a narrowing of our vision is conducive to a more unified vision, so that we see more clearly and directly and wholly, if not more largely. Life is seen consistently from one point of view; and seen thus, life falls into an integrated pattern without loose ends. Such is the gift of the aesthetic vision.

Of these various sources of pleasure in wit comedy, the one which requires special consideration is the vicarious satisfaction of our egoism, malice, sexuality, and skepticism. The moralistic critics have always been most severe on these seemingly negative elements in wit comedy, and perhaps there may be some dubiety as to their salutary effect.

The best statement of the point of view I am suggesting is the theory of catharsis, formulated by Aristotle in the *Poetics*, and applied to comedy in the *Tractatus Coislinianus*.[5] A modern restatement is that of Freud in his *Wit and Its Relation to the Unconscious*, in which he develops the thesis that since society does not sanction the direct expression in

[5] In Cooper, *An Aristotelian Theory of Comedy*, p. 224.

public of such primitive tendencies as sex and hostility, the individual finds vicarious satisfaction through wit. There is pleasure in skeptical, malicious, and sexual wit because our repressed tendencies are satisfied by the short cut provided by wit; and such relief from restraint is conducive to mental health. According to this theory, the vicarious satisfaction of our sexual, malicious, and cynical tendencies through wit comedy will make us less likely to express these tendencies directly, and perhaps dangerously, among our fellow men.

Such a purgative theory, however, is not to be taken as a complete explanation of how wit comedy affects us: in its cruder form, as psychic and emotional purgation, it merely indicates the biological function of art. It is not this medicinal theory but the theory of catharsis as purification which is much sounder as a description of the aesthetic effect.

A work of art produces in us a feeling of purification and well-being: there is, at once, a sense of the immediacy and intensity and novelty of a pleasurable experience, as well as the absence of any practical demands or consequences. In the aesthetic experience, the nexus between us and the practical world is weakened, and we live for a moment more abundantly, vigorously, and intensely than we normally do.

Wit comedy produces this sense of well-being because it presents to us a meaningful world where a definite order prevails and definite values exist. The world of wit comedy is not a simple fairyland where the laws of cuckoldry have replaced those of matrimony; it is not quite so topsy-turvy, nor so simple. It is rather a world reduced to harmony through the dramatist's witty apprehension of life. The great issues of life, the great sorrows and noble gestures of tragedy, do not interfere here with our single, harmonious vision of life; nor is there room for involvements of a strongly emotional nature, or for the practical interests of the actual world. Rather, life is seen as a witty enterprise, where the illusions of the world are pricked by the pin of wit, and the bubble of dog-

The Aesthetics of Wit Comedy

matism and conventional morality is treated as mercilessly as the bubble of vice and hypocrisy. The witty muse flits over the surface of things, hitting those who take life too seriously —or too frivolously.

Where, one might well ask, is the principle by which the witty muse lives? Is it manners, decorum, license, or is it the *élan vital* of Bergson? But the witty muse answers not; it only mocks at such impertinent questions. If we try to label it the fanciful spirit, it retreats to the realm of decorum. If we seek to identify it with pure reason, it answers with fanciful sophistry. If we seek to brand it as immoral, it points out its services to morality in its exposure of hypocrisy and bigotry. If we call it the civilizing spirit of laughter, it mocks us with its cynical and sexual rejoinders. The witty muse is mercurial and elusive and indefinable; it pretends to no practical purpose, for it is concerned chiefly with pleasure. But beneath the constantly changing surface, it is always playful (though often with a mixture of seriousness in its levity). It sits gracefully in the company of sophisticated men and women, with its head cocked to one side, and over its features plays a sprightly and malicious smile like a bright flame. It is the soul of irreverence, and respects no man and no thing. But to those who keep it company, it is kind indeed, for it bestows on them both freedom and pleasure. This perhaps suggests something of the effect of wit comedy.

* * * * *

Structure is the second point to consider in the aesthetics of wit comedy. The organization of the plays is very simple: the plot consists of an outwitting situation involving Truewits, Witwouds, and Witlesses. This is the basic *comic* situation, and by *comic* I mean principally the interaction of people on the stage which produces laughter in the audience. The elaboration of this situation takes some of these forms: the Truewit and his mistress outwit those who stand in their way (such as parents, guardians, and foolish rivals); they expose and ridicule those who are less witty than they (Witwoud and Witless); and they often try to outwit each other. A play may contain all of these outwitting situations. In *The Way of the World*, for example, Mirabell and Millamant outwit Lady Wishfort, Fainall, and Marwood, who stand in their way; they expose Witless and Witwoud in the persons of Petulant, Sir Wilfull Witwoud, and Witwoud; and at the same time, they carry on a wit contest between themselves.

In addition to the comic outwitting situation, there is considerable *wit play*—in fanciful similitudes, raillery scenes, and expressions of skeptical, sexual, and sophistical wit. This wit play is not always related to the comic situation and may exist for its own sake, but the exploitation of nondramatic wit provides considerable pleasure and is an important feature of wit comedy.

The sources of comic-witty pleasure in the plays, then, are principally two: (1) the outwitting situation (embracing plot and character), and (2) the nondramatic wit (*dianoia* and diction).[6] To this we might add *comic wit*, which is a synthesis of the two mentioned above: this occurs most often in courtship and "proviso" scenes, such as those between Dorimant and Harriet, or Mirabell and Millamant, when the couple thrust and parry with the weapon of wit in order to outwit each other. An understanding of these two elements in the structure of wit comedy involves, first, a consideration of the comic and the role of laughter, and second, a consideration of wit.

In wit comedy, when we laugh at those involved in a comic situation, we identify ourselves with the Truewit and glory

[6] The distinction between the comic situation and the wit-play is suggested by the author of the *Tractatus Coislinianus* when he notes that laughter arises from the diction and from things (in *An Aristotelian Theory of Comedy*, p. 224), and the distinction is observed also by Quintilian, who cites "words or deeds" as sources of laughter (*Institutio Oratoria*, VI, iii, tr. Butler, II, 441).

in his triumph over the inferior person (Witless, Witwoud, parents, and rivals). Such laughter is best explained by the "malicious" theory, particularly in the form in which Hobbes expounded it; for it was the most widely accepted among the writers of the period.[7] The classical definition of the comic is likewise the most relevant for wit comedy.

The comic, according to Aristotle, is to be found in some human defect, either physical or moral, which is not so extreme as to be painful. The *Tractatus Coislinianus* names the buffoon, the impostor, and the ironical man as the chief types in comedy, and these figures from classical comedy suggest, though they do not actually correspond to, Witless, Witwoud, and Truewit.[8] Witless and Witwoud are ridiculous because of a defect, intellectual, social, and aesthetic; and in laughing at them, we feel a sense of superiority, or what Hobbes described more picturesquely as a sense of "sudden glory." There is little didactic value to such laughter, since we are seldom persuaded to see our own defects; and James Sully is quite right in his observation that when we laugh at moral deformities, it is not because we see them as *moral* defects: the comic situation itself excites our risibility, and we derive pleasure from the triumph of the superior person over the inferior, whether it be in the moral, physical, or intellectual realm.[9]

The nonutilitarian and malicious character of the laughter in wit comedy is especially clear from the ridicule of the fool.

[7] Cf. Dryden, "Essay of Dramatick Poesy," *Works*, xv, 351; *A Comparison between the Two Stages*, p. 32; Charleton, *Natural History of the Passions*, pp. 146-147; Addison, *Spectator* #47.

[8] Cooper, *An Aristotelian Theory of Comedy*, p. 262. The buffoon comes closest to the Restoration comic type, in suggesting Witless (cf. the buffoon, *The Characters of Theophrastus*, tr. and ed., J. M. Edmonds, London and New York, 1929, pp. 69-71). In classical comedy, the impostor is the braggart (cf. the pretender, *The Characters of Theophrastus*, pp. 99-103). There is little resemblance between the ironical man (*Eiron*) and Truewit, except in the fact that both employ irony; for the *Eiron* is a ridiculous figure, whereas the Truewit is not.

[9] James Sully, *An Essay on Laughter*, London, 1907, p. 92.

The Aesthetics of Wit Comedy

The Truewits in the plays confess as much, and in *The Man of Mode*, Lady Townley is quite explicit on this point:

L. TOWN: 'Tis good to have an universal taste; we should love Wit, but for Variety be able to divert our selves with the Extravagancies of those who want it.

MEDLEY: Fools will make you laugh.

EMILIA: For once or twice! but the repetition of their Folly after a visit or two grows tedious and unsufferable.

L. TOWN: You are a little too delicate, *Emilia*.

(*Enter a Page.*)

PAGE: Sir *Fopling Flutter*, Madam, desires to know if you are to be seen.

L. TOWN: Here's the freshest Fool in Town, and one who has not cloy'd you yet. Page!

PAGE: Madam!

L. TOWN: Desire him to walk up.

DORIMANT: Do not you fall on him, *Medley*, and snub him. Sooth him up in his extravagance! he will shew the better.

MEDLEY: You know I have a natural indulgence for Fools and need not this caution, Sir! (III, ii)

So the incorrigible Sir Fopling Flutter walks into the trap, to be exposed to the malicious laughter of the Truewits—and of the audience. In *The Country Wife*, Horner voices the sentiments of his fellow Wits toward fools when he says, "In short, I converse with 'em, as you do with rich fools, to laugh at 'em and use 'em ill" (III, ii); and Mrs. Joyner, in *Love in a Wood*, observes that "every wit has his cully"—to serve as a foil (I, i). Addison agreed with Hobbes, in the *Spectator* #47, that men laughed out of a sense of superiority, and consequently found fools a satisfying object of ridicule.

The fool is ludicrous because of a defect, usually that of ignorance. In the *Philebus*, Plato suggested that the ridiculous arises from ignorance—from "the vain conceit of beauty, of wisdom, and of wealth."[10] Of these three forms of conceit, the most common in wit comedy are "conceit of beauty," as

[10] Plato, *Philebus*, 48-50, in *Dialogues*, tr. B. Jowett, Boston and New York, 1871, III, 187-188.

The Aesthetics of Wit Comedy

in Sir Fopling and Monsieur Paris, and the "conceit of wisdom," as in Witwoud and Dapperwit. This defect of ignorance characterizes the five orders of fools enumerated by the
Marquess of Halifax: blockhead, coxcomb, vain blockhead,
grave coxcomb, and the half-witted fellow.[11] These types are
not mutually exclusive, of course, and in wit comedy the
basic distinction is between Witless (the stupid blockhead or
boor) and Witwoud (the pretender to wit). Coxcomb is a
generic term applicable to any silly, conceited person; and the
fop is a fool who manifests his ignorance by excessive addiction to senseless fashions. Our laughter at such fools is malicious, but at the same time, it preserves its aesthetic character
insofar as we are not practically concerned with them.

The second element in the structure is the wit-play, as distinguished from the comic situation. Wit differs from the
comic in two ways: objectively, in the content; and subjec-
tively, in the effect. Wit has to do with ideas and words rather
than with people and action. Further, it titillates the mind
without arousing real laughter, and often it leads us by a
short cut to a destination which we had not expected at all.
As an explanation of wit, the incongruity theory of Kant and
Schopenhauer is probably the most pertinent, though it was
not a widely accepted theory in the seventeenth century. But
in the conception of wit as fancy, and especially in the stress
on brevity, quickness, novelty, and surprise, writers like
Hobbes, Addison, and Dryden do show a familiarity with the
point of view represented by Kant's description of the peculiar
psychological impact of wit. This element I have discussed
more extensively in chapter two.

Finally, in comic wit, we have a fusion of the comic (involving character and action) and the witty (involving words and
ideas). Wit becomes "an attitude or manner of behaviour,"[12]

---

[11] Halifax, "Moral Thoughts and Reflections," *The Complete Works*,
p. 234.
[12] Sully, *An Essay on Laughter*, pp. 354-355.

as the Truewits utilize the whole arsenal of wit to outwit others and to cope effectively with the world about them. Comic wit results from the collision of a witty mind with people and circumstances which it can treat playfully. It is not merely the result of a critical and dispassionate observation of life, since wit, in this sense, implies the ability, not only to perceive the incongruities of human action and thought, but to be master of them in a playful manner. Hence the Wit is usually an ironic person who treats life with a mixture of "levity and seriousness."

As the central figure in wit comedy, the Truewit is the master of the comic situation, the artist of verbal wit, and the source of comic wit. His witty temper is grounded in skepticism, and he is usually a man critical of dogmatism or "enthusiasm." He is against the idealist who considers man divine, and consequently he lays himself open to the charge of cynicism. However, he is equally the enemy of the practical man whose only ideal is prudence and worldly success; and thus, as an enemy of the prudential view, he is charged with frivolity. Likewise, the Wit is opposed to the moralist who condemns pleasure, and consequently he exposes himself to the charge of immorality. The Wit suffers, then, from accusations of cynicism, frivolity, and immorality. The essential character of the Wit, however, is his freedom, for he refuses to be committed to a dogmatic position, and he believes in the free exercise of the human intelligence.

In this spirit, the Wits of the Restoration attacked what they considered dogmatic and false: they criticized what they thought the pretenses of religion and morality, and they warred against what they believed to be hypocritical and unnatural. The motive for such witty attacks was sincere: it was a desire for truth and honesty. The Wit who indulged in skeptical, cynical, and sexual wit did so from a feeling that the moral and religious conventions observed by the majority of men were artificial (and unnatural), and that in refusing

The Aesthetics of Wit Comedy

to recognize the sexual, malicious, and selfish nature of man, society was hypocritical. The Wits believed in being true to nature, and they poked witty fun at artificiality wherever they found it, whether in religious and moral observances or in social conventions. It is indeed ironic that these enemies of artificiality should today be considered the authors of an artificial comedy and the proponents of an artificial code of manners.

As to whether such witty criticism is dangerous, there is no real argument. Wit is playful in its criticism, and since it is more concerned with mockery than persuasion, it can affect only those who are already predisposed to such criticism. The enemies of wit were answered pretty effectively, I think, by the Earl of Shaftesbury. Wit, he declared, is an enemy of "enthusiasm" and dogmatism;[13] it is a critical weapon in the service of reason;[14] and it is a means of freeing the human mind of error and pretension.[15] He was also of the opinion that there is less to be feared from the Wits than from the bigots, who would smother truth.[16] And, indeed, the greatest enemies of truth are the dogmatists and fanatics, who are so convinced that they possess the truth that they will suppress all beliefs but their own. But truth is a woman with a thousand beautiful faces, and wit, with its skepticism, keeps us from being seduced by one fair face.

The point brought up by John Harrington Smith has been answered, I think.[17] On the ethical side, the standard in wit comedy is naturalistic; and the sexuality and malice of the characters are not offensive if we remember that the witty authors tried to present people as true to life, in accordance with their bias. At the same time, we have no reason to reject their constant criticism of pretension, artificiality, hypocrisy,

[13] Shaftesbury, "A Letter concerning Enthusiasm" (1708), in *Characteristicks*, I, 18.
[14] Shaftesbury, "Advice to an Author" (1710), *Characteristicks*, II, 260.
[15] Shaftesbury, "Sensus Communis," *Characteristicks*, I, 60.
[16] *Ibid.*, pp. 96-97.   [17] See above, p. 59.

The Aesthetics of Wit Comedy

vanity, avarice, exaggeration, boorishness, and folly, nor the implicit praise of naturalness, reason, moderation, sincerity, and truth. Furthermore, the naturalistic depiction of the Truewits is rendered palatable for most readers, I think, by the beauty of the language and the standard of decorum which governs their speech and conduct. Above all, wit comedy introduces us to a harmonious, graceful, and free world where the playful judgment can be exercised, and it provides a satisfying experience, at once vivid, complete, and pleasurable. There can be no question, therefore, of the sanity and value of wit comedy; and this can be demonstrated by examining in some detail the works of Etherege, Wycherley, and Congreve.

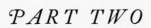

PART TWO

V

SIR GEORGE ETHEREGE

Sɪʀ Gᴇᴏʀɢᴇ Eᴛʜᴇʀᴇɢᴇ is generally credited with having
originated a new type of comedy, and this belief need not be
challenged, though there is reason to question modern opinion
as to the type of comedy he inaugurated. To determine the
nature of his contribution, however, we should first find out
what sort of man he was. And here we are fortunate in having
the *Letterbook*, the epistolary record of his last years at
Ratisbon. From these letters, both personal and official, and
also from contemporary records, there emerges a clear picture
of Etherege as a Truewit—libertine, skeptical, naturalistic,
and more concerned with wit than with morality or "manners."

Unfortunately, Etherege has suffered the same misinter-
pretation as have his comedies, and at present his true features
are obscured by the descriptions of the censorious and of the
"manners" critics. On the one hand, he is called "the most
irresponsible rake of all," "an atrocious libertine" who could
be fierce and vindictive under passion, and a man whose life
is "a sordid story."[1] On the other hand, he is described by
the "manners" critics as " a brilliant butterfly, alighting only
upon such things as attract him; a creature without much
depth, but of an extraordinary charm and a marvellous surety
of touch."[2] He is called "a delicate painter who loved subtle
contrasts in 'rose-colour and pale grey' ";[3] and he is said to
have encountered gracefully the one problem of his genera-

---

[1] Elwin, *The Playgoer's Handbook to Restoration Drama*, pp. 12-13;
Dr. Doran, *"Their Majesties' Servants": Annals of the English Stage, from
Thomas Betterton to Edmund Kean*, New York, 1865, I, 140; Felix E.
Schelling, *English Drama*, London and New York, 1914, p. 259.
[2] Dobrée, *Restoration Comedy*, p. 58.   [3] *Ibid.*, p. 76.

tion, that of style, "whether it was fighting the Dutch, defeating the policy of Achitophel, tying a riband, or writing a play."[4] The world of his plays is described as a frivolous one, where Strephon bends on one knee to Chloe fanning the pink blush on her painted cheek, while Momus peeps out at them—"an engaging trio, *mais ce n'est pas de la vie humaine.*"[5]

Of these two schools, the moralistic critics have at least a more colorful conception of Etherege than his apologists, who emasculate both the man and his art. But neither gives a credible nor faithful picture of the witty dramatist who created such intelligent and convincing people as Harriet and Dorimant. What is needed is an examination of Etherege's ideas and personality to determine to what extent he was affected by the currents of naturalism, skepticism, and libertinism, and how his comedies are an aesthetic expression of the Truewit's attitude toward life. Once we have a clear picture of Etherege as a human being, and of the connection between the man and his art, we shall not dismiss him casually as a brilliant butterfly or a mere rake, nor regard his plays as creating only the illusion of life.

The accounts of his contemporaries do not harmonize with either of the descriptions given above of Etherege. By Oldys he was called "a celebrated Wit," and he was praised by Langbaine as "a Gentleman sufficiently eminent in the Town for his Wit and Parts, and One whose tallent in sound Sence, and the Knowledge of Wit and Humour, are sufficiently conspicuous."[6] The Earl of Rochester, in "A Trial of the Poets for the Bays," credited Etherege with "fancy, sense, judgment and wit"—virtues which are not all suggested in the "manners" description. The charming, yet rather malicious, character of

---

[4] Palmer, *Comedy of Manners*, p. 91.

[5] Edmund Gosse, "Sir George Etheredge," in *Seventeenth Century Studies*, New York, 1897, p. 283.

[6] John Oldys, "Sir George Etherege," in *Biographia Britannica*, London, 1747-1766, III, 1841. Gerard Langbaine, *An Account of the English Dramatick Poets*, Oxford, 1691, p. 186.

his wit is evident from his comedies (particularly in such passages as the raillery between Dorimant and Harriet), the rallying letter to Buckingham, and some "smart lampoons" on Nell Gwynn with which Theophilus Cibber credited him.[7] In his writings there was a grace, delicacy, and courtly air that made them attractive;[8] and this, with his affable and courteous deportment, and his sprightly and generous temper, gained him the character of "Gentle" George and "Easy" Etherege.[9] By virtue of these qualities, he gained ready access to the best company, and soon became a popular companion of aristocratic Wits like Buckingham, Rochester, Sir Car Scroope, Sedley, and Henry Savile.[10] They constituted an intimate circle with similar tastes: they were all men of wit and pleasure, all naturalistic, libertine, and skeptical; they were occasionally amateur men of letters, now and then diplomats, and sometimes rakes, but always Truewits. With them Etherege had his share of writing, diplomacy, and dissipation. He wrote three plays and some verse, served as secretary to the English ambassador at Constantinople, created some scandal, and in late life found himself the King's envoy at Ratisbon.

There is not much need to linger over the more scandalous events of his life, such as his part, with Rochester, in the notorious Downes affair in which Downes was killed,[11] his squabble with Buckley,[12] his championing of the actress Julia which upset the staid citizens of Ratisbon,[13] or his keeping a

---

[7] Theophilus Cibber, *The Lives of the Poets of Great Britain and Ireland to the Time of Dean Swift*, London, 1753, III, 37-38.

[8] Dennis, *Original Letters, Familiar, Moral and Critical*, London, 1721, p. 52.

[9] Oldys, "Sir George Etherege," *Biographica Britannica*, III, 1844.

[10] *Ibid.*, III, 1841. Cf. also, Cibber, *The Lives of the Poets*, III, 33; Charles Gildon, *The Lives and Characters of the English Dramatick Poets*, London, 1699, p. 53.

[11] *Correspondence of the Family of Hatton*, 1878, ed. Edward M. Thompson, I, 133-134.

[12] *The Rochester-Savile Letters, 1671-1680*, ed. John Harold Wilson, Columbus, Ohio, 1941, p. 52.

[13] Etherege, *The Letterbook*, ed. Rosenfeld, pp. 388-389.

wench and getting diseased.[14] He was, as Cibber said, as great
a libertine "in speculation as in practice."[15] Such libertinism
was the product of an unsettled age, when the Civil Wars
created political and social chaos, and the "new philosophy"
induced skepticism among thinking men. Etherege belonged
to a younger generation, described by Clarendon as having
no respect for authority or religion, which had seen conventional notions discarded and family relations destroyed.[16] He
passed through an unsettled youth in unsettled times, and
though of gentle birth, he seems to have had little or no university training, and went early into France to escape the Civil
Wars in England.[17]

The libertinism of Etherege consisted of a witty, naturalistic attitude born of such conditions, rather than of settled
principles arrived at through speculation. There is a poem
by him entitled "The Libertine" which sums up the easy
carpe diem philosophy by which he lived:

> Since death on all lays his impartial hand,
> And all resign at his command,
> The Stoic too, as well as I,
> With all his gravity must die:
> Let's wisely manage the last span,
> The momentary life of man,
> And still in pleasure's circle move,
> Giving t'our friends the days, and all our nights to love.

> CHORUS
> Thus, thus, whilst we are here, let's perfectly live,
> And taste all the pleasures that nature can give;
> And fill all our veins with a noble desire.

In this and the remaining stanzas, there is a touch of disillusionment and cynicism, a sense of the brevity and vanity of
this "momentary life of man"; but this is buoyed up by the
witty irreverence for conventional notions, and a zestful relish

[14] *Ibid.*, pp. 383-384.   [15] Cibber, *The Lives of the Poets*, III, 37.
[16] Clarendon, *Life*, II, 39-49.   [17] Cibber, *op. cit.*, III, 33.

for "all the pleasures that nature can give," such as friendship, gaming, wine, women, and wit.

His easy libertinism and his naturalistic bias are expressed also in his letters from Ratisbon. Like his friend the Earl of Rochester, Etherege pursued the pleasures of "wine and women,"[18] and he found himself "often very hearty" with a "plain Bavarian,"[19] though he complained that the handsome young ladies were difficult because "their unconscionable price is marriage."[20] To a man who had been "bred in a free nation / With liberty of speech and passion,"[21] it must have been extremely painful to curtail the natural indulgence of sexual passion, which he believed good and necessary. " 'Tis a fine thing," he exclaimed, "for a Man, who has been nourish'd so many Years with good substantial Flesh and Blood, to be reduc'd to Sighs and Wishes, and all those airy Courses which are serv'd up to feast a belle Passion."[22] But at least there was the divertissement of "le traîneau où l'on se met en croupe de quelque belle Allemande,"[23] and for a time there was also Julia, "a comedian no less handsome and no less kind in Dutchland than Mrs. Johnson was in England."[24] At times, after over-indulgence, he confessed himself more epicurean than libertine: "tout d'un coup je suis devenu disciple d'Épicure, je me tien, dans ma petite retraite, et je me suis établi pour maxime que la plus grand volupté consiste dans une parfaite santé."[25]

His philosophy was a worldly and sensible one arrived at through experience and observation, and he was never overly interested in anything transcendental or theoretical. Speaking of his epicureanism, he declared: "je n'ai pas le loisir de m'étendre sur un si digne sujet; pour ces atomes ils ne me rompent guère la tête." Metaphysics and the atoms of Democritus were beyond his scope: "Par la grâce de Dieu je sais

[18] *Letterbook*, p. 304. [19] *Ibid.*, p. 190. [20] *Ibid.*, p. 304.
[21] *Ibid.*, pp. 62-63. [22] *Ibid.*, p. 422. [23] *Ibid.*, p. 55.
[24] *Ibid.*, p. 328. [25] *Ibid.*, p. 264.

Sir George Etherege

où mon esprit est borné et je ne me mets guère en peine de savoir de quelle manière ce monde ici a été fait ou comment on se divert dans l'autre."[26] Like the skeptical St. Evremond, Etherege regarded such metaphysical speculations as futile and sterile.

His skeptical and naturalistic temper is evident also in his references to religion. In such matters he confessed, " 'tis indifferent to me whether there be any other in the world who thinks as I do; this makes me have no temptation to talk of the business."[27] As the boon companion of free-thinkers like Sedley and Rochester, Etherege probably had a commonsensical, and perhaps deistic, attitude toward religion, and he no doubt accepted the hereafter as another of the possible hazards of existence. In a letter to a friend he said that the only quarrel that Mme. de Crecy had with them was that they were "heretics,"[28] and Hughes reported the Count to have said of Etherege, "Ce que je trouve de plus pire en lui que toutes ses débauches est, qu'il est profane et voudrait persuader tout le monde d'être de son sentiment."[29] There is no proof that Etherege was atheistic, but he was at least anticlerical and as Erastian as Hobbes, for he wrote of the clergy: "The mischief they daily do in the world makes me have no better an opinion of them than Lucian had of the ancient philosophers; their pride, their passion, and their covetousness makes them endeavour to destroy the government they were instituted to support, and, instead of taking care of the quietness of our souls, they are industrious to make us cut one another's throats."[30]

As a Truewit he accepted the vicissitudes of this life with equanimity, and without too much anxiety about the future. Of his attitude toward life he wrote:

> Humble to fortune, not her slave,
> I still was pleas'd with what she gave;

[26] *Ibid.* [27] *Ibid.*, p. 305. [28] *Ibid.*, p. 310.
[29] *Ibid.*, pp. 386-387. [30] *Ibid.*, p. 337.

Sir George Etherege

And, with a firm, and cheerful mind,
I steer my course with every wind,
To all the ports she has design'd.[31]

He accepted life as it is, without complaint, because he had experienced enough of it to know what its limitations are. After all, this life is brief, and there is the disillusionment of knowing that "our Gayety and Vigour leaves us so soon in the lurch, . . . Feebleness attacks us without giving us fair Warning, and we no sooner pass the Meridian of Life but begin to decline."[32] He was not dazzled by the sham prizes of this world; and when James Fitzjames, the king's natural son, received a dukedom, Etherege wrote him that such honors are of no intrinsic value—"nevertheless the glittering favours of fortune are necessary to entertain those who, without examining any deeper, worship appearances."[33] This is the wisdom of a Truewit who has seen enough of the world to know that titles are baubles, of no intrinsic value to men of sense, yet useful in impressing the foolish, with whom the world abounds. When Etherege was praised too highly by Lord Dover, he wrote back: "The life I have led has afforded me little time to turn over books, but I have had leisure sufficient while I idly rolled about the town to look into myself and know when I am too highly valued."[34] He was not swayed by popular opinion or rumor, and upon hearing that Prince Herman of Baden, who was coming to Ratisbon, was an intolerably proud person, Etherege wrote to his superior in London, "I know the injury report generally does to mankind and therefore will not give you his character by hearsay, but stay till I have seen him and know him a little myself."[35] He showed manliness and generosity, if not prudence, in defending the actress Julia against the irate citizens of Ratisbon,[36] and he remained loyal to King James to the end of his life.

This is hardly the superficial "butterfly" depicted by the

[31] *Ibid.*, p. 63.
[32] *Ibid.*, p. 415.
[33] *Ibid.*, p. 187.
[34] *Ibid.*, pp. 301-302.
[35] *Ibid.*, p. 284.
[36] *Ibid.*, p. 119.

"manners" critics. Though never profound in his thinking, Etherege had the sensible worldliness of an Augustan like Horace. He was not overly interested in speculative matters like religion and philosophy, and he lived for this world in an epicurean spirit, in accordance with his naturalistic bias; but he was tolerant of others' beliefs, affectionate toward his friends, and capable of loyalty. He accepted this life, according to his judgment, without illusions, and he lived it as sensibly and pleasantly as a Truewit could, suffering neither envy at the fortunes of others nor regret for his libertine existence.

Toward women he had the naturalistic bias of most Truewits: he regarded them as affected, hypocritical, vain, and dissembling creatures, useful principally for venereal pleasures. From Constantinople, during his secretaryship there, he wrote of the Sultana: "though women here are not so polite and refin'd as in Christendome, yet shee wants not her little arts to secure her Sultan's affections, shee can dissemble fondness and jealousy and can swoone at pleasure."[37] He probably agreed with Dryden when the latter wrote to him from London, "Ask me not of love, for every man hates every man perfectly and women are still the same bitches."[38] To Buckingham he wrote a witty account of how a grief-stricken widow, a "Pattern of Conjugal Fidelity," had eloped with a young ensign, after being persuaded that immoderate sorrow would be ruinous to her beauty, and had thus proved herself a modern example of the Widow of Ephesus.[39] Toward matrimony he could scarcely be charitable in view of his own unhappy marriage to a widow, gently described by an anonymous writer as "a Bitch, / A Wizard, wrincled Woman, & a Witch."[40] In a poem "To a lady, asking him how long he would love her," he declared that a man and woman should be constant to each other, freely and naturally, only so long

---

[37] *Ibid.*, p. 406.   [38] *Ibid.*, p. 357.   [39] *Ibid.*, pp. 417-421.
[40] Quoted by H. F. Brett-Smith, intro. to *The Dramatic Works of Sir George Etherege*, I, xxix.

as love endured between them; any such yoke as marriage was an unnatural imposition on human nature, and a commitment to love one another when love had ceased to exist.

Being a Truewit, he was opposed not only to marriage but to business; and as the King's envoy at Ratisbon he conducted himself more like a Wit than a diplomat, though he discharged his duties creditably. He was encouraged in this attitude by his superior and friend Lord Middleton, who wrote, "I hope in a little time we may hear something of your diversions as well as your business, which would be much pleasanter, and perhaps as instructive."[41] Following such advice, Etherege referred lightly to political matters, and to a friend he wrote, "The business of the Diet for the most part is only fit to entertain those insects in politics which crawl under the trees in St. James's Park."[42] Yet, to the Duke of Buckingham he confessed to a greater aptitude for business than he had suspected,[43] and his lucid reports of the political situation in the Empire and of its relations with France show his mastery of affairs. Though he challenged Dryden's title to the province of idleness,[44] he turned out a voluminous official correspondence, as well as many personal letters, three comedies, and some verse. One suspects that his "noble laziness of mind" was a pretense, especially when he described himself ironically as an idle fellow at the end of a lengthy official communication that runs to some three printed pages.[45] Etherege was closer to the truth when he said, "I am too lazy and too careless to be ambitious."[46]

At Ratisbon, he longed for cheer, company, and late hours —some such evening as Dryden described so happily in his dedication of a play to Sedley: "We have, like them our genial nights, where our discourse is neither too serious nor too light, but always pleasant, and, for the most part, instructive; the raillery, neither too sharp upon the present,

[41] *Letterbook*, p. 344.   [42] *Ibid.*, p. 210.   [43] *Ibid.*, p. 413.
[44] *Ibid.*, p. 167.   [45] *Ibid.*, p. 67.   [46] *Ibid.*, p. 139.

nor too censorious on the absent; and the cups only such as will raise the conversation of the night, without disturbing the business of the morrow."[47] But at Ratisbon, Etherege found that the men were so addicted to drinking that it destroyed the pleasures of conversation.[48] The ceremony of the place also made convivial gatherings rare; and often he was condemned "To make grave legs in formal fetters, / Converse with fops, and write dull letters."[49] Wittily Etherege exposed the absurd formality with which the Diet conducted even the trifling business of arranging to see a farce that had come to town,[50] and he exercised his wit in a malicious portrait of the Count de Windisgratz, the most pompous of them all.[51] He kept the wittiest and easiest company he could find—the French ambassador the Count de Crecy, described by Etherege as "a *bel esprit*"; the Count de Lamberg, a gentleman who knew how to live; and Monsieur Schnolsky, so much a Wit that no one could distinguish "between his jest and earnest."[52] He remembered with regret the bitter frosty night when he and Dorset carried "two draggle-tailed nymphs" over the Thames to Lambeth,[53] and in his letters he asked to be remembered to all his friends at the Rose and "the lily at the bar."[54] He was cheered to hear that his friend Sedley, who "had always more wit than was enough for one man," had produced a successful play in *Bellamira*.[55] Himself he compared to Ovid at Pontus,[56] and epigrammatically he dismissed the bourgeois society in which he was stranded: "London is dull by accident but Ratisbon by nature."[57] The person mirrored in these letters is, indeed, a Truewit—genial, witty, skeptical, worldly, and easy.

As a writer, Etherege displayed the same careless, playful attitude, and of his literary success he wrote to Dryden:

---

[47] Dryden, Dedication of *The Assignation, or Love in a Nunnery*, in *Works*, IV, 351.

[48] *Letterbook*, p. 414. [49] *Ibid.*, p. 62. [50] *Ibid.*, p. 117.

[51] *Ibid.*, pp. 103-104. [52] *Ibid.*, p. 290, p. 142, p. 309. [53] *Ibid.*, p. 240.

[54] *Ibid.*, p. 325. [55] *Ibid.*, p. 227, p. 212. [56] *Ibid.*, p. 293.

[57] *Ibid.*, p. 278.

Sir George Etherege

"Though I have not been able formerly to forbear playing the fool in verse and prose I have now judgment enough to know how much I ventured, and am rather amazed at my good fortune than vain upon a little success; and did I not see my own error the commendation you give me would be enough to persuade me of it. A woman, who has luckily been thought agreeable, has not reason to be proud when she hears herself extravagantly praised by an undoubted beauty. It would be a pretty thing for a man who has learned of his own head to scrape on the fiddle to enter the list with the greatest master in the science of music."[58] Yet, Etherege was the man of whom Dryden said in 1687, "I will never enter the lists in prose with the undoubted best author of it which our nation has produced."[59] That this high praise is merited is evident if we compare the rather heavy and labored wit of Dryden's letter with the sprightly ease and wit of Etherege's reply.[60] There was ease and carelessness in Etherege's attitude toward writing, but he was by no means an artless writer. In his library at Ratisbon he had copies of *Critiques sur Horace* (5 volumes), Rymer's *Tragedies of the Last Age*, and *Reflections on Aristotle's Treaty of Poesy*;[61] and as a Truewit, Etherege was also committed to the principle of decorum (wit), which called for naturalness, an easy elegance, and propriety. What he objected to was the labored writing that savored of the pedant or the professional writer, as one may gather from his censure of the Count de Crecy for meticulously polishing and repolishing the expressions in his memorial.[62]

As a writer Etherege seems to have been interested in wit in all its manifestations. In the prologue he wrote for Dryden's *Sir Martin Mar-all*, he lamented the fact that the age was no

---

[58] *Ibid.*, p. 168.   [59] *Ibid.*, p. 355.
[60] Dryden to Etherege, February 16, 1687; Etherege to Dryden, March 10/20, 1686/7. Letters 13 and 14, in *The Letters of John Dryden*, ed. Charles E. Ward, Durham, 1942.
[61] *Letterbook*, pp. 376-378.   [62] *Ibid.*, p. 289.

longer content with wit, but wanted gaudy sights. From Ratisbon, he requested a copy of Shadwell's *Squire of Alsatia* that he might know what fools were prevalent.[63] In his own comedies, what contemporaries praised was the witty, naturalistic depiction of coxcombs and Truewits, and Dryden wrote in "MacFlecknoe":

> Let gentle George in triumph tread the stage,
> Make Dorimant betray, and Loveit rage;
> Let Cully, Cockwood, Fopling, charm the pit,
> And in their folly show the writer's wit.

Oldys, in fact, attributed Etherege's success as a dramatist to his witty dialogue and to his naturalistic representation of Truewits: "These applauses arose from our Author's changing the study after old copies, and chimerical draughts from ungrounded speculation, which is but painting with dead colours, for those, taken directly from the freshest practise and experience in original life. . . . He has also spirited his dialogues, especially in the courtship of the fair sex, for which he is distinguished by Mr. Dryden and others, with a sparkling gaiety which had but little appeared before upon the stage, in parts pretending to the character of modish Gallants; and to judge his figures according to the rules of true resemblance, he will appear a masterly hand; but strictly to examine them, by the rules of honour, morality, and the principles of virtue, where none are seriously professed . . . would be a severity."[64]

This is as clear a statement as one can find anywhere of what constitutes the salient features of Etherege's comic writing: witty dialogue, especially between the gallant and his mistress in raillery and "proviso" scenes, a naturalistic view of man (and a consequent disregard of conventional morality), and realistic technique. These are the points in which Etherege excelled as a writer, though not every critic

[63] *Ibid.*, p. 338.
[64] Oldys, "Sir George Etherege," *Biographia Britannica*, III, 1842.

approved, as one gathers from Captain Alexander Radcliffe's censure of Etherege for being too photographic in his realism, "So what he writes is but Translation / From Dog and Partridge conversation."[65] What we should look for in Etherege's comedies, then, is not interest in "manners," but such features of wit comedy as witty dialogue, naturalistic content, and realistic technique. We should also expect malicious laughter at fools, and the expression of a skeptical and libertine philosophy in witty form.

His first comedy, *The Comical Revenge, or Love in a Tub* (1664),[66] has most of these elements, though in rather rudimentary form. Evelyn described the play as "a facetious comedy," and Pepys observed that it was "very merry, but only so by gesture, not wit at all, which methinks is beneath the House."[67] Both Langbaine and Downes record that the play was a success,[68] and we have Oldys' statement that "the fame of this play," dedicated to the witty Lord Buckhurst, helped Etherege gain the friendship of the aristocratic Wits.[69]

But despite its warm reception, the play reveals an ambiguity of purpose on Etherege's part, and a consequent lack of unity; and at best, it represents only a groping toward what later became the comedy of wit. In the prologue, Etherege lamented the fact that political bias, and not wit, determined the merit of a play. Yet one cannot say that he succeeded in writing a witty play, nor in wholly excluding political bias. The title of the play suggests an outwitting situation; and the three comic plots are indeed of this nature: Wheadle and Palmer setting plots against Sir Nicholas Cully,

[65] Radcliffe, "News from Hell," in Dryden, *Miscellany Poems*, London, 1716, II, 101.

[66] The edition used for this and subsequent plays is *The Dramatic Works of Sir George Etherege*, ed. H. F. Brett-Smith, 2 vols., Oxford, 1927.

[67] Evelyn, *Diary*, April 27, 1664; Pepys, *Diary*, January 4, 1664/5.

[68] Langbaine, *An Account of the English Dramatick Poets*, p. 187. Rev. John Downes, *Roscius Anglicanus, or, an Historical Review of the Stage*, London, 1789, p. 35.

[69] Oldys, *op. cit.*, III, 1841.

only to be outwitted themselves by the Truewit; Betty exposing Dufoy; and Sir Frederick and the Widow trying to outwit each other in a series of "comical revenges." But in these situations, the comical element is more in evidence than the witty; and the opening scenes could hardly have impressed the audience. In the first scene, Dufoy, with a plaster on his head, is complaining that his master Sir Frederick has broken his head:

DUFOY: dis Bedlamé, Mad-cape, diable de matré, vas drunké
de last night, and vor no reason, but dat me did advisé him to
go to bed, begar he did striké, breaké my headé, Jernie.
CLARK: Have patience, he did it unadvisedly.
DUFOY: Unadvisé! didé not me advise him justé when he did
ité? (I, i)

When Sir Frederick appears, the wit is not much better. Upon Dufoy's showing his plastered head, Sir Frederick remarks lamely, "Thou hast a notable brain" (I, ii).

The embryonic character of this first comedy of wit by Etherege is most apparent from an examination of the Truewits in the play. Sir Frederick, who dominates the outwitting situations, is such a man as is described in *The Character of a Town-Gallant*—a drinker of wine, an assailer of the watch, and a breaker of windows.[70] His wildness reminds us of the author's own frolics. The night prior to the first scene, Sir Frederick has been out drinking, crying "whore" at the door of a kept mistress, and he has come home drunk and broken Dufoy's head. There are coachmen, link-boys, and fiddlers to be paid after the night's debauch. There is a rather sophomoric quality about his escapades; and by the standards of Dorimant or Mirabell, Sir Frederick could hardly qualify as a Truewit. Noise, bustle, the breaking of windows, and the beating of the watch gradually came to be regarded as signs of false wit; and in later wit comedies, these came to be the marks of Witwoud rather than of the Wit. Sir Frederick

---

[70] *The Character of a Town-Gallant*, p. 6.

conforms to a rather callow conception of the Truewit, though Etherege distinguished between his gallant wildness and the stupid, witless wildness of Sir Nicholas (iv, iii).

Though he is a poor specimen of a Truewit by comparison with Dorimant, Sir Frederick satisfies the Widow's taste for "the prettiest, wittiest, wildest Gentleman about the Town." He has traveled abroad in France; he has the easy courage of a Truewit who does not take life, death, or love too seriously; and he can bear with "the inconveniences of honest Company," if there is freedom of conversation. He speaks lightly of virtue, and is inclined to be cynical about women and matrimony. He believes that "Women, like Juglers-Tricks, appear Miracles to the ignorant; but in themselves th' are meer cheats" (i, ii); and when he disposes of his kept mistress Lucy to Sir Nicholas, he tells the cully: "And, give her her due, faith she was a very honest Wench to me, and I believe will make a very honest Wife to you" (v, v). As a Truewit he also shares the naturalistic belief that love is only lust, and when informed by Beaufort that the Widow loves him, he exclaims, "What? the Widow has some kind thoughts of my body?" (i, ii). He has honesty enough to save Sir Nicholas from being cheated by Wheadle, but he has malice enough to marry off Sir Nicholas to his own kept mistress, and to couple Wheadle with Grace, and Palmer with Grace's maid.

There is no doubt that Sir Frederick possesses vivacity, some degree of perspicacity, and malice—all marks of the Truewit. But he hardly conforms to the standard of decorum, nor displays much novelty or fineness of fancy. In fact, he can even be gross in his *double-entendre*, as on the occasion of his disturbing the Widow's household late at night:

MAID: Sir *Frederick*, I wonder you will offer this; you will lose her favour for ever.
SIR FRED: Y'are mistaken; now's the time to creep into her favour.

MAID: I'm sure y'ave wak'd me out of the sweetest sleep. Hey
  ho—
SIR FRED: Poor girl! let me in, I'le rock thee into a sweeter.
  (III, ii)

In his solitary efforts he is seldom striking, and for the Widow
he has this rather jejune similitude: "Some Women, like
Fishes, despise the Bait, or else suspect it, whil'st still it's
bobbing at their mouths; but subtilly wav'd by the Angler's
hand, greedily hang themselves upon the hook" (I, ii).[71]
Again, the double hyperbole of his remark on Jenny the maid
lacks novelty: "Sh'as made more noise than half a dozen
Paper-mills: *London*-bridge at a low water is silence to her"
(I, ii). Even the most frequently quoted of his witticisms
comes off poorly when read in its context:

MAID: Unhand me; are you a man fit to be trusted with a
  woman's reputation?
SIR FRED: Not when I am in a reeling condition; men are now
  and then subject to those infirmities in drink, which women
  have when th' are sober. Drunkenness is no good Secretary,
  Jenny; you must not look so angry, good faith, you must not.
  (I, ii)

The author spoils the wit by not knowing when to stop; and
Sir Frederick, after a witty stroke at women, tumbles into a
feeble apology to a maid. Sir Frederick's wit splutters now and
then, but is never sustained.

The liveliest wit is to be expected in the courtship scenes,
but here again, we usually find tricks rather than comic wit.
Part of this defect is due to the fact that the heroine suffers
under the handicap of being a widow. Sir Frederick assumes
that her marital experiences have only sharpened her sexual
appetite, and the Widow Rich conforms to his expectations by

[71] Cf. Etherege's use of the same figure in Act I, sc. iii, where Wheadle
is speaking of Sir Nicholas Cully: "How eagerly did this half-witted fellow
chap up the bait? Like a ravenous Fish, that will not give the Angler leave
to sink his Line, but greedily darts up and meets it half way." This reveals
a somewhat indiscriminate distribution of wit among the characters in the
play.

betraying more eagerness than a witty woman should. She is obviously in love with him from the beginning; and when he pretends to be dead, in order to trick a confession of love from her, she weeps with genuine grief and exclaims in blank verse: "Unhappy woman! why shou'd I survive / The only man in whom my joys did live? / My dreadful grief!" (iv, vii). Though she laughs at Sir Frederick a moment later to prove she saw through his trick, her show of emotion is too genuine to be laughed away so easily. She is too warm and generous for a Truewit: she feels sorry for Dufoy and orders him released from the tub, and she also sends money to free Sir Frederick when she hears he has been arrested for his debts. In these episodes she shows a lack of perspicacity which makes her the dupe of others. It is evident that the Widow lacks the perspicacity and the malice of a Truewit, so that she is no ready match for Sir Frederick. Because of this initial disadvantage under which the Widow labors, there can be no real wit combat between her and Sir Frederick such as we find in later comedies by Etherege. Furthermore, the combats between the two very often degenerate into tricks ("comical revenges"), such as Sir Frederick's having himself borne in on a bier or his sending word that he has been arrested. It is then up to the Widow to penetrate his trick, and thus expose him.

It is in these encounters, however, that we have the best repartee in the play. There is not a great deal of wit in these exchanges, but they do show some spirit. On their first meeting the two are wary of each other but amiable, and they rally one another sharply, though with more humor than wit:

> SIR FRED: Widow, I dare not venture my self in those amorous shades; you have a mind to be talking of Love I perceive, and my heart's too tender to be trusted with such conversation.
>
> WID: I did not imagine you were so foolishly conceited; is it your Wit or your Person, Sir, that is so taking?
>
> SIR FRED: Truly you are much mistaken, I have no such great

thoughts of the young man you see; who ever knew a Woman have so much reason to build her Love upon merit? Have we not daily experience of great Fortunes, that fling themselves into the arms of vain idle Fellows? Can you blame me then for standing upon my guard? (II, i)

Sir Frederick and the Widow are too good-natured for sharp raillery, and his disparagement of himself at the same time that he rallies the Widow shows a man of humor as much as a man of wit. On another occasion, when he pounds her door at night to prove his wit, we have this characteristic passage of repartee:

> SIR FRED: Can you in conscience turn a young man out of doors at this time o'th' night, Widow? Fie, fie, the very thought on't will keep you waking.
> WID: So pretty, so well-favour'd a young man; one that loves me.
> SIR FRED: Ay, one that loves you.
> WID: Truly 'tis a very hard-hearted thing. (She sighs.)
> SIR FRED: Come, come, be mollifi'd. You may go, Gentlemen, and leave me here; you may go. (To the Masquers.)
> WID: You may stay, Gentlemen; you may stay, and take your Captain along with you: You'l find good Quarters in some warm Hay-loft.
> SIR FRED: Merciless Woman! Do but lend me thy Maid; faith I'le use her very tenderly and lovingly, even as I'd use thy self, dear Widow, if thou wou'dst but make proof of my affection. (III, iii)

The Widow's wit is sarcasm of no very high order, and her speech, with its "Hay-loft," is too homely for a city Wit. The raillery lacks polish and point; and Sir Frederick can be smutty but not very witty. Now and then the Widow may bristle up and exclaim, "I have seen e'ne as merry a man as your self, Sir *Frederick*, brought to stand with folded arms, and with a tristful look tell a mournful tale to a Lady" (II, ii); but more often, Sir Frederick adopts a domineering tone toward her, and cries, "Widow, May the desire of man keep thee waking till thou art as mad as I am" (IV, vii).

Sir George Etherege

It is evident that Pepys's criticism of the play as "merry by gesture, not wit," is largely justified. The play has occasional flashes of wit, but they are never sustained. The two Truewits lack the polish and brilliance of a Dorimant and Harriet. They are promising young fledglings not yet come of age, and their wit necessarily shows a somewhat callow quality. Sir Frederick at least has the buoyancy and carefree attitude toward life characteristic of the Truewit, but his interests are still too physical, such as playing tricks on the Widow, creating disturbances at night, and chasing maids. He has not yet arrived at a refined taste in women or in wit.

The naturalistic temper in the play is much more consistently maintained than the wit, particularly in the comic scenes involving the minor figures. There are such naturalistic passages as Dufoy jesting about being "clap'd":

CLARK: Methinks the wound your Master gave you last night, makes you look very thin and wan, Monsieur.
DUFOY: Begar you mistake, it be de voundé dat my Metresse did give me long agoe.
CLARK: What? some pretty little English Lady's crept into your heart?
DUFOY: No, but damn'd littel English whore is creepé into my bone begar, me could vish dat de Diable vould také her vid allé my harté. (II, i)

In appreciating such scenes, we need not be as squeamish as some modern critics are,[72] for such witticisms are to be expected from characters naturalistically conceived. The saucy, impertinent Dufoy is also ridiculous as an incipient Witwoud who claims he was hired for being a "man d'esprit, and of vitté," and is consequently exposed to the malicious laughter of his superiors.

The strength of the naturalistic temper is evident, too, in the Wheadle-Sir Nicholas plot. This has been described as

---

[72] Cf. Palmer: "To-day the scenes in which the plight of Dufoy is for comic purposes exploited are wholly disgusting" (*Comedy of Manners*, p. 75).

Middletonian in spirit,[73] but Etherege probably did not go back to his literary predecessor when he could copy directly from the life about him. A book published in the reign of Charles, *Proteus Redivivus: or the Art of Wheedling, or Insinuation* (1675), gives a very complete account of the contemporary practice of wheedling, and describes such persons as Wheadle and Sir Nicholas. "Wheedle" is defined as a term in the "Canting Dictionary" which "imports a subtil insinuation into the nature, humours and inclinations of such we converse with, working upon them so effectually, that we possess them with a belief that all our actions and services tend to their pleasures and profit, whereas it is but seemingly so, that we may work on them our real advantage"; and the town Wheedle is described as living off fops, whom he entices to a tavern for the purpose of swindling them.[74] He has also laid up a store of choice things to say, and has wit enough to please in conversation.[75] This picture corresponds to Sir Frederick's description of Wheadle: "one whose trade is Trechery, to make a Friend, and then deceive him; he's of a ready Wit, pleasant Conversation, throughly skill'd in men" (I, ii). Like Dufoy, Wheadle has a dry, hard wit that is part of his naturalistic make-up. When outwitted by the Truewit and forced to marry the mistress he has been keeping, he says: "Come hither, *Grace*; I did but make bold, like a young Heir, with his Estate, before it came into his hands: Little did I think, *Grace*, that this Pasty, (Stroaking her belly.) when we first cut it up, should have been preserv'd for my Wedding Feast" (v, iv). Wheadle has many of the characteristics of the Witwoud; and at the same time, he is a realistic portrayal of a familiar figure from contemporary low-life.

Sir Nicholas Cully is obviously the Witless in the play, but

[73] Lynch, *The Social Mode of Restoration Comedy*, p. 143.
[74] [Richard Head], *Proteus Redivivus: or the Art of Wheedling, or Insinuation*, London, 1675, pp. 2, 4, 198.
[75] *Ibid.*, p. 149.

like Wheadle, he is an imperfect copy of what eventually became a type figure in wit comedy. He is ridiculous not only because of his stupidity and boorishness but because he has Puritan antecedents. He is described by Sir Frederick as "one whom *Oliver*, for the transcendent knavery and disloyalty of his Father, has dishonour'd with Knight-hood; a fellow as poor in experience as in parts, and one that has a vain-glorious humour to gain a reputation amongst the Gentry, by feigning good nature, and affection to the King and his Party" (i, ii).

Though neither Sir Nicholas nor Wheadle are perfect examples of Witless and Witwoud, they fit into the normal pattern of wit comedy. Wheadle, as Witwoud, plays with Sir Nicholas Cully; but he overrates his wit (cleverness), and is exposed at the end by Sir Frederick, the Truewit, who forces him to marry Grace. Wheadle and Sir Nicholas, along with Dufoy, are naturalistically conceived, and they contribute to the comic side of the play, since they are all exposed to the malicious laughter of the Truewits.

Of the main plot, which is heroic and serious, I have said nothing, because it is out of keeping with the rest of the play. Aurelia puts her finger on the essential difference between it and the rest of the play when she says: "But we by Custom, not by Nature led, / Must in the beaten paths of Honour tread" (ii, ii). The characters in the comic portion follow nature because of their naturalistic bias, and a person like Sir Frederick never considers honor; but the people of the Graciana-Beaufort world act according to custom and honor. Yet the heroic world is not insulated against the currents of skepticism and naturalism; and even Graciana recognizes the fact that men admire women who can conceal their love, and contend with them on equal terms (ii, ii), though she herself is incapable of profiting from this knowledge, as the Widow Rich does. The two worlds in the play are irreconcilable; and Etherege, perhaps unintentionally, shows the absurdity and artificiality of the code by which the honorable, custom-bound half lives and suffers.

Etherege's second play, *She Would if She Could*, opened on February 6, 1668, to a capacity audience which included Wits like Charles, Buckingham, Buckhurst, and Sedley. Pepys, who was also there, wrote in his *Diary*, "Lord! how full was the house, and how silly the play, there being nothing in the world good in it, and few people pleased in it"— to which he added, "all the rest did, through the whole pit, blame the play as a silly, dull thing, though there was something very roguish and witty; but the design of the play, and end, mighty insipid." Dennis observed many years later that despite its poor reception on the first performance, "it was esteem'd by the Men of Sense, for the trueness of some of its Characters, and the purity and freeness and easie grace of its Dialogue."[76]

The story of the overeager woman frustrated is not very original, and is familiar to us from pre-Restoration plays like Shirley's *Lady of Pleasure* (1635). But the picture of the lustful woman in Lady Cockwood is an extremely fine naturalistic study. She serves several purposes in the play: first, she exemplifies the author's naturalistic belief that women are, at bottom, as sensual as men; second, she gives pleasure to the audience by serving as the butt of its malicious laughter; and third, through her, the dramatist wittily exposes the conventional notion of honor. It is a mistake to think of her as "a woman of social pretensions whose attempted illicit amours are wrecked by the pressure of a social standard which she lacks intelligence to comprehend."[77] She has no social pretensions because she is evidently on good terms with the modish people of her group. Nor is she "a female Tartuffe, a woman of loud religious pretensions, who demands respect and devotion for her piety, and who is

[76] Dennis, "A Large Account of the Taste in Poetry" (1702), in *The Critical Works*, I, 289.

[77] Lynch, *op. cit.*, p. 154.

really engaged, all the time, in the vain prosecution of a disgraceful intrigue."[78] Neither the "manners" nor the moralistic interpretation can explain her character and her role in the play. She is actually an unhappily married woman whose strong sexual desires are frustrated because her unmanly husband shuns his marital duties.

In the naturalistically conceived role of the frustrated wife, Lady Cockwood becomes ridiculous only because of her over-eager efforts to satisfy her sexual desire, and, at the same time, her refusal to recognize the natural fact that she has physical needs. Since she has other faults such as impertinence, inordinate fondness, vanity, and jealousy—all marks of the female Witwoud—she is also ridiculed for aspiring to the love of a Truewit. But her chief flaw is her pretending to the principles of conventional morality: she declares that she loves her husband fondly, and she professes to be the very soul of honor. Since she is at the same time striving to satisfy her desires extramaritally, she speaks euphemistically, from hypocrisy or self-delusion, of Courtall's "generous passion." Even in her relations with her maid Mrs. Sentry, she cannot put off her tarnished dress of honor; and following an interview alone with Courtall, which she desired, Lady Cockwood admonishes her maid:

> LA. COCK: What a strange thing is this! will you never take warning, but still be leaving me alone in these suspicious occasions?
> SEN: I was but in the next room, Madam.
> LA. COCK: What may Mr. *Courtall* think of my innocent intentions? I protest if you serve me so agen, I shall be strangely angry: you should have more regard to your Lady's Honour. (II, ii)

This is not social satire, as the "manners" critics would suggest, for Lady Cockwood is not criticized because of her failure to conform to a social mode: she is ridiculed because

---

[78] Gosse, "Sir George Etheredge," p. 271.

of her self-delusion, her hypocrisy, and her cant about honor. On the other hand, this is not conventional moral satire; for though Etherege may prefer sincerity to hypocrisy, he is not concerned with virtue or with exposing vanity and hypocrisy for the usual moral reasons. In fact, Lady Cockwood will undoubtedly take Courtall's advice at the end to "entertain an able Chaplain," as the best means of satisfying her sexual appetite circumspectly. She remains as obdurate as ever in her lust and reforms only so far as to solace herself with a chaplain rather than a gallant; and there is no suggestion that Etherege condemns her for having adulterous desires. As her name implies, she is a naturalistically conceived woman who would follow nature and fornicate, if she could stop pretending that she lives by honor. Through her, Etherege wittily exposes the conventional notion of honor, since it is only a ridiculous female coxcomb like her that professes it.

In this naturalistic world, Sir Oliver Cockwood and Sir Joslin Jolly are quite at home: they are a pair of Witlesses who set off each other's folly and expose themselves to the malicious laughter of the Truewits. Sir Oliver and Lady Cockwood, in the familiar role of Witless and Witwoud, are also involved in an outwitting situation in which the more stupid is exposed to laughter. Sir Oliver pretends to be a "taring Blade" but is cowardly at heart, and as a husband, he is not only uxorious and hen-pecked, but lacks the where-withal to satisfy his wife. Above all, he is a stupid oaf who believes in his wife's fidelity, and says fatuously, "Never man was so happy in a vertuous and loving Lady!" (v, i). Sir Joslin Jolly is equally a Witless. His merriment smacks of the coarse boisterousness of the country, and his speech is larded with sexual references, horse and hare similitudes, and country snatches; and he thinks that low creatures like the pimp Rake-hell and the whores that Rake-hell brings to their parties are the finest company in the world. These two Wit-lesses are ridiculous because they lack sense and judgment, they are boorish in their fun, and they lack perspicacity to see through the deception of others.

Pepys's comment on the mediocrity of the plot and the unoriginal ending applies to the pursuit of the young girls by the gallants as much as to the Cockwood story, for the courtship is left pretty much to chance, and the final agreement among the lovers is due principally to accident and opportunity. The outwitting plot serves as a framework, however, for the wit play of a quartet of Truewits consisting of the two gallants and their mistresses.

Courtall and Freeman are "two honest Gentlemen of the Town" in pursuit of wine, women, and wit. Of the two, Courtall is not only the wittier and more perspicacious but the bolder, and he takes the lead in the intrigue to outwit Lady Cockwood and gain the favors of the young women. When Freeman fears that the girls mistrust them, Courtall exclaims, "Never fear it; whatsoever women say, I am sure they seldom think the worse of a man, for running at all, 'tis a sign of youth and high mettal, and makes them rather piquee, who shall tame him" (III, i). With his ready tongue, he rallies the Exchange women, who are fond of him for his wit; and he plays with Lady Cockwood, wittily pretending that it is his virtue and her honor that stand in the way of their affair:

> Cour: Oh, 'tis impossible, Madam, never think on't now you have been seen with me; to leave 'em upon any pretence will be so suspitious, that my concern for your honour will make me so feverish and disordered, that I shal lose the taste of all the happiness you give me.
>
> La. Cock: Methinks you are too scrupulous, heroick Sir. (III, i)

This is Truewit using Lady Cockwood's own cant about honor to outwit a hypocritical woman for whom he has no real taste. Courtall rallies her ironically at times: "The truth is, Madam, I am a Rascal; but I fear you have contributed to the making me so" (iv, ii). He is cynical about marriage, and exclaims, "a Wife's a dish, of which if a man once surfeit, he shall have a better stomach to all others ever after" (iii, iii). In a conversation with Sir Oliver, he also expresses his libertinism and skepticism:

> Sir Oliv: Well a pox of this tying man and woman together, for better, for worse! upon my conscience it was but a Trick that the Clergy might have a feeling in the Cause.
>
> Cour: I do not conceive it to be much for their profit, Sir *Oliver*, for I dare lay a good wager, let 'em but allow Christian Liberty, and they shall get ten times more by Christnings, than they are likely to lose by Marriages. (i, i)

Freeman is less witty than his friend, and is less inclined to indulge in skeptical wit, though now and then he can handle a witty antithesis cleverly: "I have an appointment made me without my seeking too, by such a she, that I will break the whole ten Commandments, rather than disappoint her of her breaking one" (iv, ii). But more often he plays second fiddle to his friend:

> Cour: I have been so often balk'd with these Vizard-Masks, that I have at least a dozen times forsworn 'em; they are a most certain sign of an ill face, or what is worse, an old Acquaintance.
>
> Free: The truth is, nothing but some such weighty reason, is able to make women deny themselves the pride they have to be seen. (ii, i)

In the witticisms of these two gallants, there is nothing very striking, aside from an occasional hit at matrimony and Courtall's ironical pretense to virtue. Sometimes they even fall into such labored similitudes as the following, when they meet unexpectedly:

> Cour: What unlucky Devil has brought thee hither?
>
> Free: I believe a better natur'd Devil then yours, *Courtall*, if a Leveret be better meat then an old Puss, that has been cours'd by most of the young Fellows of her country: I am not work-

ing my brain for a Counterplot, a disappointment is not my
bus'ness.

COUR: You are mistaken, *Freeman*: prithee be gone, and leave
me the Garden to my self, or I shall grow as testy as an old
Fowler that is put by his shoot, after he has crept half a mile
upon his belly.

FREE: Prithee be thou gone, or I shall take it as unkindly as a
Chymist wou'd, if thou should'st kick down his Limbeck in
the very minute that he look'd for projection. (IV, ii)

The wit play of the two gallants alone, though spirited, shows
no great merit: not only is there an absence of original similitudes, but there is little of the elegance and epigrammatical
quality of fine wit. What chiefly distinguishes the two as
Truewits is their carefree attitude, their naturalistic temper,
and their contempt for Witlesses like Sir Oliver and Sir
Joslin.

Of the two girls, Gatty is the only real Truewit: she is
almost as fine a figure as Harriet, and she is superior to
Courtall. On their first appearance, Gatty reveals herself as
a Truewit, and Ariana as something less. Gatty cries, "How
glad am I we are in this Town agen," while Ariana regrets
the pleasures of the country—"the benefit of the fresh Air,
and the delight of wandring in the pleasant Groves" (I, ii).
Gatty is also rebellious against the restraints imposed by their
"grave Relations," and wants to partake freely of the pleasures of the town. She is wild and free, and has the freshness
of the country about her; if she does not always show the
decorum of a fine town lady, she has the verve of a young
filly romping about the pasture. She is not above a homely
country simile: to the young gallants she says, "Our Company
may put a constraint upon you; for I find you daily hover
about these Gardens, as a Kite does about a back-side, watch-
ing an opportunity to catch up the Poultry" (IV, ii). But this
is part of her carefree, witty attitude toward life. She likes
freedom and sincerity, and when Ariana reproves her for
singing a wanton love-song, she exclaims, "I hate to dissemble

when I need not." With true naturalistic bias, she ridicules Platonic love, and she rallies her sister for being melancholy out of love: "Now art thou for a melancholy Madrigal, compos'd by some amorous Coxcomb, who swears in all Companies he loves his Mistress so well, that he wou'd not do her the injury, were she willing to grant him the favour, and it may be is Sot enough to believe he wou'd oblige her in keeping his Oath too" (v, i). To a woman, nothing can be more serious than love, but she will jest about it nevertheless. Gatty has the virtue of maintaining the character of a Truewit throughout the play, without falling into flat similitudes or ever losing her witty attitude toward life.

It is hardly sound, then, to suggest, as Dobrée does, that "the full-blooded boisterousness of Sir Joslin Jolly and Sir Oliver Cockwood" is incompatible with "Ariana's fragile world."[79] Actually there is no such fragile and artificial world of the sort the "manners" critics imagine, for the world of Ariana and Gatty is full-blooded and naturalistic. The two girls are happy-go-lucky in their attitude toward life; and after so serious an episode as Sir Oliver and Courtall fighting, the girls are next door, "laughing and playing at Lantre-lou." Though Ariana expresses too much sentiment in her earlier appearances, neither of the girls weeps and trembles over the future, as do Graciana and Aurelia in the preceding play. They are a charming pair of Truewits, with a touch of naïveté, but with sufficient perspicacity to see through the hypocrisy of Lady Cockwood and the coxcombry of Sir Oliver. There is more good-nature than malice in their raillery, and their frank delight in the pleasures of courtship is unspoiled by satiety or experience.

Separately, the four young Truewits do not approach the highest wit. The courtship scenes, however, provide passages that Pepys found "very roguish and witty." When the quartet meet, they usually engage in what Gatty calls "a little harm-

[79] Dobrée, *Restoration Comedy*, p. 65.

Sir George Etherege

less Raillery betwixt us." Their first encounter is marked by a long passage of sustained repartee which has the character of a tour de force:

> Cour: By your leave, Ladies—
> Gatty: I perceive you can make bold enough without it.
> Free: Your Servant, Ladies—
> Aria: Or any other Ladys that will give themselves the trouble to entertain you.
> Free: 'Slife, their tongues are as nimble as their heels.
> Cour: Can you have so little good nature to dash a couple of bashful young men out of countenance, who came out of pure love to tender you their service?
> Gatty: 'Twere pity to baulk 'em, Sister.
> Aria: Indeed methinks they look as if they never had been slip'd before.
> Free: Yes faith, we have had many a fair course in this Paddock, have been very well flesh'd, and dare boldly fasten.
> (ii, i)

The speeches are quick and short, and the repartee has verve. Despite the absence of balanced epigrams and of real malice, the remarks are witty, and Freeman's *double-entendre* is superior to anything in the preceding play.

As they grow more familiar and develop a little pique toward each other, the comic wit improves; and when the girls encounter the men, who they believe have audaciously forged letters from them, there is some sharp repartee:

> Gatty: I suppose your Mistress, Mr. *Courtall*, is always the last Woman you are acquainted with.
> Cour: Do not think, Madam, I have that false measure of my acquaintance, which Poets have of their Verse, always to think the last best, though I esteem you so, in justice to your merit.
> Gatty: Or if you do not love her best, you always love to talk of her most; as a barren Coxcomb that wants discourse, is ever entertaining Company out of the last Book he read in.
> Cour: Now you accuse me most unjustly, Madam; who the Devil, that has common sense, will go a birding with a Clack in his Cap?

ARIA: Nay, we do not blame you, Gentlemen, every one in their
way; a Huntsman talks of his Dogs, a Falconer of his Hawks,
a Jocky of his Horse, and a Gallant of his Mistress.

GATTY: Without the allowance of this Vanity, an Amour would
soon grow as dull as Matrimony. (IV, ii)

Here are fine "turns" and some pointed rejoinders. Finally,
in an incipient "proviso" scene, there is one fine passage, at
once balanced and paradoxical, when Courtall says to Gatty:
"Now shall I sleep as little without you, as I shou'd do with
you" (V, i).

She Would if She Could is superior to the first play in
every respect. Yet the wit is not always of the highest: there
is often a lapsing into flat similitudes; there is not much of
the malicious and skeptical wit that gives so much vitality to
wit comedy; and there is little of the elegance and fine balance of language which is the mark of high wit. The comic
wit sparkles at times, but principally because of the zest and
high spirit of the young Truewits rather than because of an
original play of ideas. The Truewits are, in fact, extremely
young, and display more fancy than judgment in their speech
and conduct. Finally, the wit in the play does not always
spring from the dramatic action, nor is the wit of the different
characters often distinguished, since the witticisms are assigned
somewhat indiscriminately to the several Truewits. The best
thing in the play is the naturalistic portrait of Lady Cockwood, and Etherege's witty use of her to deflate the notion
of honor.

His last play, *The Man of Mode, or Sir Fopling Flutter*
(1676), is one of the best examples of the comedy of wit. In
the prologue Sir Car Scroope implied that one would find
"Nature well drawn and Wit" in this comedy; and Langbaine commended its naturalism: "This Play is written with
great Art and Judgment, and is acknowledg'd by all, to be
as true Comedy, and the Characters as well drawn to the
Life, as any Play that has been Acted since the Restauration

of the *English* Stage."[80] The contemporaries of Etherege noted particularly this fact of realistic portraiture, and there was much speculation as to the originals of characters like Dorimant, Sir Fopling, and Medley.

It is a failure to appreciate the realistic technique and the naturalistic basis which has led to an underestimation of the play's true merits. On the one hand, we have Steele's moralistic censure of the play, in the *Spectator #65*, as "a perfect contradiction to good manners, good sense, and common honesty," and of Dorimant as "a direct knave in his designs, and a clown in his language." On the other hand, we have the "manners" view that the play is "a more exquisite and airy picture of the manners of that age than any other extant."[81] Neither of these estimates does justice to the comedy, for they both fail to appreciate the essential character of the play and the two main elements in it—the wit and the naturalistic characterization. *The Man of Mode* is a comedy of wit, with the usual outwitting situations involving naturalistically conceived characters.

Among the major figures, Dorimant is perhaps the least appreciated by modern readers, largely because the naturalistic characterization is not recognized. He is too often dismissed as a cruel and selfish rake; whereas he is actually a superb portrait of a Truewit. Dennis, in his defence of the play, pointed out that "*Dorimont* is a young Courtier, haughty, vain, and prone to Anger, amorous, false, and inconstant," because this is the true nature of young men as described by Aristotle in his *Rhetoric*, and the dramatist must be true to life (that is, be a naturalistic writer).[82] Dennis also pointed out that Rochester was the model for the part: "all the World was charm'd with *Dorimont*; and . . . it was

[80] Langbaine, *An Account of the English Dramatick Poets*, p. 187.
[81] Hazlitt, *Lectures on the English Comic Writers*, in *The Collected Works*, VIII, p. 129.
[82] Dennis, "A Defence of Sir *Fopling Flutter*," *The Critical Works*, II, 245-247.

unanimously agreed, that he had in him several of the Qualities of *Wilmot* Earl of *Rochester*, as, his Wit, his Spirit, his amorous Temper, the Charms that he had for the fair Sex, his Falshood, and his Inconstancy; the agreeable Manner of his chiding his Servants . . . ; and lastly, his repeating, on every Occasion, the Verses of *Waller*, for whom that noble Lord had a very particular Esteem."[83] Jacob says further that "the Character of *Dorimant* was drawn in Compliment to the Earl of *Rochester*."[84]

Dorimant embodies all the virtues of the masculine True-wit, and he is what Dean Lockier called "the genteel rake of wit."[85] Every term of this description deserves emphasis: Dorimant is genteel, as a Truewit who observes decorum ought to be; he is a rake, because his principles are libertine; and above all, he is a Wit, for he values intellectual distinction above other virtues. This is a far better description than Hazlitt's, which makes Dorimant "the genius of grace, gallantry, and gaiety"[86]—and sacrifices accuracy to alliteration. The gallantry of Dorimant is more predatory than courtly, in keeping with his naturalistic bias; and his gaiety is subdued, for there is a dark streak in his nature, compounded of the intellectuality, cynicism, and passion of his original. He is not easy to understand because he has considerable depth, and unlike Courtall and Freeman, he is not open and frank about his inner life. He is a man of strong passions, but is Wit enough to have control over them; his fancy is tempered by judgment; and he possesses higher intellectual qualities than the average Truewit.

On the more superficial side, he is the embodiment of elegant ease—a ready Wit, a cultivated man who has Waller on his lips, and an easy conversationalist with "a Tongue . . .

---

[83] *Ibid.*, p. 248.

[84] Giles Jacob, *The Poetical Register*, London, 1719, p. 96.

[85] Rev. Joseph Spence, *Anecdotes, Observations, and Characters, of Books and Men*, London, 1858, p. 47.

[86] Hazlitt, *op. cit.*, VIII, 68.

would tempt the Angels to a second fall." He has histrionic talents, and can adopt the proper tone for every occasion: with Lady Woodvill, he ironically plays the role of the formally courteous Mr. Courtage; with his fellow Wits he is the railler; with Belinda he is gallantly amorous and ardent; and with the Orange Woman and the Shoemaker, he adopts a tone of rough raillery and easy superiority. Possessing the superior perspicacity and cleverness of a Truewit, Dorimant can see through the devices of others, and at the same time, dissemble well enough so that others cannot see through him. His histrionic talents are also displayed in mimicry of others, a talent which Harriet shares with him. He does it grossly and sarcastically with Loveit, in his imitation of Sir Fopling, or ironically and maliciously, as in his mimicry of Harriet. Dorimant can please anyone when, and if, he wishes to do so, because he possesses the virtues of versatility, ease, and perspicacity.

As a Truewit, he also has a tongue as sharp as a rapier— and the raillery of Dorimant is seldom gentle, since he has malice enough to be cutting. Yet it has point and originality enough to be pleasing. It can be as fine as his repartee with Harriet on their first encounter:

DOR: You were talking of Play, Madam; Pray what may be your stint?

HAR: A little harmless discourse in publick walks, or at most an appointment in a Box bare-fac'd at the Play-House; you are for Masks, and private meetings, where Women engage for all they are worth, I hear.

DOR: I have been us'd to deep Play, but I can make one at small Game, when I like my Gamester well.

HAR: And be so unconcern'd you'l ha' no pleasure in't.

DOR: Where there is a considerable sum to be won, the hope of drawing people in, makes every trifle considerable.

HAR: The sordidness of mens natures, I know, makes 'em willing to flatter and comply with the Rich, though they are sure never to be the better for 'em.

DOR: 'Tis in their power to do us good, and we despair not but at some time or other they may be willing.

HAR: To men who have far'd in this Town like you, 'twoud be a great Mortification to live on hope; could you keep a Lent for a Mistriss?

DOR: In expectation of a happy Easter, and though time be very precious, think forty daies well lost, to gain your favour. (III, iii)

His raillery can also be as sarcastic as his retort to Pert, "Oh Mrs. *Pert*, I never knew you sullen enough to be silent" (II, ii); or as good-naturedly rough as his remark to his servant, "Take notice henceforward who's wanting in his duty, the next Clap he gets, he shall rot for an example" (I, i).

As a Truewit, Dorimant professes naturalistic principles, and he is cynical about women. He has known enough women to be certain that they are vain, hypocritical, and affected creatures; most complaisant when they seem most to resist; and jealous and demanding when won. A striking example of his raillery, malice, his libertinism, frankness, and wit is his passage with Mrs. Loveit:

LOVEIT: Is this the constancy you vow'd?

DOR: Constancy at my years! 'tis not a Vertue in season, you might as well expect the Fruit the Autumn ripens i'the Spring.

LOVEIT: Monstrous Principle!

DOR: Youth has a long Journey to go, Madam; shou'd I have set up my rest at the first Inn I lodg'd at, I shou'd never have arriv'd at the happiness I now enjoy.

LOVEIT: Dissembler, damn'd Dissembler!

DOR: I am so, I confess; good nature and good manners corrupt me. I am honest in my inclinations, and wou'd not, wer' not to avoid offence, make a Lady a little in years believe I think her young, wilfully mistake Art for Nature; and seem as fond of a thing I am weary of, as when I doated on't in earnest.

LOVEIT: False Man!

DOR: True Woman!

LOVEIT: Now you begin to show your self!

Dor: Love gilds us over, and makes us show fine things to one another for a time, but soon the Gold wears off, and then again the native brass appears. (II, ii)

He is professedly libertine, and lives according to naturalistic principles.

If there is any fault in Dorimant as a Truewit, it is his over-sophistication, which makes his wit a little too self-conscious; for now and then his wit is a trifle forced, as in his raillery on the young woman whom the Orange Woman reports to him: "This fine Woman, I'le lay my life, is some awkward ill fashion'd Country Toad, who not having above Four Dozen of black hairs on her head, has adorn'd her baldness with a large white Fruz, that she may look sparkishly in the Fore Front of the Kings Box, at an old Play" (I, i). Harriet, who is a keen judge of wit, observes of Dorimant, when Young Bellair praises him for his ease and naturalness, "He's agreeable and pleasant I must own, but he does so much affect being so, he displeases me" (III, iii). Dorimant has too much judgment to indulge in fanciful wit, so that he does not provide the most natural and spontaneous display of wit. But he is a Truewit because he is libertine in his principles, perspicacious and malicious, he observes decorum in his speech and conduct, and he detests coxcombs like Sir Fopling.

His friend Medley has the more fanciful wit of the two, and he serves, therefore, as a foil to Dorimant's more solid wit. When he is "rhetorically drunk," he is a great elaborator of fancies; and he rallies the ladies with a pleasant account of a fictitious book, "written by a late beauty of Quality, teaching you how to draw up your Breasts, stretch up your neck, to thrust out your Breech, to play with your Head, to toss up your Nose, to bite your Lips, to turn up your Eyes, to speak in a silly soft tone of a Voice, and use all the Foolish French Words that will infallibly make your person and conversation charming, with a short apologie at the end, in behalf of young Ladies, who notoriously wash, and paint, though they have naturally good Complexions" (II, i). Medley rallies everyone, but with much less malice than Dorimant, and he lets his tongue run freely on everyone and everything.

It is also he, rather than Dorimant, who voices most of the skeptical wit in the play; and this is done with a much more natural, if less fine, carelessness than Dorimant is capable of. He is a skeptic in matrimony as well as religion, and he rallies Young Bellair on his intended marriage: "You have a good strong Faith, and that may contribute much towards your Salvation. I confess I am but of an untoward constitution, apt to have doubts and scruples, and in Love they are no less distracting than in Religion; were I so near Marriage, I shou'd cry out by Fits as I ride in my Coach, Cuckold, Cuckold, with no less fury than the mad Fanatick does Glory in *Bethlem*" (i, i). When Dorimant gets a letter from Molly the whore asking for a guinea to see the "Opery," Medley exclaims, "Pray let the Whore have a favourable answer, that she may spark it in a Box, and do honour to her profession" (i, i). He also gives the rallying advice to the witty Shoemaker: "I advise you like a Friend, reform your Life; you have brought the envy of the World upon you, by living above your self. Whoring and Swearing are Vices too gentile for a Shoomaker" (i, i). Though Dorimant is the finer Wit, with more malice, perspicacity, and judgment, Medley, with his fanciful and skeptical wit, is often more original and entertaining.

The one other important Truewit in the play is Harriet, who has much in common with Dorimant. Compared to her sisters Gatty, Ariana, and the Widow Rich, Harriet is endowed with a much more solid wit; and her perspicacity, sound sense, and fine self-control make her a formidable person. She is, as Dorimant says, "Wild, witty, lovesome, beautiful and young," but tempering these qualities is sound judgment and sincere feeling. Her exceptional physical beauty is the least part of her merits, and it speaks well for Dorimant that he is interested in her wit (i, i).

Sir George Etherege

Like Dorimant, she has histrionic talents and the ability to dissemble, and there are excellent scenes of comic wit when she and Dorimant take each other off on their first meeting, and when she and Young Bellair dissemble before their parents, by pretending to be in love. She displays a roguish wit, as when she tells Young Bellair, "I know not what it is to love, but I have made pretty remarks by being now and then where Lovers meet" (iii, i). Or when she is merry at her mother's expense, by exclaiming in the presence of Dorimant, who is unknown to Lady Woodvill, "I would fain see that *Dorimant*, Mother, you so cry out of, for a monster; he's in the *Mail* I hear" (iii, iii). But there is good-nature at bottom in Harriet, and the occasional malice of her tongue is due to some deeper feeling which she wishes to conceal. She is a Truewit with sufficient self-control to treat her lover and her emotion playfully; and if her emotion breaks through, it is perceptible only in her sharper and more malicious wit:

HAR: I did not think to have heard of Love from you.
DOR: I never knew what 'twas to have a settled Ague yet, but now and then have had irregular fitts.
HAR: Take heed, sickness after long health is commonly more violent and dangerous.
DOR: I have took the infection from her, and feel the disease spreading in me— (Aside.)
Is the name of love so frightful that you dare not stand it? (To her.)
HAR: 'Twill do little execution out of your mouth on me, I am sure.
DOR: It has been fatal—
HAR: To some easy Women, but we are not all born to one destiny; I was inform'd you use to laugh at Love, and not make it.
DOR: The time has been, but now I must speak—
HAR: If it be on that Idle subject, I will put on my serious look, turn my head carelessly from you, drop my lip, let my Eye-lids fall and hang half o're my Eyes— Thus— while you buz

a speech of an hour long in my ear, and I answer never a word! why do you not begin? (iv, i)

Such raillery is a fine weapon in her capable hands.

Her wit is charming because it springs from sincere feeling and sound judgment. She has sensible views, untainted by cynicism; and though she may say of a husband, "I think I might be brought to endure him, and that is all a reasonable Woman should expect in a Husband," she adds significantly, "but there is duty i'the case," implying thereby that were not duty involved (as there must be in an arranged marriage), a woman might reasonably dote on her husband (iii, i). As a Truewit she is an enemy of all that is affected, dull, and formal, and speaking of Hyde Park, she says, "I abominate the dull diversions there, the formal bows, the Affected smiles, the silly by-Words, and amorous Tweers, in passing" (iii, iii). She has passions, and will not conceal them under an affected softness (iv, i). In fact, she loves naturalness so much that she criticizes even Dorimant for not being natural enough in his wit (iii, iii). And she exclaims against all pretenders— "That Women should set up for beauty as much in spite of nature, as some men have done for Wit!" (iii, i). At its best, her wit is first-rate because it is unpretentious: her witticisms are never forced, and her speech is free of labored similitudes. Only she is capable of wit at once so sensible and whimsical as the following:

DOR: Is this all—will you not promise me—
HAR: I hate to promise! what we do then is expected from us, and wants much of the welcom it finds, when it surprizes.
DOR: May I not hope?
HAR: That depends on you, and not on me, and 'tis to no purpose to forbid it. (v, ii)

It must be her speeches in particular that Dennis had in mind when he said of *The Man of Mode*: "the Dialogue is the most charming that has been writ by the Moderns: That with

Purity and Simplicity, it has Art and Elegance; and with Force and Vivacity, the utmost Grace and Delicacy."[87]

As foils to the three Wits discussed so far, there are the several characters who fall short of being Truewits. Of these Emilia and Young Bellair are the most attractive, but like Graciana and Beaufort in the first play, they belong to an honorable world which is out of harmony with the dominantly naturalistic temper of the play. Young Bellair is described by Dorimant as "Handsome, well bred, and by much the most tolerable of all the young men that do not abound in wit" (i, i); and Emilia, according to Medley, "has the best reputation of any young Woman about Town, who has beauty enough to provoke detraction; her Carriage is unaffected, her discourse modest, not at all censorious, nor pretending like the Counterfeits of the Age" (i, i). What alone makes them tolerable to the Truewits is their naturalness and lack of affectation; as lovers, they lack fire and spirit, and theirs is a conventional affair, with the usual obstacles and hazards of honorable courtship and marriage.

Aside from Bellinda, who is a rather foolish young woman, the other foils to the Truewits are all objects of malicious laughter in the play. Mrs. Loveit has some beauty and wit, but she is absurd because of her unnatural jealousy and affectation. Lady Woodvill and Old Bellair, "their Gravities" of a past age, are minor objects of ridicule. Old Bellair is laughable because of his unnatural love for a young girl, for such fond love at his age is a sure sign of dotage or impotent lechery. Lady Woodvill is "a great Admirer of the Forms and Civilities of the last Age," when beauties were courted in proper form, with a due regard for the conventions of Platonic love. "Lewdness is the business now," she says with regret, "Love was the bus'ness in my Time" (iv, i). She does not realize that the new world in which she is so out of place

---

[87] Dennis, "A Defence of Sir *Fopling Flutter*," *The Critical Works*, ii, 243.

is naturalistic in its principles, and that young couples like Emilia and Young Bellair who carry on in the approved fashion of her age are passé.

The chief foil to the Truewits is Sir Fopling, but so much has been said about him by critics that further commentary seems superfluous. It is important, however, to note that he is not chiefly an object of social satire, as is commonly supposed: he is laughed at principally because he is deficient in wit. His pretension to fashion and taste in clothes reveals the poverty of his mind, and it is this mental defect that exposes him to laughter. He is such a person as the Marquess of Halifax described—a superfine gentleman whose understanding is so appropriated to his dress that his fine clothes become his sole care.[88] After the Truewits have ironically ridiculed his supposed fine taste in clothes, they mercilessly condemn him as a fool:

MED: a fine mettl'd Coxcomb.
DOR: Brisk and Insipid—
MED: Pert and dull.
EMILIA: However you despise him, Gentlemen, I'le lay my life he passes for a Wit with many.
DOR: That may very well be, Nature has her cheats, stum's a brain, and puts sophisticate dulness often on the tasteless multitude for true wit and good humour. (III, ii)

Undoubtedly there is some element of social satire in the ridicule of the fop, but the "manners" approach which makes Sir Fopling a mere conglomeration of fine clothes misses the whole point of his being Witwoud. Furthermore, the "manners" view which finds him a superfluous accessory to the plot fails to grasp the unity of the play. It is quite evident that in this comedy of wit he occupies the role of the Witwoud who is exposed by his intellectual superiors, and that he is not

---

[88] Halifax, "Some Cautions offered to the Consideration of those who are to chuse *Members* to serve for the Ensuing *Parliament*," in *The Complete Works*, p. 153.

only a foil to the Truewits but the butt of their malicious laughter.

In his three wit comedies, Etherege shows a progressive development in his art. *The Comical Revenge,* his first attempt at the comedy of wit, shows an uncertain mastery: the heroic-moral world is not properly subordinated, Wheadle and Dufoy are not perfect Witwouds, and Sir Nicholas is not a very amusing Witless. The Truewits are also deficient: Sir Frederick, with his callow interest in frolics, and the Widow, with her over-ready show of feeling, are not yet capable of the brilliant comic wit to be found in later plays. But the naturalistic temper is prominently displayed. In the second comedy, *She Would if She Could,* Etherege successfully poked witty fun at the conventional notion of honor, in the person of Lady Cockwood, and he brought together a quartet of spirited Truewits. The wit in the play, however, seldom reaches a very high level: the repartees are characterized more by high spirits than by an original exchange of ideas; there is a preponderance of wit play over comic wit; and the Truewits are not properly distinguished in their wit, for the difference between Courtall and Freeman, for example, is that the former is the bolder of the two.

The last play, *The Man of Mode,* is superior in every respect. Not only does it have a fine Witwoud in Sir Fopling Flutter, but it has three notable Truewits, in Dorimant, Harriet, and Medley, who are carefully distinguished by Etherege in terms of their wit: Dorimant is characterized by malice and judgment, Medley by fanciful and skeptical wit, and Harriet by natural, spontaneous wit. In Dorimant and Harriet, we see to what an extent Etherege succeeded in making the wit significant and dramatic: not only does the wit of Harriet probe deeper into human absurdities; it is more thoroughly a part of the dramatic action, as well as an expression of her true character. Dorimant and Harriet also have an intellectual solidity and depth of feeling which make them far more human and substantial than their predecessors. These two Truewits are both lovers of fine wit; they have penetration enough to see through the affectation and folly of others, and wit enough to dissemble with the world; enough judgment to act sensibly at all times; a sufficiently playful attitude toward life not to be swept away by their own emotions; and an easy and elegant superiority to everyone else by virtue of these qualities. They are intelligent without being over-intellectual, worldly without being disillusioned with life, and witty without being superficial or frivolous.

Dorimant and particularly Harriet represent the finest expression of Etherege's witty attitude toward life—his good sense, elegance, and libertinism; and his scorn of fools, ceremony, and artificiality. As Truewits they belong to a free world—and a world which is neither corrupt as the moralistic critics affirm, nor superficial as the "manners" critics would have us believe. It may not have the breadth of Dante's universe because the supernatural is excluded, but there is much in this world of the Truewit that is valuable, such as elegance, intellectual distinction, clarity of thought, absence of artificial formality, freedom from cant about honor, and a graceful and natural acceptance of this life on earth.

VI

WILLIAM WYCHERLEY

As with Etherege, there are certain misconceptions about William Wycherley which must be dispelled before we can properly understand the man and his work. Perhaps the most serious of these is the belief that Wycherley differed from Etherege and Congreve in being a fierce, and often misanthropic, satirist. This misconception has been fostered to a great extent by modern apologists for Restoration comedy, who seem to find special gratification in the belief that Wycherley is one shining example in the age of a major comic writer with a serious moral purpose. Surprisingly, too, this notion is indebted principally to the "manners" critics, who have always insisted most strongly that morality should not be considered in any appraisal of Restoration comedy.

Word has got around that Wycherley was a moralist in temper, and that though he participated in the libertine life of the age, he actually loathed it at heart.[1] This conception of the reluctant rake has its origin in descriptions like Palmer's: "Fundamentally he was a Puritan. Superficially, in his life and writing, he accepted the pageant and portrayed it; but frequently the moral fury of a satirist breaks violently through the fine gentleman."[2] This is outdone by Dobrée's description of Wycherley as a sort of Quaker: "For this John Fox masquerading in the habiliments of a Charles Sedley— or should it be the other way round?—seems very strange. He is like a Dante strayed into the gardens of Boccaccio, but unable to forget for a moment the plague raging every-

---

[1] Cf. Montague Summers, *The Playhouse of Pepys*, London, 1935, p. 313.
[2] Palmer, *Comedy of Manners*, pp. 93-94.

William Wycherley

where."[3] This picture of Wycherley as a Puritan or Quaker is hardly credible, and would no doubt have puzzled the affable Truewit who ridiculed Gripe for his Puritan sympathies.

Those who stress Wycherley's moral fervor, and assert that he loathed the life he led, overlook the consistent libertinism of his life and thinking. In the 1704 and 1728 editions of his poetry there are a great many libertine verses such as only a Truewit could have written. Some of these were composed earlier, but at no time in his life does he seem to have disapproved of them. The *Miscellany Poems* of 1704, for example, contains poems like the following: "To a fine young Woman, who being ask'd by her Lover, Why she kept so filthy a thing as a Snake in her Bosom; answer'd, 'Twas to keep a filthier thing out of it, his Hand"; "Upon a Lady's Fall over a Stile, gotten by running from her Lover; by which She show'd Her Fair Back-side, which was Her best Side, and made Him more Her pursuer than He was before"; "Upon a Fine Woman's Fine Breasts"; and "To a Lady, who wore Drawers in an Ill Hour."

This is not to deny that Wycherley was sometimes a satirist; for there is contemporary praise of his satirical writings by critics like Dryden,[4] and there are undoubtedly some satirical poems in the 1704 and 1728 editions of his verse. There is no serious objection to calling even *The Plain Dealer* a satirical play (as long as one does not confuse this with conventional moral satire). Yet one does have to reject the main argument for considering Wycherley a satirist: that he supposedly represented himself in the figure of Manly in *The Plain Dealer*. Since Manly's extreme misanthropy is ridiculed in that play, this identification seems untenable.

The seeming contradiction of these statements is resolved if we examine the basis of Wycherley's "satire." We must remember that he was always a Truewit, and that, consequently,

[3] Dobrée, *Restoration Comedy*, p. 80.
[4] Dryden, "Author's Apology for Heroic Poetry and Poetic License," *Works*, v, 115.

William Wycherley

his criterion was not a Christian system of ethics. As a True-wit, he wittily exposed the unnatural and the affected on the basis of his naturalistic philosophy; and when the conventional observance of Christian morality produced an artificial relationship, as in arranged marriages, he exposed conventional morality. The Christian dogmas were called into question by Wycherley, as in the criticism of "the old philosophy" in *The Plain Dealer* (III, i), and the clergy was frequently the butt of the author's wit for its failings. The only standard that Wycherley accepted was the naturalistic one, according to which the one great sin is the sin against nature. Thus, his "satire" was directed against "preciseness" (a punctilious insistence on honor), false wit, and coxcombry, rather than against violations of morality. At the same time, in accordance with his allegiance to the standards of true wit, Wycherley utilized the resources of wit and tempered the sharpness of his criticism with urbanity.

Before differentiating Wycherley from Congreve and Etherege, we must also consider his great interest in skeptical and sexual wit, in comic wit and raillery, and his own reputation as a Wit. An examination of his life and work reveals him as a Truewit—libertine, skeptical, naturalistic, and as much devoted to true wit as Etherege. The preponderant evidence, it seems to me, is against treating him as a fierce satirist and moralist, though one cannot deny that the satirical temper is strong in his works, especially in the form of ironic wit.

His early life and education prepared him for the role of a Truewit in later life. At fifteen, he was sent to France, where he came into close contact with Mme. de Montausier, one of the leading figures among the *précieux*. This group was interested in wit, polished conversation, gallant pursuits, and decorum, and it no doubt left a strong impression on his young mind. At any rate, the characteristic response of a Truewit is evident in his remark to Dennis years later that, "young as he was, he was equally pleas'd with the Beauty of her Mind, and with the Graces of her Person."[5] Upon his return to England just before the Restoration, Wycherley tried the university and then the Middle Temple, but abandoned them shortly for the life of a Wit. Charles had returned to Whitehall with his courtiers, and a pleasanter career lay open to a young man of wit and talent. "But making his *First Appearance* in Town," says his friend Major Pack, "in a *Reign* when Wit and Gaiety were the *Favourite Distinctions*, He soon left the *Dry Study* of the Law, and gave into *Pursuits* more *Agreeable* to *His own* Genius, as well as to the *Taste* of the Age."[6] He very shortly produced a witty play which brought him the acquaintance of "the most celebrated wits, both of the court and town," and also the favor of the Duchess of Cleveland.[7]

The manner of his entrance into the gay Whitehall circle is particularly significant, in revealing Wycherley's chief qualifications—his wit and personal charm. Dennis has left us an amusing account of how Wycherley was accosted in the Mall by the Duchess of Cleveland, after the performance of his first play, and how she thrust herself half out of her coach and complimented him by calling him "son of a whore," in witty reference to a song in the play.[8] His friendship with the Duke of Buckingham was also due to his wit and charm. His familiarity with the Duchess having aroused the jealousy of her cousin Buckingham, Rochester and Sedley intervened; the Duke was persuaded to meet the dramatist, and was soon charmed by his wit.[9] Charles was also "extremely *Fond* of him upon account of his *Wit*,"[10] and often "chose him for a Companion at his leisure Hours, as *Augustus* did

[5] Dennis, "To the Honourable Major Pack," *Original Letters, Familiar, Moral and Critical*, p. 215.

[6] Richardson Pack, "Some Memoirs of Mr. Wycherley's Life," *The Whole Works of Major Richardson Pack*, London, 1729, p. 182.

[7] Theophilus Cibber, *The Lives of the Poets*, III, 249.

[8] Dennis, *Original Letters*, pp. 215-217.

[9] *Ibid.*, pp. 218-220.

[10] Pack, *op. cit.*, p. 184.

William Wycherley

Horace."[11] Very quickly, then, by virtue of his wit and charm, Wycherley found his way into the company of Wits, among whom he would hardly have ventured had he been a Puritan at heart.

Among his witty friends, Wycherley seems to have been admired for his manliness, his good nature, and his wit (which meant his judgment also). Dennis rallied him amiably "as a Man sent purposely into the World to charm the Ears of the wittiest Men, and to ravish the Hearts of the most beautiful Women."[12] Lord Lansdowne has left us an account of Wycherley which pretty well dispels the modern notion of the dramatist as a fierce misanthrope: "To judge by the Sharpness and Spirit of his Satyr, you might be led into another Mistake, and imagine him an ill-natur'd Man: But what my Lord *Rochester* said of Lord *Dorset*, is as applicable to him—*The best good Man, with the worst-natur'd Muse*. As pointed and severe as he is in his Writings, in his Temper he has all the Softness of the tenderest Disposition; gentle and inðffensive to every Man in his particular Character."[13] Wycherley was generous, gentle of manners, and good-natured, though impatient at hearing a friend calumniated.[14] He was also "of a Wit sprightly, entertaining, and inoffensive, a valuable Companion, and a sincere Friend," unassuming and modest in conversation, who "wou'd never be wiser than his Company."[15] This is corroborated by an examination of his personal letters, for among them one searches in vain for sharp raillery of the sort that one often finds in Etherege's letters. This is not the Puritan or Quaker painted by some

[11] Lord Lansdowne, "A Character of Mr. *Wycherly*," in *The Genuine Works in Verse and Prose of the Right Honourable George Granville, Lord Lansdowne*, London, 1732, I, 435.

[12] Dennis, *The Select Works of Mr. John Dennis*, London, 1718, II, 490-491.

[13] Lansdowne, *op. cit.*, p. 434.   [14] Pack, *op. cit.*, p. 186.

[15] Charles Gildon, *Memoirs of the Life of William Wycherley, Esq; with a Character of his Writings by the Right Honourable George, Lord Lansdowne*, London, 1718, p. 22.

modern critics, but rather a cultivated Truewit who was affable toward all, witty without malice, and entertaining in his
conversation.

At the same time, there was an inwardness and reserve
about Wycherley which we do not find in the extroverted
Etherege. Gildon tells us that Wycherley "knew how to be
Civil over a Glass to Mr. *Durfey* as well as to Mr. *Dryden*,
but this was no mark of his Friendship or Intimacy"; and "he
was all his life besides more cautious of his Friendships, the
Brightest and the most Excellent always esteem'd him, and
he reciprocally them, having all along a Contempt for pretending Coxcombs."[16] As a Truewit, Wycherley chose friends
who were men of wit and taste, and his intimates included
gifted Wits like Dryden, Etherege, Dorset, Buckingham,
Rochester, Butler, Dennis, and toward the end of his life,
Pope, whom he affectionately called his "Deare Little Infal-
lible." Pope noted that "Wycherley was a very genteel man;
and had the nobleman-look as much as the Duke of Buckingham."[17]

An examination of Wycherley's ideas corroborates the view
that he was a Truewit—libertine, skeptical, and naturalistic—
with a strong interest in wit. According to Pope, "Wycherley
used to read himself asleep o'nights, either in Montaigne,
Rochefoucault, Seneca, or Gracian; for these were his favor-
ite authors"[18]—and these men, significantly, were rationalistic,
shrewdly realistic in their appraisal of men, and sometimes
skeptical. Rochefoucault stressed the egoism of man; and
even Gracián had maxims like the following in his *Oraculo
Manual*: "A shrewd man knows that others when they seek
him do not seek *him*, but their advantage in him and by
him" (CCLIII). Wycherley was probably indebted to them
in the writing of his own maxims, which reveal his naturalistic
bias. He was no doubt influenced, too, by Montaigne, the

[16] *Ibid.*, p. 20, p. 17.
[17] Spence, *Anecdotes*, p. 215.　　　　[18] *Ibid.*, p. 150.

William Wycherley

great skeptic and naturalistic thinker of the Renaissance; for like Montaigne in his "Apology for Raymond de Sebonde," Wycherley questioned the superiority of mankind over animals in a piece entitled, "Upon the Impertinence of Knowledge, the Unreasonableness of Reason, and the Brutality of Humanity; proving the Animal Life the most Reasonable Life, since the most Natural, and most Innocent." The reasonable life is equated with the natural life, and Wycherley advises men to follow nature.

Because of this naturalistic bias, Wycherley was skeptical about the supernatural, though, like the Marquess of Halifax, he was undoubtedly a deist rather than an atheist. In a poem "To a University-Wit, or Poet," he sharply criticized the church:

> ... Faith i'th' Church, is more, as Reason less;
> Where oft it is, Religion, to be dull,
> And to be Faithful, to be Fanciful;
> Nay Nonsense, Sacred, in the Pulpit is,
> Where Clergy-Fictions, Lay-men dare not hiss,
> Railing, or Damning, dare not take amiss.[19]

Wycherley began life as a Protestant, was converted to Catholicism in his youth, then was reconverted to Protestantism, but died a Catholic—a fact which shows that if he was not devout, at least he was not indifferent to religion. What he no doubt desired was a faith compatible with reason. As a Truewit, he was anticlerical in his sentiments, and among his maxims are remarks like the following: "Churchmen but believe that they believe, and so make others believe what they themselves do not; since their Actions contradict their Faith, and the Flesh is generally observ'd to get the better of the Spirit" (ccxciii). "Parsons are a Sort of Spiritual Mountebanks, who poison themselves with their own false Doctrines, that they may put them the better on other People,

[19] Wycherley, *The Complete Works of William Wycherley*, ed. Montague Summers, Soho, 1924, III, 69.

and make them swallow, by their swallowing the same before them" (CCLXX). But Wycherley was critical of the clergy rather than of true faith, for he also wrote maxims like the following: "The best Receipt to live every way long, and well, is not to consult too many Doctors, either of the Soul or Body; since those of the latter, by tampering with our Constitutions, often fling us into a Weakness; and those of the former, by practising on our Faith, as often unsettle it, if not leave us none at all" (LXI).

In accordance with his naturalistic bias, Wycherley also accepted the relativism of Hobbes, and he observed, "Nothing is good, or bad, to Us as it is in itself, but as it is taken by us" (IX). In other maxims, he accepted the naturalistic view that man is egoistic: "The Friendships we shew to our Acquaintance, are often more out of Love to our selves than the Persons we call Friends; and we do Benefits, as Usurers lend Money, not so much for the Borrower's Service as our own Interest, which is rather exacting a Kindness than doing one, so more properly taking our Revenge than giving our Assistance" (CCLXXVI). "Men have no Faith in others, but to beget theirs in them; have no Friendship but out of Interest; and no Complacency for others but out of Self-Love"(CXIV). But such ideas, as with Hobbes, are not evidences of misanthropy; and they did not prevent Wycherley's enjoying the sincere friendship of worthy men like Dennis and Dryden, nor his trying to help the neglected poet Samuel Butler. In fact, contemporary testimony shows that Wycherley was loved as a generous and sincere friend; and he appears to have been an egoist in principle rather than in practice.

Wycherley also professed libertine principles, railed as heartily as Etherege against matrimony, and maintained the merits of free love. There is "A Disswasive to his Mistress, on her resolving to turn Nun," in which he ironically advised her to marry if she would be a true penitent. In a poem "To a Lady, an Advocate for Marriage," he declared that marriage is just a mode of bartering love, a dull tenure sold by the church, and argues distrust on the part of the woman; the greatest favors are those granted "most voluntary, frank, and free," and the virgin who stands on no wedlock terms is "the most honourable Mistress." In a poem "On Orpheus's Descent to Hell," he observed wittily that hell is a place "Whither most Husbands to this Day, 'tis said, / More by their Wives than other Whores are led." There is also an ironical poem "To the most Honourable Match-Maker, a Bawd, call'd J.C.—; proving Free Love more Honourable, than Slavish, Mercenary Marriage." In "A Consolation to Cuckolds," he wittily urged the merit of bastards, as in the song from *Love in a Wood* to which the Duchess of Cleveland referred at their first meeting. Yet Wycherley could not have been a complete enemy of matrimony, since he himself married a widow. But where marriage, supported by conventional notions of honor, went contrary to nature, Wycherley let his wit playfully pluck at the foundations.

His hedonic attitude toward life ranged from libertinism to mild epicureanism. In "Honour, an Enemy to Love," he attacked that "false Idol Honour," which stands in the way of love's fulfilment. In a poem "To his Unconsenting Mistress," he urged her to follow nature and enjoy the pleasures of love; and in "The Various Mix'd Life," he spoke of love as life's chief blessing and joy, but a joy to be found only in variety. Like Etherege, he was definitely antistoical, and he wrote in a maxim, "The *Stoicks* seem the Reverse of old *Deucalion*'s Fable, since the Latter was for turning Stones into Men; but the Former, by their Philosophy, would turn Men into Stones" (cxix). Apparently he believed that men are human by virtue of their feelings and their appetites, and that the suppression of these natural desires destroys man's humanity. At other times, he spoke up for moderation, and in another maxim he remarked, "Our Luxury should teach us a Lesson of Temperance, since Pleasures turn to Surfeits by their Multiplicity; and too much of any thing makes us satisfied with nothing" (LXVII). At his most reflective, Wycherley expressed a moderate and wise *modus vivendi* which is epicurean in the best sense. In a poem "To an Ingenious young Man, so sollicitous for the Future, that he neglected the Present," Wycherley advised the young man to live the present life well, and let the future take care of itself.

As a writer, he also displayed the marks of a Truewit. He remained a "Gentleman-Writer" and was never a "Trader in Wit."[20] Gildon observed that "he writ not for Benefit, or ever made it his Livelyhood";[21] and Lansdowne believed that Wycherley would not have written at all, "if it had been a Trouble to him to write."[22] In this respect, Wycherley had much in common with Etherege, who was an amateur in art, and with Congreve, who preferred being a Truewit to being a mere dramatist.

Wycherley's virtues as a witty writer differ, however, from those of Etherege. He was frequently praised for his "pointed Wit, and Energy of Sense."[23] But more often, he was commended by contemporaries for his judgment: his "strict Enquiries into Nature" and his "close Observations on the several Humours, Manners, and Affections of all Ranks and Degrees of Men."[24] Critics found the highest wit in his "observation" of human nature, that is, in the naturalistic depiction of figures like Manly, Olivia, Pinchwife, Lady Fidget, Horner, and the Widow Blackacre. Wycherley himself valued sound judgment and naturalness above fancy, and he declared, "Wit without Judgment is like a Ship at Sea without Rudder or Ballast, fluctuating at random, and ever in Danger from its unsteady lightness" (XCIII). In a

---

[20] Rochester, "The Sessions of the Poets."

[21] Gildon, *Memoirs*, pp. 11-12.

[22] Lansdowne, "A Character of Mr. *Wycherly*," *Genuine Works*, I, 434.

[23] Elijah Fenton, "Epistle to Mr. Southerne," *Poems on Several Occasions*, London, 1717, p. 72.

[24] Lansdowne, *op. cit.*, I, 434. Cf. also, Gildon, *Memoirs*, p. 6; Dennis, Preface to *Miscellanies in Verse and Prose*, London, 1693.

letter to Pope he remarked, "they . . . who have most Wit or Money, are most sparing of either."[25] Wit, he thought, is best when most unassuming and simple;[26] for "Nature transcends Art" (XIII), and both wit and beauty can be lessened by too much art (LI). Wycherley believed that the best wit carries with it a large element of judgment and restraint, and that in being least artificial, it is the most acceptable to Truewits.

Because of these predilections, he had nothing but contempt for coxcombs who, though deficient in judgment, set up for Wits in spite of nature. "Half-witted Fools," he wrote, "are harder to be dealt with, by sensible or honest Men, than thorough-pac'd Knaves" (XVII). Fortunately, fools can at least afford malicious pleasure to Truewits, for they are "the fittest to make Men and Women Sport."[27] Accordingly, in his comedies, Wycherley ridiculed coxcombs like Dapperwit and Novel, who are absurd because of their labored attempts to be witty and their complete lack of judgment in the display of their trivial wares.

Sound judgment and fidelity to nature—these are the criteria of wit for Wycherley; and these are the basis of his characterization and also of his "satire." In his plays, then, we can expect an emphasis on naturalism and sound judgment, in addition to the more familiar ingredients of wit comedy, such as outwitting situations, comic wit, raillery, and sexual and skeptical wit.

His first play, *Love in a Wood, or St. James's Park* (1671),[28] brought him the friendship of the court Wits and the favors of the Duchess of Cleveland, and it no doubt de-

---

[25] Pope, *Mr. Pope's Literary Correspondence for Thirty Years; from 1704 to 1734*, London, 1735, I, 19.

[26] Wycherley, Postscript to *Miscellany Poems*, in *The Complete Works*, III, 14.

[27] Wycherley, "Upon the Discretion of Folly," *The Complete Works*, III, 27.

[28] The edition used for Wycherley's plays is *William Wycherley*, ed. W. C. Ward (Mermaid Series).

serves some praise as a witty play. It has several characters who are ostensibly Truewits, it has typical Witwouds in Dapperwit and Lady Flippant, and a Witless in Sir Simon Addleplot, and several outwitting situations in which these characters are involved. But, as with Etherege's first attempt, the play is more notable for the expression of a naturalistic temper and for isolated instances of wit than for a successful integration of the various elements that constitute a comedy of wit.

The most original and entertaining character in the play is Lady Flippant, who might almost qualify as a Truewit, were it not for her affectation and lack of judgment. She is like Lady Cockwood in her eager pursuit of men, but she is far bolder and franker in speech. In fact, she is almost masculine in her conduct, and it is she who sings the song referred to by the Duchess:

> When parents are slaves,
> Their brats cannot be any other;
> Great wits and great braves
> Have always a punk to their mother.

She is a naturalistic creature, anticonventional and sexual, and she is almost convincingly witty at times:

L. FLIP: Though I did so mean a thing as to love a fellow, I would not do so mean a thing as to confess it, certainly, by my trouble to part with him. If I confessed love, it should be before they left me.

LYD: So you would deserve to be left, before you were. But could you ever do so mean a thing as to confess love to any?

L. FLIP: Yes; but I never did so mean a thing as really to love any.

LYD: You had once a husband.

L. FLIP: Fy! madam, do you think me so ill bred as to love a husband?

LYD: You had a widow's heart, before you were a widow, I see.

L. FLIP: I should rather make an adventure of my honour with a gallant for a gown, a new coach, a necklace, than clap my husband's cheek for them, or sit in his lap. I should be as ashamed to be caught in such a posture with a husband, as a brisk well-bred spark of the town would be to be caught on his knees at prayers—unless to his mistress. (III, iv)

Her wit rings false because, despite her professed abhorrence of love and marriage, she is husband-hunting in earnest; and we have the double pleasure of her witticism, and the author's ironic exposure of her insincerity. The passage is dramatic and ironic—a characteristic mark of Wycherley's wit. She is not as fine a creation as Lady Cockwood, however, because she is less consistent in her coxcombry, and her false wit is often too contrived, as in the remark, "I abominate honourable love, upon my honour" (II, i).

The Truewits in the comedy are less striking than Lady Flippant, and they also reveal defects of one sort or another. Ranger is the boldest gallant of all: he can be witty in his repartee with Lydia and contemptuous of a Witwoud like Dapperwit; and his ironical treatment of Lady Flippant is reminiscent of Courtall's encounters with Lady Cockwood. Yet he is deficient in judgment, and consequently he is discredited and made to appear ridiculous in his pursuit of Christina. His opinion that "Women are poor credulous creatures, easily deceived" (I, ii), is also disproved. At the end he repents of his infidelity to Lydia, and reforms. "Lydia, triumph!" he exclaims, "I now am thine again. Of intrigues, honourable or dishonourable, and all sorts of rambling, I take my leave; when we are giddy, 'tis time to stand still" (IV, v).

His friend Vincent comes closer to being a Truewit. He is properly described by Ranger as a person with "more courage than wit, but wants neither" (I, ii); and as a plain dealer and a hater of pretense, he is a rough draft of Manly. When Dapperwit rails at Ranger, he rebukes the Witwoud sharply:

VIN: Detracting fop! when did you see him desert his friend.
DAP: You have a rough kind of raillery, Mr. Vincent. (I, ii)

William Wycherley

Like Eliza in *The Plain Dealer*, Vincent seems to represent a middle ground of common sense and honesty, as opposed to the extremism of the others; and he is characterized by sound judgment rather than by any distinction of speech. He rebukes Ranger for his low opinion of women, and he serves as a moderating influence on both Ranger and Valentine.

Of the other Truewits little need be said. Lydia is ostensibly a Truewit, but her role of the neglected and scorned woman at the beginning makes her an object of ridicule. When Ranger disappoints her, she tells him, "You mistake me; but you shall not lessen any favour you do to me. You are going to excuse your not coming to me last night, when I take it as a particular obligation, that though you threatened me with a visit, upon consideration you were so civil as not to trouble me" (iii, iv). Such sarcasm shows more presence of mind than real wit. She is better, though not much more distinguished in her speech, when she is rallying Dapperwit, who thinks he is being gallant with his insipid similitudes. The remaining couple, Valentine and Christina, though major figures, are as out of place in wit comedy as Aurelia and Bruce in Etherege's first play; for they belong equally to a world governed by honor and custom. If they have redeeming features, it is that Christina has considerable judgment, and Valentine an occasional distinction of speech, as in the remark on his mistress: "If she be innocent, I should be afraid to surprise her, for her sake; if false, I should be afraid to surprise her for my own" (iv, v). Aside from such occasional expressions of wit, the Truewits in the play are not a memorable group.

Of the two masculine coxcombs in the play, Dapperwit is the more original, in the familiar role of the Witwoud. He is almost up to Gripe's description of him as "an idle, loitering, slandering, foul-mouthed, beggarly wit" (v, vi). But he is, more properly, "a little wit, a modest wit," as Mrs. Crossbite says, "and they do no such outrageous things as your great wits do" (III, i). Dapperwit displays some of the characteristic attitudes of the Truewit, and at times he is almost clever enough in his speech to be mistaken for a real Wit, as when he exclaims, "A pox! I think women take inconstancy from me worse than from any man breathing" (III, ii). But this is only after he has been cast off by Lucy and rendered ridiculous. The long passage in which he explains to Lydia the variety of Wits is a tour de force, and exposes his labored, and hence, affected wit. Likewise, he is absurd when he thinks he is being wittily satirical in speaking ill of the people he meets. He is actually "a brisk, conceited, half-witted fellow of the town," who would rather lose his mistress than a similitude. Above all, he is deficient in judgment, so that he is exposed to the ridicule of the Truewits. When he believes he has outwitted Witless by stealing his mistress, Dapperwit finds himself married to a young woman some months gone with another man's child. He is a great talker, like most of Wycherley's Witwouds, but frequently he is simply verbose without being amusing in his half-wit—which is a reflection on the author's wit.

Sir Simon Addleplot, as his name implies, is the Witless in the play. His activities are limited pretty much to pursuing supposed women of fortune, and to being the butt of those more intelligent than he. He is called coxcomb, gull, and fop, and Ranger describes him as "That spark, who has his fruitless designs upon the bed-ridden widow, down to the suckling heiress in her pissing-clout" (I, ii). As Witless, he is patronized and deceived by Dapperwit, who tolerates him because every Witwoud must have his cully. But Sir Simon, with his mannerisms, his "faith and troth," is too stupid and unoriginal a figure to be particularly amusing.

The most striking feature of the play is not the wit of the main plots, but the naturalistic temper, prominently displayed in the scenes involving Gripe, Mrs. Joyner, and Mrs. Crossbite. These scenes are also significant for what they reveal of Wycherley's art. Characteristically, they are used for the expression of his naturalistic ideas, and they are consequently not well integrated with the rest of the comedy. They are also the most misunderstood passages in the play. The first scene in which Gripe appears is described by Perry as "gruesome," and is cited as evidence of Wycherley's "horror of diseased souls."[29] This is hardly justified.

Gripe is "seemingly precise, but a covetous, lecherous, old Usurer of the city," and Mrs. Joyner is "A Match-maker, or precise city bawd." What the two have in common is their "preciseness," that is, their punctilious insistence on virtue; and like Lady Cockwood, they are ridiculed because their "preciseness" is a mere pretense. There is an extended passage of ironic raillery in the first scene, where the two praise each other's "virtue"; and though this passage is not good dramaturgy because it is out of keeping with their characters, it makes perfectly clear Wycherley's intention of exposing their "preciseness." Gripe is also ridiculed because he is a Puritan, a "commonwealth's man," a hater of bishops and Wits, and "a censorious rigid fop" (i, i). This is usually mistaken for conventional moral satire, but I cannot see much difference between Wycherley's witty exposure of Gripe and Etherege's exposure of Lady Cockwood. Both are witty in treatment, and both represent a naturalistic point of view: a disparagement of virtue (as commonly mouthed by people like Gripe and Lady Cockwood), and an advocacy of honesty instead. The author's naturalistic "satire" is evident in a remark like Gripe's about Lucy, in which false piety and lechery are equally mingled: "There can be no entertainment to me more luscious and savoury than communion with that little gentlewoman.—Will you call her out? I fast till I see her" (iii, iii). Dobrée remarks of these naturalistic scenes: "The scabrous passages seem badly aimed, as though Wycherley himself did not quite know with what object they were

[29] Perry, *Comic Spirit in Restoration Drama*, p. 38.

William Wycherley

there."[30] It is apparent that as a Truewit, Wycherley was wittily exposing that "false Idol Honour."

Love in a Wood is very uneven work, as one might well expect from the dramatist's first attempt. The Truewits in the play do not consistently maintain their roles, Dapperwit is sometimes more offensive than amusing, and Sir Simon is too stupid as Witless. But Lady Flippant, as a female coxcomb, provides some passages of good comic wit, and the Gripe scenes reveal Wycherley's predilection for expressing his naturalistic views with mordant wit.

The next play, *The Gentleman Dancing-Master* (1672), is also uneven: it has some good passages of wit, but the play as a whole is too farcical to give rise to the highest comic wit. The one respect in which it is definitely superior to the first play is in its structure. The plot is well-defined, and consists of a comic situation in which the two young Truewits, Gerrard and Hippolita, successfully outwit her father and aunt, and also expose the coxcombry of the Witwouds.

Of the two Truewits in the play, Hippolita is the more original character, and also one of the most misunderstood of Wycherley's creations. There is not much one need say about Gerrard because he is a more conventional figure: a Truewit who has been in France, and shows it in his mien, without ostentation; a man who, according to even Paris, is "witty, brave, and *de bel humeur*, and well-bred," with good sense and judgment (I, i). He admires Hippolita for her wit (II, ii); and he can be witty with her in repartee, and ironic toward her father Don Diego. There is nothing very complicated or ambiguous about his character.

Hippolita, on the other hand, is complex enough to be misunderstood by some very good critics. Perry says of her, "Hippolita wants a man (she doesn't care much who)," and Dobrée remarks, "there is a hatred Wycherley has for Hip-

---

[30] Dobrée, *Restoration Comedy*, p. 81.

polita because she has the desires natural to the animal."[31] Neither of these statements is true. Hippolita must not be confused with such forward and coarse creatures as Miss Prue and Hoyden: she is a Truewit interested only in a man with wit. Before she has ever met Gerrard, she remarks that if he has not wit, he would not be welcome (i, i); and later, when she meets him, she is afraid for a moment that he loves her but is dull (ii, ii). Likewise, her repugnance for her fiancé Paris springs entirely from the fact that he lacks wit (i, i).

Wycherley himself realized that critics might condemn her for her rather unwomanly role of the pursuer at the beginning; and consequently, with tongue in cheek, he put into the play a defense of Hippolita by herself: "I am thinking if some little, filching, inquisitive poet should get my story, and represent it to the stage, what those ladies who are never precise but at a play would say of me;—that I were a confident, coming piece, I warrant, and they would damn the poor poet for libelling the sex. But sure, though I give myself and fortune away frankly, without the consent of my friends, my confidence is less than theirs who stand off only for separate maintenance" (v, i). Though this is poor dramaturgy because it destroys the dramatic illusion, it shows Wycherley's partiality for Hippolita. Then, to make the point doubly clear, he made another witty defense of her character in the epilogue.

Hippolita is not a successful artistic creation, however. She is, rather, a character who exemplifies the author's ideas. She is a sophisticated ingenue, with a peculiar mixture of native wisdom and naïveté, and her motivation is not always plausible. No doubt she would seem less bold if her age were not given as fourteen; but she is a Truewit, eager for freedom from parental domination, rebellious against unnatural restraint, and common-sensical in her views. When Mrs. Caution rails against the libertine age, Hippolita retorts, "By what

[31] Perry, *op. cit.*, p. 40. Dobrée, *op. cit.*, p. 85.

William Wycherley

I've heard, 'tis a pleasant, well-bred, complaisant, free, frolic, good-natured, pretty age: and if you do not like it, leave it to us to that do" (i, i). This probably echoes Wycherley's own sentiments, and it seems to disprove those critics who think he loathed the age.

Above all, Hippolita is a sensible girl who embodies Wycherley's naturalistic views on matrimony: she wants a love-marriage, as against a conventional arranged marriage; and the justification of her conduct, in eloping, is to be found in a song of which she approves very highly:

> The match soon made is happy still,
>   For only love has there to do.
> Let no one marry 'gainst her will,
>   But stand off when her parents woo,
> And only to their suits be coy:
>   For she whom jointure can obtain,
> To let a fop her bed enjoy,
>   Is but a lawful wench for gain. (ii, ii)

How sensible she is, is evident, too, from her rejection of her maid's cynical advice to marry Paris:

Hip: Would'st thou have me marry a fool, an idiot?
Prue: Lord! 'tis a sign you have been kept up indeed, and know little of the world, to refuse a man for a husband only because he's a fool! Methinks he's a pretty apish kind of a gentleman, like other gentlemen, and handsome enough to lie with in the dark, when husbands take their privileges; and for the day-times, you may take the privilege of a wife. (i, i)

Hippolita tells Gerrard that a marriage between Truewits must be based on equality and trust, and be free of jealousy (v, i)—a point developed at length in *The Country Wife*. She wishes to marry to obtain freedom and love, and these she can find only with a Truewit like Gerrard.

The two Witwouds in the play are Monsieur Paris and Don Diego. Paris is vain and frivolous and affects French manners; Don Diego is formal and grave and affects Spanish manners; and they serve to set off each other's folly. Both of them are deficient in judgment; and the criticism of a "manners" critic like Perry is hardly sound, it seems to me, when he says, "The weakness in the character of Paris satirically considered is that his worst misfortunes do not come directly from his chief weakness, an affectation of French manners."[32] As with Sir Fopling, the absurd addiction to French manners is a sign of defective judgment, and Paris is exposed to the malicious laughter of the Truewits and of the audience for this deficiency. Don Diego and Paris carry the comic burden in the play, but they are usually too mechanical in their behavior to be very amusing. Furthermore, the farcical outwitting plot, with its stress on mistaken identity, is hardly conducive to either the best comic wit or even half-wit.

The most striking and original feature of the play is the solid naturalistic substratum and the anticonventional wit which springs from it. Mrs. Caution appears in the naturalistically conceived role of "an impertinent precise old woman"; and through her Wycherley introduces the problem of sexual wit and of true modesty. Though she harps on virtue and modesty, she is the most lubricious-minded of all, and voices much of the sexual *double-entendre* in the play. Like many another "precise" character, she expresses detestation of sex as a filthy thing, and yet constantly suggests sexual ideas to her young charge. When Hippolita says she will be a good scholar to the dancing-master, Mrs. Caution retorts, "As kind as ever your mother was to your father, I warrant" (IV, i). Upon discovering how Hippolita and Gerrard have outwitted her, she exclaims, "Nay, young man, you have danced a fair dance for yourself, royally; and now you may go jig it together till you are both weary. And though you were so eager to have him, Mrs. Minx, you'll soon have your bellyful of him, let me tell you, mistress" (V, i). There is a comic scene

[32] Perry, *op. cit.*, p. 41.

in which Mrs. Caution's "preciseness" is exposed, when she condones sexual dreams as opposed to the actual deed (ɪ, i). This question of sexual wit and modesty must have been of some concern to Wycherley, for the epilogue contains an ironic defense of sexual wit by Flirt, a common woman of the town:

> The ladies first I am to compliment,
> Whom (if he could) the poet would content,
> But to their pleasure then they must consent;
> Most spoil their sport still by their modesty,
> And when they should be pleased, cry out, 'O fy!'
> And the least smutty jest will ne'er pass by.

Wycherley implied that everyone enjoys sexual wit, but that "precise" women are hypocritical enough to pretend that it offends their modesty. "The Affectation of Modesty is the greatest Impudence," he observed in a maxim; "and as real Modesty is the Beauty of the Mind, so an Affectation of it as much disgraces a perfect Mind, as Art, and an affected Dress, do a perfect Face" (xxvɪɪɪ).

The Truewit's naturalistic ideas also find other forms of expression in the play. There is some anticlerical wit, of which the most obvious is the following:

DON DIEGO: but are you sure my daughter has not seen a man since my departure?

MRS. CAUT: No, not so much as a churchman.

DON: As a churchman! *voto*! I thank you for that; not a churchman! not a churchman!

MRS. CAUT: No, not so much as a churchman; but of any, one would think one might trust a churchman.

DON: No, we are bold enough in trusting them with our souls, I'll never trust them with the body of my daughter, look you, *guarda*! You see what comes of trusting churchmen here in England; and 'tis because the women govern the families, that chaplains are so much in fashion. Trust a churchman!—trust a coward with your honour, a fool with your secret, a gamester with your purse, as soon as a priest with your wife or daughter. (ɪɪ, i)

In other passages there are witty hits at the avarice of parsons, who "for a guinea or two care not what mischief they do," and also at their fear of death (v, i).

One of the wittiest passages in the play is an attack on conventional marriages, and an ironic holding up of "keeping" as a more honorable institution, in a parody of the "proviso" scene:

> Mons: Well, Flirt, now I am a match for thee: now I may keep you.—And there's little difference betwixt keeping a wench and marriage; only marriage is a little the cheaper; but the other is the more honourable now, *vert* and *bleu*! . . . Come, come, I am thine; let us strike up the bargain: thine, according to the honourable institution of keeping.—Come.
>
> Flirt: Nay, hold, sir; two words to the bargain; first, I have ne'er a lawyer here to draw articles and settlements.
>
> Mons: How! is the world come to that? A man cannot keep a wench without articles and settlements! Nay, then 'tis e'en as bad as marriage, indeed, and there's no difference betwixt a wife and a wench. (v, i)

Then Flirt proceeds to the settlements, which provide for no cohabitation, separate maintenance, a house in town, a separate coach, lusty footmen, privacy and freedom, pin money, etc.— all the things that make most marriages no better than keeping. This is a wittier restatement of the idea expressed in the Hippolita-Gerrard story, and it represents the Truewit's exposure of conventional marriages and all that is unnatural and false.

The Gentleman Dancing-Master is not first-rate wit comedy because its plot is too farcical and its characters are neither very original nor very plausible. Even Hippolita is not a consistent Truewit because her sensible views and solid judgment are obscured at times by her whimsical changes of mood. One notices, too, how Wycherley is beginning to subordinate the dramatic presentation of character and action to the expression of his own naturalistic views. The characters are frequently mouthpieces for Wycherley, and the play is wittiest as a vehicle for the author's ideas. Through Mrs. Caution he exposes "precise" people who are libertine in their thinking but pretend to modesty. There is also some anticlerical wit and hits at conventional marriage in scenes involving minor characters. Most effectively, through Hippolita, Wycherley expresses his belief that marriage must be a natural union based on love and equality, and not an artificial contract that gives social sanction to mercenary bartering and libertine conduct.

The third play, *The Country Wife* (1673), is the most mature product of Wycherley's mind, and it restates in wittier form ideas expressed earlier. The main characteristics of this play are those of wit comedy, for its plots consist of outwitting situations, with Truewits in Horner and Harcourt, Witwoud in Sparkish, and Witless in Sir Jasper. The three stories in the play are also utilized for the witty expression of Wycherley's views on "preciseness" and on marriage and jealousy.

Of these, the Horner-Lady Fidget story is the most effective and the wittiest, but it is also the most difficult for some readers to accept, principally because of Horner's pretense of being impotent. I do not think we need to question the probability of the situation at the beginning,[33] for this pretense is a premise on which the author bases the play, and it also springs naturally from Horner's character. It is, after all, a witty intrigue by a Truewit, intended not only to satisfy his appetite, but to expose the "preciseness" of women like Lady Fidget. This basic situation is hardly "the most atrocious in all Restoration comedy."[34] Nor is Horner the "grim, nightmare" figure that Dobrée pictures.[35] "Un joyeux libertin," says M. Perromat,[36] but this description errs in the opposite direction. Steele, despite his incorrigible sentiment, got closer to

[33] Cf. Dennis, *Original Letters*, pp. 37-38.

[34] George Henry Nettleton, *English Drama of the Restoration and the Eighteenth Century*, New York, 1914, p. 80.

[35] Dobrée, *op. cit.*, p. 94.

[36] Charles Perromat, *William Wycherley Sa Vie—Son Oeuvre*, Paris, 1921, p. 201.

William Wycherley

Horner than any modern critic when he described him, in *The Tatler* #3, as "a good Representation of the Age in which that Comedy was written; at which Time Love and Wenching were the Business of Life, and the Gallant Manner of pursuing Women was the best Recommendation at Court." The one flaw in this description is that Steele failed to mention the witty character of Horner's intrigue, and thus made him too physical in his pursuit; for though Horner is naturalistically conceived, he is at the same time a Truewit much concerned with wit.

Horner's preoccupation with his witty intrigue obscures his more attractive qualities, and we ought to stress these, because Wycherley obviously intended him to be a human and convincing Truewit. Margery Pinchwife found him "a curious fine gentleman." And if we consider her opinion biased, we must remember that his fellow Wits treat him amiably at all times, despite a supposed infirmity that would soon expose a lesser man to ridicule. Horner values wit in women, and he is undoubtedly sincere when he says, "But methinks wit is more necessary than beauty; and I think no young woman ugly that has it, and no handsome woman agreeable without it" (i, i). In his own speech he is witty and pointed, as when he remarks, "Let me alone; if I can but abuse the husbands, I'll soon disabuse the wives" (i, i). I think we should believe Horner when he says he prefers the pleasures of good fellowship and friendship over love and wenching, for the former are "lasting, rational, and manly" (i, i). He is not without a sense of decency, for he shields Margery when the sudden arrival of friends prevents her departure from his lodgings (v, iv). Likewise, when he believes Harcourt has lost Alithea to Sparkish, he is sincerely moved by his friend's loss:

HORN: I'm sorry for't.
PINCH: How comes he so concerned for her? (Aside.)
SPARK: You sorry for't? Why, do you know any ill by her?

HORN: No, I know none but by thee; 'tis for her sake, not yours, and another man's sake that might have hoped, I thought.

SPARK: Another man! another man! what is his name?

HORN: Nay, since 'tis past, he shall be nameless.— (Aside.) Poor Harcourt! I am sorry thou hast missed her.

PINCH: He seems to be much troubled at the match. (Aside.) (IV, iii)

Finally, it is quite unfair to describe Horner as "the type of all that is most unselectively lecherous."[37] He has no designs upon Alithea, a Truewit loved by his friend Harcourt and the most attractive young woman in the play; and it must be remembered, too, that the men whom Horner cuckolds, Pinchwife and Sir Jasper, deserve their fate, and that the women with whom he lies are either "precise" or not overly virtuous.

Horner is like Manly in hating the unnatural and affected, and in his taste for plain dealing; and as a Truewit he has only contempt for "all that force nature," like Sparkish (I, i). For this reason, he is led to prey on women like Lady Fidget, who are virtuous in public but libertine in private. His attitude is clear from his remarks to the Quack:

QUACK: But do civil persons and women of honour drink, and sing bawdy songs?

HORN: O, amongst friends, amongst friends. For your bigots in honour are just like those in religion; they fear the eye of the world more than the eye of Heaven; and think there is no virtue, but railing at vice, and no sin, but giving scandal. They rail at a poor, little, kept player, and keep themselves some young, modest pulpit comedian to be privy to their sins in their closets, not to tell 'em of them in their chapels. (IV, iii)

At that moment Lady Fidget walks in, and Horner's contempt for such a "woman of honour" is quite evident. This hatred of the unnatural and the hypocritical is a common trait

[37] Dobrée, *op. cit.*, p. 94.

in Wycherley's Truewits, and it is the motivating force behind Horner's ironic deeds and words.

In other respects, Horner is a more conventional Truewit. His business in life is pleasure, and he confesses to Lady Fidget that he is "a Machiavel in love." He thinks that "a marriage vow is like a penitent gamester's oath"; and when he has an appetite he prefers to fall to without ceremony, at "an ordinary" if necessary. He has a mordant wit that is sharp and masculine. On occasion, he plays with Sir Jasper, as in a passage of ironic *double-entendre* like the following: "Well, Sir Jasper, plain-dealing is a jewel; if ever you suffer your wife to trouble me again here, she shall carry you home a pair of horns; by my lord mayor she shall" (iv, iii). When he is annoyed, he can be very biting, as in his witty retort to Pinchwife:

> PINCH: I will not be a cuckold, I say; there will be danger in making me a cuckold.
> HORN: Why, wert thou not well cured of thy clap? (iv, iii)

There is also the notorious "china" scene, in which Horner exercises his wit by indulging in sexual *double-entendre*. Horner's wit may be too blunt and frank for some readers, but there is nothing "grim" or "nightmarish" about his character.

Lady Fidget, who is coupled with Horner, is the "precise" woman: she objects to the bare word "naked," and like Olivia, considers Horner's "very name obscenity" (ii, i). The meretricious character of Lady Fidget is evident in her anxiety, when he makes advances to her, that he be anatomically sound. "But, indeed, sir," she asks, "as perfectly, perfectly the same man as before your going into France, sir? as perfectly, perfectly, sir?" When assured by him that he is not impotent, she tells him, "Nay, then, as one may say, you may do your worst, dear, dear sir" (ii, i). Yet, like Lady Cockwood, so ingrained is her pretense to honor that she cannot leave off even then, and she begs Horner, "But first, my dear sir, you must promise to have a care of my dear honour" (IV, iii). At the end, in a drinking scene, she is properly exposed, along with Mrs. Squeamish and Mrs. Dainty Fidget, whom Horner describes as "pretenders to honour, as critics to wit, only by censuring others" (II, i). Some critics fail to grasp Wycherley's witty exposure of "preciseness," and how grievously some err we can see from a remark like Archer's: "The women's drinking-bout in the last scene adds a finishing touch to the loathesomeness of what is surely the most bestial play in all literature."[38]

The point of the Pinchwife story is the naturalistic view that marriage must be based on equality and be free of jealousy—an idea expressed in the preceding play through Hippolita. Pinchwife is a coxcomb who declares that women are "dough-baked, senseless, indocile animals" (IV, iv); that "good wives and private soldiers should be ignorant" (I, i); and that "if we do not cheat women, they'll cheat us, and fraud may be justly used with secret enemies, of which a wife is the most dangerous" (IV, ii). Such views are obnoxious to a Truewit like Horner, and he retorts: "Well, but let me tell you, women, as you say, are like soldiers, made constant and loyal by good pay, rather than by oaths and covenants" (I, i). And "good pay," most Truewits would agree, would be in the form of equality, freedom, sexual satisfaction, and perhaps even love. The jealous coxcomb who marries an ignorant girl and tries to keep her in seclusion because he wants a woman of his own to lie with, is soon rewarded with a pair of horns, as he deserves. Like Etherege, Wycherley believes a marriage will endure only so long as the couple love each other naturally and freely.

Margery, a pleasure-loving and unaffected girl from the country, is simply a pawn in this witty plot, but she provides

[38] William Archer, *The Old Drama and the New*, New York, 1929, p. 193.

William Wycherley

some excellent comic wit. There is such effective understatement as the following, in her love letter to Horner: "Be sure you love me, whatsoever my husband says to the contrary, and let him not see this, lest he should come home and pinch me, or kill my squirrel" (IV, iii). Or the unintentional ironic wit of the passage with Alithea:

MRS. PINCH: He says he won't let me go abroad for fear of catching the pox.
ALITHEA: Fy! the small-pox you should say. (II, i)

Pinchwife probably meant "pox" (syphilis), because he is afraid of being cuckolded by some gallant.

The third plot of the play, the Alithea-Harcourt affair, is a variation on the theme of marriage. Alithea is bound in the beginning by an unnatural engagement to Sparkish, but is properly won at the end by Harcourt, a Truewit who outwits the Witwoud. Ostensibly, too, Alithea's affections are turned away from Sparkish because he displays extreme jealousy, a fault of which no Truewit would be guilty. The courtship of the two Truewits is marred, however, by Alithea's somewhat strict notions of honor; and though she is described as having "wit too, as well as beauty," there is little evidence of it in the play, aside from the fact that she appreciates Harcourt's wit and leads the active social life of a Truewit. She seldom utters any striking witticism, and she is quite overshadowed by her maid Lucy, who, like most servants in wit comedy, is opportunistic, skeptical, sensual, and contemptuous of conventions. Lucy exclaims against honor as but "a disease in the head" (IV, i); she makes reflections against parsons, with their "canonical smirk" and "filthy palm" (IV, i); and she thinks, like Hippolita's maid, that a woman ought to marry a fool so that she can enjoy her freedom and pleasures without detection (III, ii). Wycherley is to blame, perhaps, for making Lucy wittier than her mistress, but the fault is not so much that Lucy is too witty as that Alithea is not witty enough.

William Wycherley

The play has its usual contingent of Witless and Witwoud in Sir Jasper Fidget and Sparkish, but neither is a very original nor striking creation. Sir Jasper is a stupid, credulous coxcomb with an absurd concern for business. "Business," he says, "must be preferred always before love and ceremony with the wise, Mr. Horner" (i, i). Meanwhile, Horner is taking care of his wife's business. Sparkish is another of those talkative coxcombs who appear so often in Wycherley's plays. He imagines himself "a gentleman of wit and pleasure about the town," because he talks against matrimony, honor, and virtue. He makes labored attempts to be witty, and when he thinks he has made a lucky hit, he is not content unless he exclaims, " 'Gad, I am witty, I think" (iv, iii).

The Country Wife, like its predecessor, is an obvious vehicle for Wycherley's witty ideas, for unlike Etherege, he wants to stick his head out from the wings to see that his point has got across to the audience. The main themes of the play have been stated before, but this play is superior to his others in the successful accommodation of the ideas to the dramatic action. In Horner he has also created his most striking Truewit—a plain-dealing, yet ironic Wit, mordant and blunt in his speech, libertine in his principles, skeptical in temper, and rationalistic. Horner is neither corrupt nor wholly cynical, for he believes in something better than what he discovers about him. As a Truewit, he believes in honesty and plain dealing, in common sense, in wit (judgment), and in fidelity to nature. Surveying the society about him, which is full of affected, unnatural creatures, he wittily plays with the coxcombs and "precise" women, and exposes them for his own malicious pleasure. This provides some scenes of excellent comic wit. Principally through Horner, Wycherley expresses his naturalistic views; and the play is clearly a witty and often mordant statement of the Truewit's attitude toward life. Frankness, truth to nature, sound judgment, and wit are praised, while pretense to honor, unnatural jealousy, and stupidity are ridiculed.

Wycherley's last work, *The Plain Dealer* (1674), is ranked very high among his plays by virtue of its "satirical" vigor and forceful characterization. But it is inferior as a play and also as a comedy of wit. The large element of farce in the play and the contrived situations are hardly conducive to the best comic wit, and the dramatic action is often subordinated to the expression of Wycherley's wit. The high regard in which the play is held, despite these flaws, is due in large part to the identification of the author with the vituperative Manly and the belief that this play is a fierce satire on the corruptness of mankind. The belief that Wycherley expressed himself through Manly is, I believe, quite wrong; for though contemporaries referred to him as "Manly," it was principally in tribute to his masculinity and frankness rather than for any virulent hatred of mankind. This identification represents a complete misconception of Wycherley the Truewit and a total misunderstanding of the play.

Palmer set the fashion in our century for this identification, and for regarding *The Plain Dealer* as a furious satire on mankind. Of it he wrote: "it is the deliberate attempt of a ferocious moralist to expose the vices of nature for our disgust. It is the unhappy protest against life of a man who lived semi-consciously against the grain of his nature."[39] To Dobrée, "the play reads like a cry of despair";[40] and Perry describes the author as a "vicious" satirist who "looks about the world, sees evil everywhere, and at once comes to the conclusion that the man who forswears human society is the man of sense and poise."[41]

I do not think that Wycherley drew himself in Manly, or that Manly was his *"beau ideal,"* "a paragon of all the masculine virtues."[42] The study of Wycherley's personality reveals

[39] Palmer, *Comedy of Manners,* pp. 134-135.
[40] Dobrée, *op. cit.,* p. 92.   [41] Perry, *op. cit.,* p. 51.   [42] *Ibid.,* p. 52.

an entirely different temper. Though there was a strong streak of the plain dealer in him, he was always a Truewit, affable and courteous, even to coxcombs, and very much a believer in moderation and good sense. Moreover, unlike Manly, he was never one to reject society and good fellowship, such as he found in the company of Dennis, Dryden, and Pope.

As keys to *The Plain Dealer*, the prologue, the ironic dedication, and the motto prefixed to the play are particularly significant. In the motto, Wycherley preferred ridicule to severity, as any Truewit would; and in the play, the severity of Manly, in his extreme misanthropy, is contrasted unfavorably with the ridicule that Eliza and Freeman resort to, which is more effective in exposing coxcombs. In the prologue, Manly expresses his mistaken opinion that fine women are all mercenary jilts, and friends all unfaithful; but he is proved wrong, and he recants on this score at the end of the play. Finally, in the ironic dedication of the play to the notorious bawd Mother Bennet, Wycherley, again with tongue in cheek, speaks out against hypocrisy and the false honor of "precise" ladies who are meretricious enough to find *double-entendres* everywhere. In an ironic tone, and yet urbanely and wittily, Wycherley repeats points made earlier. The Wycherley who speaks here in his own person is not a vicious or fierce satirist lashing out against all humanity, and this impression of the ironic and urbane Truewit is probably a more accurate one than any pieced together from the diatribes of Manly.

Obviously, the crucial character in this play is Manly, for upon our understanding of him depends our understanding of the whole play. In the *dramatis personae* he is described as "of an honest, surly, nice humour," a man who chose a sea life to avoid the world; while Freeman, who serves as his foil, is described as "a complier with the Age." It would be a mistake to assume that Wycherley was all for Manly and quite against Freeman. In the very first scene, where

most authors try to create the proper impression of a pro-
tagonist, Manly is revealed as a rough and irascible seaman,
blunt and plain dealing, and lacking in the graces of a Truewit. To be sure, he has some of the traits of a Wit. He speaks
out against the "old philosophy," which is incompatible with
reason; he makes reflections on the avarice and cowardice of
chaplains; he is cynical about women, and rails against their
folly; and he detests coxcombs like Lord Plausible and
Novel. He even has his share of similitudes. But these are
rather labored and unoriginal, as in his repartee with the
Widow:

> WID: You are as troublesome to a poor widow of business, as a
> young coxcombly rhyming lover.
> MAN: And thou art as troublesome to me, as a rook to a losing
> gamester, or a young putter of cases to his mistress or
> sempstress, who has love in her head for another. (I, i)

Fidelia believes he has wit, but Olivia observes rightly that
he rails at all mankind, and that such railing is no more a sign
of wit than cruelty is of courage (IV, ii). In his behavior there
is too much surliness, and not enough grace and decorum; and
his speeches, even when expressive of a Truewit's attitude,
are too verbose and formless to be witty or striking.

Manly becomes an object of ridicule because he is deficient
in wit, particularly in perspicacity. Olivia puts her finger on
his vulnerable point when she observes of him, "No; he
that distrusts most the world, trusts most to himself, and is
but the more easily deceived, because he thinks he can't be
deceived" (IV, ii). Manly is grievously mistaken when he
thinks he sees through men. He tells Freeman, with proud
assurance, that he judges a man by his intrinsic worth, and
will not take counterfeit honor (I, i). But he discovers, to his
chagrin, that Vernish and Olivia, whom he trusted completely
because of their pretended plain dealing, are false; and that
Freeman and Fidelia, whom he suspected of being sycophants
because they professed their love for him, are his true friends.

William Wycherley

At the end, he confesses his mistake to his friends: "I will believe there are now in the world / Good-natured friends, who are not prostitutes, / And handsome women worthy to be friends" (v, iv). Thus, like his original Alceste, in Molière's *Le Misanthrope*, Manly is exposed to ridicule for his extreme misanthropy, and his vituperations are shown to be exaggerated. He has revealed a deficiency in perspicacity and decorum; yet he is not beyond redemption as a Truewit because, at bottom, he suffers from a mistaken misanthropy rather than from a complete lack of judgment.

Freeman is more of a Truewit than Manly. He never takes life too seriously, and is never aroused to anger by the hypocrisy in the world, nor depressed by the vicissitudes of fortune. Though he is an opportunist, and goes the way of the world, he is capable of honesty and fidelity, and he is quite sincere in his friendship for Manly. At times he can be as much the plain dealer, in his ridicule of coxcombs like Major Oldfox and Novel. But unlike Manly, Freeman is Truewit enough to take pleasure in exposing fools and knaves, a sport with which his friend has no patience:

> MAN: Why the devil, then, should a man be troubled with the flattery of knaves if he be not a fool or cully; or with the fondness of fools, if he be not a knave or cheat?
> FREE: Only for his pleasure: for there is some in laughing at fools, and disappointing knaves. (III, i)

Freeman is no doubt the wittiest figure in the play, but he is deficient in decorum and reminds us a little of Etherege's Sir Frederick. He says he is "an old scourer, and can naturally beat up a wench's quarters that won't be civil" (v, ii); and his courtship of the Widow is conducted at times in the fashion of Sir Frederick: "But you have no business a-nights, widow; and I'll make you pleasanter business than any you have. For a-nights, I assure you, I am a man of great business; for the business—" (II, i). His verbal wit generally lacks distinction, though now and then he expresses an original, if inelegant, similitude, as in his reference to Jerry and his mother: "Steal away the calf, and the cow will follow you" (III, i).

The most important figure in the play, as Wycherley's *beau ideal*, is Eliza rather than Freeman or Manly: she is principally a mouthpiece for the author, without any real part in the dramatic action. She is a Truewit by virtue of her judgment; as for verbal wit, she has little to her credit. She is realistic in her attitude, and though aware of the follies of this world, like any Truewit she accepts this life:

> OLIV: Ah, cousin, what a world 'tis we live in! I am so weary of it.
> ELIZA: Truly, cousin, I can find no fault with it, but that we cannot always live in't, for I can never be weary of it.
> OLIV: O hideous! you cannot be in earnest sure, when you say you like the filthy world.
> ELIZA: You cannot be in earnest sure, when you say you dislike it. (II, i)

Eliza's attitude is more representative than Manly's of Wycherley's own feelings, and it is a restatement of Hippolita's remark to Mrs. Caution. Eliza is the author's mouthpiece in other respects: she defends *The Country Wife* and its "china" scene, and she also censures Novel and Olivia for their senseless railing spree. She is obviously a foil for her cousin Olivia, and she at least displays a great deal of judgment if not much distinction of speech.

The play is superior in its gallery of Witwouds than in its Truewits. Of these, the most prominent and the most complex is Olivia. But as a female coxcomb, she is a somewhat inconsistent creation. On the one hand, she is the "precise" but lustful woman who pretends to have an aversion to sex and "filthy" plays, and yet has a furious sexual appetite that must be indulged clandestinely. In this naturalistically conceived role, she is sometimes perspicacious and frank, and displays some judgment. When she quarrels with Manly only to be rid of him, she observes to herself: "Well, we women, like the rest of the cheats of the world, when our cullies or creditors have found us out, and will or can trust no longer, pay debts and satisfy obligations with a quarrel, the kindest present a man can make to his mistress, when he can make no more presents" (ii, i). In the pursuit of sexual satisfaction, she is as bold as any man, and she can even be witty on such occasions: "So, I have at once now brought about those two grateful businesses, which all prudent women do together, secured money and pleasure; and now all interruptions of the last are removed. Go, husband, and come up, friend; just the buckets in the well; the absence of one brings the other. But I hope, like them too, they will not meet in the way, jostle, and clash together" (iv, ii).

On the other hand, as an affected female Witwoud who loves malicious raillery, she is rather stupid and is easily exposed to ridicule. In the long railing scene with Novel, she monopolizes the conversation, and yet says naïvely, "Ay, those fops who love to talk all themselves are of all things my aversion" (ii, i). The scenes with Eliza in which her coxcombry is exposed through her own remarks are inconsistent with other scenes in which she displays her perspicacity. Olivia is obviously intended as a female Witwoud, but Wycherley fails to observe decorum in her characterization.

The other coxcombs in the play are more consistently portrayed because they are simpler creations. Novel is a Witwoud with two failings. First, he mistakes mere novelty for wit, since wit is characterized by novelty; and as Olivia observes, he "affects novelty as much as the fashion, and is as fantastical as changeable, and as well known as the fashion; who likes nothing but what is new, nay, would choose to have his friend or his title a new one" (ii, i). Second, he mistakes railing and noise for wit, and is sometimes amusing as a loud, talkative coxcomb:

Nov: Prithee when did you ever find me want something to say, as you do often?

MAN: Nay, I confess thou art always talking, roaring, or making a noise; that I'll say for thee.

Nov: Well, and is talking a sign of a fool?

MAN: Yes, always talking, especially too if it be loud and fast, is the sign of a fool.

Nov: Pshaw! talking is like fencing, the quicker the better; run 'em down, run 'em down, no matter for parrying; push on still, sa, sa, sa! No matter whether you argue in form, push in guard or no.

MAN: Or hit or no; I think thou always talkest without thinking, Novel.

Nov: Ay, ay; studied play's the worse, to follow the allegory, as the old pedants say. (v, ii)

His companion Major Oldfox is "an old impertinent Fop" who values "that facetious noble way of wit, quibbling." Lord Plausible is Witless, a person of "supercilious forms, and slavish ceremonies," who "libels everybody with dull praise." These are rather conventional figures, and they are usually too impertinent or too stupid to be very amusing, for Wycherley's contempt for coxcombs seems to have been too great to permit an airy treatment of them such as we find in Etherege's comedies.

The Plain Dealer reveals signs of careless writing, and it lacks the elegance and decorum necessary for the best wit comedy. On one occasion, Manly says that Olivia has disdained "the gaudy fluttering parrots of the town, apes and echoes of men only, and refused their common-place pert chat, flattery and submissions, to be entertained with my sullen bluntness, and honest love" (I, i). In the next act, Freeman uses almost the same words in speaking to Manly of Olivia: "Faith, pardon her, captain, that, since she could no longer be entertained with your manly bluntness and honest love, she takes up with the pert chat and commonplace flattery of these fluttering parrots of the town, apes and echoes of men only" (II, i). This is symptomatic of one of Wycherley's chief weaknesses, his repetitiousnness and his constant harping on a few themes. This is what contemporaries might have called "a lack of invention." The play is also weak in such scenes as the raillery passage of Novel and Olivia and the conversations between Olivia and Eliza, for these are non-dramatic and are intended solely to expose a Witwoud's coxcombry and hypocrisy.

In the play there is not much comic wit of a high order, for there is no pair of witty lovers. The repartee of Freeman and the Widow is frank but lacking in elegance; and Olivia's rallying of Manly is sarcastic rather than witty: "And then, that captain-like carelessness in your dress, but especially your scarf; 'twas just such another, only a little higher tied, made me in love with my tailor as he passed by my window the last training-day; for we women adore a martial man, and you have nothing wanting to make you more one, or more agreeable, but a wooden leg" (ii, i). The Witwouds in the play, Novel in particular, provide some amusement as butts of the Truewits; but there is nothing comparable to the wit of the earlier plays. *The Plain Dealer*, which contemporaries praised for its wit, is principally witty in the sense that it expresses Wycherley's sound judgment: his sensible acceptance of this world; his ironic commentary on life; and his detestation of the coxcombry of Olivia, the extreme misanthropy of Manly, and the folly of Novel and Lord Plausible.

In the four plays, the dominant impression we have of Wycherley is of a Truewit who is ironic and intellectual. There are frequent ironies of situation and of speech, which give rise to *double-entendres*; and the wit in the plays has a mordant quality. Perhaps the finest expression of this side of his temper is the character of Horner, whose plain dealing, like the author's, is so ironic that it is misunderstood by the victims. In the plays there is a strong impression also of Wycherley's intellectual power, but this is due not so much to originality of thought as to mere vigor and repetition and frequent intrusion *in propria persona*. Further, the wit of

William Wycherley

Wycherley is characterized by a preponderance of judgment over fancy. The result of these tendencies is a lessening in the gaiety of wit comedy, and an increase in the mordancy of tone. Instead of the raillery of Dorimant and Harriet, we have more often the ironic laughter of Horner enjoying the spectacle of Witwoud, Witless, or knaves wriggling on the hook of their own folly. At the same time, we must remember how often Wycherley has his tongue in cheek, and how easily his ironic wit can be mistaken for savage indignation.

The most striking feature of Wycherley's plays is the Truewit's philosophy, as expressed through character and action, and the consistency with which he maintained his naturalistic and witty point of view from first to last. In *Love in a Wood*, Wycherley effectively ridiculed a female coxcomb in Lady Flippant, and exposed the "preciseness" of Gripe and Mrs. Joyner. In *The Gentleman Dancing-Master*, he took off the "precise" woman in Mrs. Caution, expressed his anti-conventional and anticlerical wit through minor figures, and, most important, through Hippolita, he wittily criticized conventional marriages and defended the hedonic age. In *The Country Wife*, he successfully ridiculed "preciseness," in Lady Fidget; and in the Pinchwife and the Harcourt-Alithea stories he expressed his naturalistic view that marriage must be based on freedom and equality. Finally, in *The Plain Dealer*, Wycherley exposed the coxcombry of Olivia and Novel and the exaggerated misanthropy of Manly, and through Eliza, and partly through Freeman, he expressed the Truewit's sensible and easy attitude toward life.

Basic to this witty exposure of "preciseness," coxcombry, and pretense, is the naturalistic point of view, which recognizes the egoism of man and the naturalness of sex. The chief criterion of conduct is fidelity to nature, and Wycherley exposes those who are false to nature in one way or another. Thus, the "precise" woman who expresses an aversion to sex and pretends to honor is exposed as a hypocrite who has as

William Wycherley

much sexual desire as anyone else. The Witwoud is likewise ridiculed as one who goes against nature by trying to be more than he is. This is not orthodox satire, and there is little reason to regard Wycherley as a fierce satirist or a Puritan at heart. He was always a Truewit, naturalistic in his standards, skeptical of the "old philosophy," an enemy to coxcombs, anticonventional in his wit, a lover of freedom and naturalness, and a believer in sound sense. What makes him a more incisive writer than either Etherege or Congreve is his ironic wit and his more intense nature.

Wycherley's world is not as carefree and gay as Etherege's, but neither is it as malicious. It is a richer world, with more diversity in the characters, and greater extremes of folly and stupidity, for Wycherley was far more aware than Etherege that there are knaves and asses in the world. But he was sufficiently a Truewit to be satisfied with wittily exposing the Witwouds, Witlesses, and knaves with whom the world abounds, and in his criticism there is little evidence of misanthropy, morbidity, or ferocity. In his writings he may not have attained the decorum of Etherege nor created such elegant and witty figures as Harriet and Dorimant; but he himself retained the intellectual and social virtues of the Truewit. This impression is corroborated by Lely's portrait of him, in which the Truewit is clearly visible—in the aristocratic bearing, the witty sparkle of his eyes, the touch of libertinism in the sensuous mouth and chin, and in the manly, urbane, and intelligent countenance.

VII

WILLIAM CONGREVE

WILLIAM CONGREVE has suffered equally with Wycherley
and Etherege at the hands of critics, who have popularized
the notion that he was a cynical writer of artificial comedies,
and that, at best, he was a brilliant stylist with nothing original to say. This view is summed up aptly in Schelling's phrase
—"Congreve's brilliant soulless dramatic art."[1]

The belief that Congreve was principally a stylist owes
much to critics like Hazlitt and Meredith, who both stressed
his style and wit.[2] The prevalence of this misconception is
evident in a suggestion like Schelling's, that for Congreve
"the glittering beads of his epigram and repartee" were the
most important element in the plays, or Palmer's statement
that the whole duty of man in Congreve's world is to talk
brilliantly.[3] For Dobrée, Congreve is a type of "pure" creator
(as distinguished from the generality of writers) who must be
judged principally as a supreme stylist.[4] This point of view
is summed up succinctly in Perry's statement that "for better
or worse Congreve's distinction as an author rests on his ability to write witty dialogue in literary form."[5] The stress on
style, at the expense of content, is evident in what he says
further about Congreve: "His work has the excellent sauce of
wit, but it lacks the body of good understanding. The surface
is so dazzling that sometimes one forgets what is lacking be-

[1] Schelling, *English Drama*, p. 307.
[2] "Every page presents a shower of brilliant conceits, is a tissue of epigrams in prose, is a new triumph of wit, a new conquest over dulness"—
Hazlitt, *Lectures on the English Comic Writers*, in *The Collected Works*,
VIII, 71.
[3] Schelling, *op. cit.*, p. 268; Palmer, *Comedy of Manners*, p. 191.
[4] Dobrée, intro. to *Comedies by William Congreve*, pp. xv-xvi.
[5] Perry, *Comic Spirit in Restoration Drama*, p. 78.

neath it, till, upon reflection, it is only too evident that Congreve never really understood the fundamental principles of human behavior. . . . He is, after all, only a professional funny man."[6] This is surprising commentary on the creator of the charming Mrs. Millamant, the elegant Mirabell, crusty old Sir Sampson, and plain-dealing Ben; and the exponent of a witty and sensible view of life.

An equally serious misconception about Congreve is that he was cynical and heartless—a view given wide currency by Palmer in his criticism of *The Way of the World*: "The cheerful wickedness of Etherege has given place to a more rounded and systematic iniquity; Congreve's characters are epicures in pleasure, exquisites in villainy. Their morality is as smoothly asserted in conduct and precept as the philosophy of Pope, which confines the universe in a couplet, and dismisses its ruler in an epigram. Congreve's muse is the full-blooded jade of Etherege and Wycherley come to discretion. Coleridge was right. Congreve's theme is often but simple wickedness, empty of pleasure or lust."[7]

This misunderstanding of Congreve arises principally from a failure to penetrate beneath the brilliant surface of the plays to the heart pulsating beneath, and from a neglect of contemporary testimony about the man. Actually, Congreve is less open to the charge of cynicism than Etherege or Wycherley, and he was, in fact, too warm-hearted and moral to be a perfect Truewit. If we examine his life and work, we discover that he also subscribed less wholeheartedly than Etherege and Wycherley to the naturalistic assumption of man's egoism. Mirabell, beside Dorimant or Horner, is extremely sensible and moral; and Mrs. Millamant, unlike Harriet, has deep feelings stirring so close to the surface that they sometimes threaten to break through. Congreve, after all, belonged, not to the Restoration, but to the age of William

[6] *Ibid.*, p. 80.
[7] Palmer, *Comedy of Manners*, pp. 191-192.

and Mary and of Queen Anne; and he was the intimate of people like Walsh, Gay, Pope, and Lady Mary Montagu rather than of libertines like Sedley, Rochester, and Buckingham. The life of Congreve was also characterized by a prudence markedly absent in the lives of Etherege and Wycherley: there were no great scandals, no drunken brawls, no surgeons to cure the "pox," and no unwise marriage to a widow. In fact, Congreve prudently remained a bachelor. The growing stress on judgment which characterized the age is also reflected in his work in a greater emphasis on sound sense, good nature, and restraint. His work is the culmination of the comedy of wit, but it is also transitional in nature, and points the way to the age of enlightenment. The carefree, witty spirit of *The Old Batchelor* ultimately gives way to the sound sense and mature philosophy of *The Way of the World*; and at that point, Congreve is not far removed from Addison, who would temper wit with morality.

Congreve remained a Truewit in many ways, nevertheless; and his career in some respects paralleled that of Wycherley and Etherege. He entered the Middle Temple, but, as Cibber observed, "the severe study of the Law was so ill adapted to the sprightly genius of Congreve, that he never attempted to reconcile himself to a way of life, for which he had the greatest aversion."[8] The author of the *Memoirs of the Life, Writings, and Amours of William Congreve* described him as having a taste too delicate, and a wit too fine, to be pleased with such "crabbed unpalatable Study; in which, the laborious dull plodding Fellow, generally excells the more sprightly and vivacious Wit."[9] He turned to the more compatible pursuit of being an amateur writer and a Wit; and after preliminary ventures in writing some verse and one short novel, he gained public recognition, like his predecessors, with a witty play.

[8] Cibber, *Lives of the Poets*, IV, 84.
[9] Charles Wilson, *Memoirs of the Life, Writings, and Amours of William Congreve*, London, 1730, p. 2.

William Congreve

Congreve also possessed personal distinction of a sort that would endear him to other Truewits. Lady Mary Wortley Montagu remembered him as the wittiest person in her father's circle, and according to Cibber, "He was sprightly as well as elegant in his manners."[10] Steele observed, too, that his wit was such that it always pleased and never offended.[11] The charm of his wit is evident from his correspondence and his nondramatic writings; and in his personal letters there is, as Cibber said, "a great deal of wit and spirit, a fine flow of language; . . . so happily intermixt with a lively and inoffensive raillery, that it is impossible not to be pleased with them at the first reading."[12] Of this nature are his letters to his friends Moyle and Dennis; and his chatty, gallant letter to Mrs. Porter, from Holland, in which he remarked, "I leave you to Judge whether Holland can be said to be wanting in Gallantry, when it is Customary there to enclose a Billet doux to a Lady, in a letter to her husband."[13] Or the warm letters to his dear friend Joseph Keally, with such Shakespearean references as, "I am grown fat; but you know I was born with somewhat of a round belly. . . . However, think of me, as I am nothing extenuate."[14] In his letters there is none of the sharp raillery and sting of Etherege's wit, for Congreve united in himself the virtues he admired in a friend—"A Clear Wit, sound Judgment and a Merciful Disposition."[15] Now and then he was capable of a piece of sharp raillery like " 'Squire Bickerstaff Detected," wittily deflating the notorious astrologer Partridge. But he was more himself when he told Dennis, "I profess my self an Enemy to Detraction";[16] and his contemporaries thought of him as "a Gentle-

[10] Spence, *Anecdotes*, p. 175; Cibber, *Lives of the Poets*, IV, 92.
[11] Richard Steele, *The Correspondence of Richard Steele*, ed. Rae Blanchard, London, 1941, p. 473.
[12] Cibber, *Lives of the Poets*, IV, 92.
[13] William Congreve, *The Mourning Bride, Poems, & Miscellanies*, ed. Bonamy Dobrée, London, 1928, p. 524.
[14] *Ibid.*, p. 495.   [15] *Ibid.*, Dedication to *Incognita*.
[16] Wilson, *Memoirs of . . . Congreve*, p. 59.

man of Wit and good Sense."[17] The wit of Congreve is more elegant and often more striking than that of either Etherege or Wycherley, but it is free of Etherege's malice and Wycherley's mordant irony.

As a man, Congreve was affectionate in temper, and he was always amiable and frank in his relations with others. Among his friends he numbered worthy men like Dryden, Steele, Dennis, Walsh, Southerne, Pope, Swift, and Sir Richard Temple. Even the usually sharp-tongued Pope paid tribute to him as one of "the three most honest hearted, real good men, of the poetical members of the kit-cat club";[18] and Gay eulogized him as "friendly *Congreve*, unreproachful man!"[19] The great John Dryden lauded his art, and at the same time commended the man: "So much the Sweetness of your Manners move, / We cannot Envy you, because we Love."[20] Equally warm and admiring is the tribute of Lord Lansdowne: "*Congreve* is your familiar Acquaintance, you may judge of *Wycherley* by him: They have the same manly way of Thinking and Writing, the same Candour, Modesty, Humanity, and Integrity of Manner. It is impossible not to love them for their own sakes, abstracted from the Merit of their Works."[21] Among literary men, Congreve was the universal peace-maker, and he tried to reconcile even those who were enemies of each other, like Dennis and Pope.[22] He appears to have been the arbiter in a short quarrel between Dryden and Tonson;[23] and it was Congreve to whom Steele wrote about

[17] Wells, *A Comparison between the Two Stages*, p. 34.

[18] Spence, *Anecdotes*, p. 35.

[19] John Gay, "Mr. Pope's Welcome from Greece," *The Poetical Works of John Gay*, ed. G. C. Faber, London, 1926, p. 166.

[20] Dryden, "To my Dear Friend Mr. Congreve, On his Comedy, call'd, *The Double-Dealer.*"

[21] Lansdowne, "A Character of Mr. *Wycherly*," in *The Genuine Works*, I, 436.

[22] Wilson, *Memoirs of . . . Congreve*, p. 135.

[23] See Dryden's letters to Tonson, August 1693; June 8, 1695; October 29, 1695. Letters 26, 33, 34, in *The Letters of John Dryden*, ed. Charles E. Ward.

his differences with Tickell: "You will please to pardon me, that I have, thus, laid this nice Affair before a Person who has the acknowledg'd Superiority to all others, not only in the most excellent Talents, but possessing them with an Equanimity, Candour and Benevolence, which render those Advantages a Pleasure as great to the rest of the World, as they can be to the Owner of them."[24]

He merited such praise by being friendly toward all, and even after becoming a successful writer, he remembered old friends like Southerne, who had been less fortunate in life.[25] He was quite without vanity, and the unjustness of Voltaire's criticism is evident from the picture Jacob paints of Congreve's later years: "Mr. *Congreve*, notwithstanding he has justly acquir'd the greatest Reputation in Dramatick Writings, is so far from being puff'd up with Vanity (a Failing in most Authors of Excellency) that he abounds with Humility and good Nature. He does not shew so much the Poet as the Gentleman; he is ambitious of few Praises, tho' he deserves numerous Encomiums; he is genteel and regular in Oeconomy, unaffected in Behaviour, pleasing and informing in his Conversation, and respectful to all."[26] In his later years, though afflicted with gout and cataracts of the eyes, Congreve maintained his urbane, cheerful temper, like the Truewit that he was.[27] In fact, there is little to substantiate Palmer's impression of a man "disdainful, delicately superior, touched with a light, fastidious irony."[28]

In Congreve there was an inwardness and reserve, born of good taste and judgment, which might have impressed strangers as a sign of coldness. But his close friends knew better, and his personal letters indeed reveal a man of strong affections.

[24] Steele, *Correspondence*, p. 517.
[25] Cibber, *Lives of the Poets*, IV, 91.
[26] Jacob, *The Poetical Register*, p. 42.
[27] Gay to Swift, in *The Correspondence of Jonathan Swift*, ed. F. Elrington Ball, London, 1910, III, 153. Also Jonathan Swift, *Journal to Stella*, ed. Harold Williams, Oxford, 1948, I, 69-70.
[28] Palmer, *op. cit.*, p. 156.

William Congreve

On the occasion of a serious accident to his intimate friend Joseph Keally, Congreve wrote, "I am sure you know me enough to know I feel very sensibly and silently for those whom I love."[29] In an earlier letter, he wrote that Keally's friends regretted his absence from London, then added, "I need not tell you that I do."[30] He desired "ease and quiet," and he confessed to Keally, "If I have not ambition, I have other passions more easily gratified. Believe me I find none more pleasing to me than my friendship for you."[31] This capacity for deep affection brought him the enduring friendship of many people, most notably of Henrietta, Duchess of Marlborough.

In keeping with his fundamentally sober temper, Congreve displayed more interest in scholarly matters than either Etherege or Wycherley. His translations of Juvenal and of Priam's lament in Homer show his excellent classical background, and his original "Discourse on the Pindarique Ode" and the letter to Dennis "Concerning Humour in Comedy" attest to his critical powers. Even as a student, he manifested his interest in critical theory by purchasing Roscommon's translation of Horace's *Ars Poetica*, Dryden's "Essay of Dramatic Poesy," and the two volumes of Hedelin's *Whole Art of the Stage*.[32] But always a Truewit, he remarked, on the occasion of the letter on humors in comedy, that he was neither able nor willing to undertake a long and labored discourse, but simply wished to communicate a few unpremeditated thoughts, as between friend and friend, without setting up for a literary dictator.[33]

In philosophical matters, he appears not to have been particularly interested in abstruse speculation, as one might well expect from a Truewit. But he showed a familiarity with

[29] Congreve, *The Mourning Bride, Poems, & Miscellanies*, p. 497.
[30] *Ibid.*, p. 486.
[31] *Ibid.*, p. 507.
[32] John C. Hodges, *William Congreve the Man*, New York, 1941, p. 28.
[33] Congreve, *Mourning Bride*, etc., p. 1.

William Congreve

naturalistic thinking by referring to Epicurus and atoms in his youthful *Incognita*.[34] In an "Epistle of Improving the Present Time," addressed to Sir Richard Temple toward the end of his life, he expressed a mild epicureanism and skepticism most characteristic of his temper:

> Come, see thy Friend, retir'd without Regret,
> Forgetting Care, or striving to forget;
> In easy Contemplation soothing Time
> With Morals much, and now and then with Rhime,
> Not so robust in Body, as in Mind,
> And always undejected, tho' declin'd;
> Not wondering at the World's new wicked Ways,
> Compar'd with those of our Fore-fathers Days,
> For Virtue now is neither more or less,
> And Vice is only varied in the Dress;
> Believe it, Men have ever been the same,
> And all the Golden Age, is but a Dream.[35]

It is not often that Congreve was actually libertine in his sentiments, as in the song beginning, "Tell me no more I am deceiv'd," and ending on the cynical note:

> You think she's false, I'm sure she's kind
> I take her Body, you her Mind,
>   Who has the better bargain?[36]

In several other poems he expressed the naturalistic view that women are inconstant, frail, and mercurial creatures.[37] But there is little reason to believe that Congreve was really cynical, or that he was a libertine in principle and practice, as Etherege was; and though there were rumors that Mrs. Bracegirdle had been kind to him, even the author of the *Memoirs* had to admit that there was no real justification for the "amours" in the title.[38]

[34] *Ibid.*, p. 29.   [35] *Ibid.*, pp. 401-402.   [36] *Ibid.*, p. 243.
[37] See remarks of Semele to Jupiter in *Semele* (ii, iii), beginning: "With my Frailty don't upbraid me, / I am Woman as you made me."
[38] See Hodges, *William Congreve the Man*, for the theory that Congreve had a liaison with the Duchess of Marlborough.

William Congreve

Congreve never professed naturalistic principles; yet he subscribed to naturalism insofar as he used nature as the standard, in censuring Witwouds and affected creatures, and also in depicting his Truewits as egoistic and libertine. In *Incognita* he might have been describing himself when he said that Aurelian abhorred anything that was conceited.[39] Writing to Dennis, he observed that "Nature abhors to be forced."[40] And in a poem entitled "Of Pleasing," he declared that the foolish and the ugly make the most ostentatious display, and he concluded:

> All Rules of Pleasing in this one unite,
> *Affect not any thing in Nature's spight.*
>
> . . . .
>
> *None are, for being what they are, in fault,*
> *But for not being what they wou'd be thought.*[41]

Hence the criticism in his plays of would-be wits, pretenders to courage, and superannuated coquettes. Congreve believed his art to be firmly founded on nature, and Steele expressed the sentiment of contemporaries when he praised Congreve's discernment "in distinguishing the Characters of Mankind."[42] The Truewits in his comedies are delineations of men who conform to nature; the Witwouds are copies of those who are false to nature. Fundamental to this distinction is their fidelity to nature. Congreve would have been very much surprised, I think, at Palmer's remark that his "comic appeal . . . rests upon the pretence that nature has been driven out; that man is emancipated from her rule."[43] He was committed, after all, to naturalism in art.

The comedies of Congreve reveal many of the qualities that we have found in the works of Etherege and Wycherley. There is the same assumption of man's egoistic, libertine nature; there are skeptical, malicious, and sexual witticisms;

---

[39] Congreve, *Mourning Bride*, etc., p. 16.
[40] *Ibid.*, p. 8. [41] *Ibid.*, p. 325.
[42] Steele, *Correspondence*, p. 473. [43] Palmer, *Comedy*, p. 40.

and there is a strong interest in wit in all its manifestations. At the same time, the growing stress on judgment and on morality produced some modification in the type of wit comedy he wrote. But an examination of his plays reveals how successfully he maintained a Truewit's sensible attitude toward life in transitional times, and how groundless is the charge of cynicism and superficiality brought against him by the "manners" critics.

His first play, *The Old Batchelor* (1693),[44] appealed to the town, according to Jacob, because of its "genteel and sprightly Wit"; and Cibber tells us that its singular success brought Congreve the acquaintance of the Earl of Halifax, "who was then the professed patron of men of wit."[45] The play is, indeed, a witty comedy. It has a group of Truewits reminiscent of Etherege's quartet in *She Would if She Could*, a Witless in Sir Joseph Wittol, and several outwitting situations. Yet Ramble, in *A Comparison between the Two Stages*, objected that there were too many quibbles in the play.[46] Bevil Higgons was more kindly in observing, "But you, too Bounteous, sow your Wit so thick, / We are surpriz'd, and know not where to pick."[47] Actually the stricture in the *Comparison* is justified, for though the play is liberally sprinkled with wit, it is often wit of a fanciful nature unrestrained by judgment. In the opening scene, for example, there is a passage of sophistical wit in which Bellmour and Vainlove play with the conceit that a wife, in choosing a lover resembling her husband, really displays her extreme love for her husband, and thereby abuses the lover rather than the husband. Such wit springs from the sprightly fancy of a youthful Truewit who now and then worried an idea to death, and these are excesses of im-

---

[44] The edition used for the plays is *Comedies by William Congreve*, ed. Bonamy Dobrée, London, 1944.
[45] Jacob, *The Poetical Register*, p. 43; Cibber, *Lives of the Poets*, IV, 87.
[46] Wells, p. 44.
[47] Higgons, "To Mr. Congreve, on his Play called *The Old Batchelor*."

maturity that Congreve did not succeed in pruning away at this stage.

The ebullient opening scene between Bellmour and Vainlove sets the tone of the play, and reveals the high spirits of these Wits. From Bellmour we have the carefree libertinism that is the mark of the Truewit: "Ay, ay, Wisdom's nothing but a pretending to know and believe more than we really do. You read of but one wise Man, and all that he knew was, that he knew nothing. Come, come, leave Business to Idlers, and Wisdom to Fools; they have need of 'em: Wit, be my Faculty, and Pleasure, my Occupation; and let Father Time shake his Glass." This is the very same philosophy by which Horner and Dorimant live, and yet how different is the spirit: Bellmour's is a joyful libertinism, without a trace of disillusionment, and the tone is effervescent and youthful and optimistic. Here, the skepticism has not hardened into cynicism, and the libertinism of spirit is not enervated by the satiety that comes of excess. Bellmour carries everything before him with his dashing wit and his youthful high spirits.

As a Truewit, he is frankly naturalistic, inconstant, and predatory, but there is no malice in his heart. He is enough of a Truewit to enjoy the spectacle of an old bachelor in love; but "Look you," he says, "*Heartwell* is my Friend; and tho' he be blind, I must not see him fall into the Snare, and unwittingly marry a Whore" (v, iii). He reminds us a little of Etherege's Courtall, except that he is more intelligent and perspicacious. Of his own activities, he remarks in a soliloquy: "Why what a Cormorant in Love am I! who, not contented with the slavery of honourable Love in one Place, and the Pleasure of enjoying some half a score Mistresses of my own acquiring; must yet take *Vainlove*'s Business upon my Hands, because it lay too heavy upon his; So am not only forc'd to lie with other Mens Wives for 'em, but must also undertake the harder Task of obliging their Mistresses—I must take up, or I shall never hold out; Flesh and Blood cannot bear it always" (I, ii). He also indulges in anticlerical wit, and observes that a soldier's dress "now-a'days as often cloaks Cowardice, as a black Gown does Atheism" (I, v). On one occasion, he assumes a Puritan's garb to go whoring, and he remarks to his servant: "I wonder why all our young Fellows should glory in an Opinion of Atheism; when they may be so much more conveniently lewd under the Coverlet of Religion" (IV, i).

In such activities, Bellmour is ably assisted by Setter, who, like most servants in wit comedy, is clever, opportunistic, and cynical. Setter has his share of anticlerical wit, and when asked by Bellmour whether he has provided the necessary garments for an assignation, he replies: "All, all, Sir; the large sanctified Hat, and the little precise Band, with a swinging long spiritual Cloak, to cover carnal Knavery—not forgetting the black Patch, which Tribulation *Spintext* wears, as I'm inform'd, upon one Eye, as a penal Mourning for the ogling Offences of his Youth; and some say, with that Eye, he first discover'd the frailty of his Wife" (III, iv). He also indulges in skeptical witticisms, as when he remarks: "*Mercury* was a Pimp too, but, though I blush to own it, at this time, I must confess I am somewhat fall'n from the Dignity of my Function, and do condescend to be scandalously imploy'd in the Promotion of vulgar Matrimony" (v, ix). Though some critics might object that Setter is too witty, his rough wit is in keeping with his character and social status. Congreve was a sufficiently conscious artist to maintain decorum in characterization; and in the letter on humor, he observed that "the Manner of *Wit* should be adapted to the *Humour*. As for instance, a Character of a Splenetick and Peevish *Humour*, should have a Satyrical Wit. A Jolly and Sanguine *Humour*, should have a Facetious Wit."[48]

Among the women, Belinda is the wittiest, in the sense of being the most fanciful and striking in her speech, though it

---

[48] Congreve, *Mourning Bride*, etc., p. 2.

appears that Congreve intended her also as an object of ridicule because of her affectations.[49] Like Olivia, she professes to loathe "that filthy, awkward, two-leg'd Creature, Man," and she exclaims to her friend, "O Gad I hate your horrid Fancy—This Love is the Devil, and sure to be in Love is to be possess'd—'Tis in the Head, the Heart, the Blood, the—All over—O gad you are quite spoil'd—I shall loath the sight of Mankind for your sake" (ii, iii). But, at the same time, she is very much attracted to Bellmour.

Yet Belinda's affectations are so spirited that they are charming; and when she meets Araminta on the street, her hyperbolical wit has great verve:

> BELIN: Oh the most inhumane, barbarous Hackney-Coach! I am jolted to a Jelly—Am I not horribly touz'd? (Pulls out a Pocket-Glass.)
> ARAM: Your Head's a little out of order.
> BELIN: A little! O frightful! What a furious Phyz I have! O most rueful! Ha, ha, ha: O Gad, I hope no body will come this way, 'till I have put my self a little in repair—(iv, viii)

She has more malice than anyone else in the play, and in her flamboyant style she wittily dissects two plump country girls she met shopping: "And t'other did so stare and gape—I fansied her like the Front of her Father's Hall; her Eyes were the two Jut-Windows, and her Mouth the great Door, most hospitably kept open, for the Entertainment of travelling Flies" (iv, viii). Belinda is, indeed, quite up to Sharper's description of her as "too proud, too inconstant, too affected and too witty, and too handsome for a Wife." With Bellmour she has some passages of high-spirited repartee:

> BELIN: Prithee hold thy Tongue—Lard, he has so pester'd me with Flames and Stuff—I think I shan't endure the sight of a Fire this Twelve-month.
> BELL: Yet all can't melt that cruel frozen Heart.
> BELIN: O Gad I hate your hideous Fancy—you said that once

---

[49] Wilson, *Memoirs of . . . Congreve*, p. 31.

before—if you must talk impertinently, for Heavens sake let it be with Variety; don't come always, like the Devil, wrapt in Flames—I'll not hear a Sentence more, that begins with an, *I burn*—Or an, *I beseech you, Madam.* (II, viii)

She has style and verve, and though her wit is fanciful and extravagant rather than judicious, it is usually entertaining.

Beside Bellmour and Belinda, Vainlove and Araminta appear far less colorful. They remind us a little of the honorable couples in the first plays of Etherege and Wycherley, for they are more emotional and thoughtful in their approach to life than most Truewits. Vainlove may be libertine in his principles, but he is a little too fastidious and precious, in his taste only for women who will be pursued without pursuing. And in the second act, when Araminta remarks on the inconstancy of men, he breaks in too feelingly with an "O Madam,"—to which she sensibly answers, "Nay come, I find we are growing serious, and then we are in great Danger of being dull" (II, vii). At bottom, Vainlove has a sober heart, and it is this, perhaps, which appeals to Araminta, since she has judgment and a refined sensibility rather than much fanciful wit.

One of the most striking figures in the play is Heartwell, a naturalistically conceived figure who would be a Truewit but for his lack of perspicacity. He is compounded of familiar ingredients: he is a plain dealer, a libertine, and a skeptic. "My Talent is chiefly that of speaking Truth," he declares; "I am for having every body be what they pretend to be; a Whoremaster be a Whoremaster; and not like *Vainlove*, kiss a Lap-Dog with Passion, when it would disgust him from the Lady's own Lips" (I, iv). He is frankly naturalistic, and has no high opinion of religion, women, or matrimony; love, for him, is a physic, and he goes whoring to purge himself. As the old bachelor in love, he is witty, though at his own expense, when he cries, "O Dotage, Dotage! That ever that noble Passion, *Lust*, should ebb to this degree—No reflux of vigorous Blood: But milky Love, supplies the empty Channels; and prompts me to the Softness of a Child—a meer Infant and would suck" (iii, x). He is etched in bold, strong lines—an old Truewit, naturalistic, libertine, and cynical, who can be witty even when he is ridiculous.

The play has the usual butts for the Truewits. But these are confined pretty much to Witlesses, since there are no real Witwouds, unless Belinda and possibly Heartwell are intended for that role. Sir Joseph Wittol is a stupid Witless not particularly amusing in his half-wit, except for one or two brief passages; and Captain Bluffe, "That Pot-Gun charged with Wind," is a discharger of cannon-phrases who affects brevity of speech and courage, like Pistol. Neither is a very original or striking creation.

The other objects of ridicule in the play are minor figures like Silvia and Fondlewife, who, in one way or another, illustrate the dramatist's ideas. Silvia, the rejected woman, is a naturalistically conceived creature reminiscent of Mrs. Loveit, and she and her maid Lucy express, and exemplify, the view that women are dissembling by nature. Fondlewife is "a kind of Mongrel Zealot," at once uxorious and pious, through whom Congreve exposes the unnaturalness of a marriage between an old fool and an amorous young woman, and also has a hit at the clergy.

The play is a comedy of wit in its outwitting situations, its characters, and its naturalistic and libertine philosophy. There is also a liberal sprinkling of fanciful wit which is pleasing because of its novelty. But in this youthful play there is more exuberance of spirit than judicious wit or decorum; and the elegance, the restraint, and the sensible views which are the mark of the maturest wit are notably absent.

Congreve's second play, *The Double-Dealer* (1694), has many characteristics of the comedy of wit, but it is a poor example of this type. In writing it, he apparently had a moral purpose in mind, if we are to believe the statement in his dedicatory epistle that he designed the moral first. Its ill-success Dryden attributed to the fact that Congreve had exposed the "Bitchery" of women too much, as well as the folly of men.[50] But the lack of success might also be due to the fact that the standards in the play are inconsistent; for not only is there the usual interest in true and false wit, but there is also a great deal of concern with barefaced villainy.

This confusion is reflected in the Truewits in the play. Mellefont is described by Congreve as "an Open-hearted honest Man, who has an entire Confidence in one whom he takes to be his Friend"—hardly an auspicious description for a Truewit. This deficiency in perspicacity is coupled with an absence of libertine principles. When approached by his aunt Lady Touchwood, Mellefont pleads honor and nearness of blood to Lord Touchwood as reasons for not satisfying her passion (I, iii). Cynthia similarly lacks the joyfulness and high spirits of the usual Truewit, for her mind is tinged with disillusionment; and when she has to tolerate a session with fools, she engages in this thoughtful soliloquy: " 'Tis not so hard to counterfeit Joy in the Depth of Affliction, as to dissemble Mirth in Company of Fools—Why should I call 'em Fools? The World thinks better of 'em; for these have Quality and Education, Wit and fine Conversation, are receiv'd and admir'd by the World—If not, they like and admire themselves—And why is not that true Wisdom, for 'tis Happiness: And for ought I know, we have misapply'd the Name all this while, and mistaken the Thing: Since / If Happiness in Self-content is plac'd, / The Wise are Wretched, and Fools only Bless'd" (III, xii). No Truewit would have such strange misgivings. But in this play, the stage is so dominated by Witlesses, Witwouds, and knaves that Truewits like Mellefont, Cynthia, and Careless are pushed into the background. How different this is in spirit from the first

[50] Letter to Walsh, 1694. Letter 28, in *The Letters of John Dryden*, ed. Charles E. Ward.

play, where the Truewits flocked joyously over the stage, and firmly put down the Witlesses when they made nuisances of themselves. The spirit of disillusionment, and the hushed awareness on the part of the Truewits of evil beyond their ken, gives the play a somber and even sad quality.

Cynthia and Mellefont are so sincerely in love from the beginning that they do not rally each other spiritedly as most lovers in wit comedy do. Instead, they have misgivings about their approaching marriage; and with as much seriousness as levity, Cynthia says to Mellefont, "What think you of drawing Stakes, and giving over in time?" After playing with the similitude for a moment, he responds with the sensible observation that though "Fortune indeed makes the Match . . . the Game depends intirely upon Judgement" (ii, iii). The two reveal an inwardness and disillusionment which make them overstep the bounds of true wit, and they are both too level-headed and too serious about life to indulge in much fanciful wit or repartee. At one point, Cynthia does show herself a Truewit by saying to Mellefont: "But 'tis but reasonable that since I consent to like a Man without the vile Consideration of Mony, he should give me a very evident Demonstration of his Wit: Therefore let me see you undermine my Lady *Touchwood*, as you boasted, and force her to give her Consent" (iv, i). Mellefont accepts this challenge, but is trapped and seriously worsted by Lady Touchwood and Maskwell—a hard fate, indeed, for a Truewit.

The evil persons in the play, Lady Touchwood and Maskwell, are naturalistically conceived, and represent the extreme manifestations of egoism. Their characters are unredeemed by any of the gaiety or playful character of wit, and they are consequently disturbing rather than pleasing or amusing figures. Lady Touchwood is the familiar scorned woman, but she is far too passionate for wit comedy. Maskwell is a perfect exponent of Hobbes' egoistic philosophy in an unmitigated form: he acts only for himself, and has no human affections;

William Congreve

and like the bastard Edmund, he has turned against a world which is against him. He is honest only out of self-interest, and he wears the mask of honor because it will the better deceive others. Joying in his superior strength and cleverness, he exclaims, "Oh, 'tis such a Pleasure, to angle for fair fac'd Fools!" Cynically he reflects:

> Why will Mankind be Fools, and be deceiv'd?
> And why are Friends and Lovers Oaths believ'd?
> When, each, who searches strictly his own Mind,
> May so much Fraud and Power of Baseness find. (II, viii)

Maskwell, as one might expect, is anticlerical, and has a hit at the clergy in his dealings with the chaplain Mr. Saygrace, an avaricious, honey-tongued sycophant.

The character of Maskwell is particularly interesting in revealing the difference between the completely naturalistic figure, in its most egoistic and cynical form, and the libertine Truewit, who is often the object of the moralist's censure. Maskwell has the Truewit's virtue of perspicacity, and he is committed to the same libertine and egoistic principles. But he carries his egoism to the point where it is destructive of society. Whatever may be charged against the Truewit, we can see, from the striking contrast between him and Maskwell, how far he is from being corrupt in his nature. Despite his libertinism, his anticlericalism, and his skepticism, the Truewit has many attractive qualities: he admires truth and honesty, he is cultivated, he is often good-natured, and he believes in the proper use of intelligence—to expose fools, knaves, and pretenders, and to give pleasure to himself and others, rather than to further his own material interests. As Shaftesbury observed, "He never *deliberates* in this case, or considers of the matter by prudential Rules of Self-Interest and Advantage. He acts from his Nature, in a manner necessarily, and without Reflection."[51] The Truewit is egoistic and libertine insofar as

[51] Shaftesbury, "Sensus Communis," *Characteristicks*, I, 13.

he is concerned with his own pleasure. But this is the natural consequence of his being young and amorous. His egoism does not preclude generosity and sincerity, and he is, by nature, incapable of calculated knavery.

In *The Double-Dealer*, this distinction may be part of "the moral." At any rate, the knavish Maskwell and the good Mellefont do not provide much comic wit. The most lively—and amusing—characters in the play are the Witwouds and Witlesses, who provide some entertaining passages of false wit. Palmer's remark that " 'manners' alone are the theme" in these passages seems dubious,[52] for these scenes are utilized by Congreve for the familiar purpose of exposing creatures without wit. Among the men, there is the usual pair of the "pert Coxcomb" and the "Solemn Coxcomb," in Brisk and Lord Froth. Brisk is "a good-natur'd Coxcomb, and has very entertaining Follies," as Mellefont says (I, iii). He is lively and talkative and devoid of judgment. "Pox on't," he exclaims, "why should I disparage my Parts by thinking what to say? None but dull Rogues *think*" (IV, v). His pretense to wit is exposed in a passage in which the plain-dealing Careless mocks him, and Mellefont ironically takes Brisk's part:

> BRISK: I'll be judg'd by *Mellefont* here, who gives and takes Raillery better, you or I. Pshaw, Man, when I say you spoil Company by leaving it, I mean you leave no Body for the Company to laugh at. I think there I was with you, ha? *Mellefont*.
> MELL: O' my Word, *Brisk*, that was a home thrust, you have silenc'd him.
> BRISK: Oh, my Dear *Mellefont*, let me perish, if thou art not the Soul of Conversation, the very Essence of Wit, and Spirit of Wine,—The Deuce take me if there were three good Things said, or understood, since thy Amputation from the Body of our Society.—He, I think that's pretty and Metaphorical enough: I'Gad I could not have said it out of thy Company,—*Careless*, ha? (I, ii)

[52] Palmer, *Comedy of Manners*, p. 185.

As the pert coxcomb, Brisk is not an original creation, but his passages, particularly with Lady Froth, have the airiness of fanciful wit that Etherege displayed in the Sir Fopling scenes.

Lord Froth, the grave coxcomb, is less versatile than Brisk, because he is more a Witless than a Witwoud. But in the first act he has an amusing scene of false wit when he says he abstains from laughter at the theatre to mortify the poets, and is rebuked, along with Brisk, by Careless:

> LD. FROTH: I assure you . . . I laugh at no Bodies Jest but my own, or a Lady's; I assure you. . . . Now when I laugh, I always laugh alone.
> BRISK: I suppose that's because you laugh at your own Jests, I'gad, ha, ha, ha.
> LD. FROTH: He, he, I swear tho', your Raillery provokes me to a Smile.
> BRISK: Ay, my Lord, it's a sign I hit you in the Teeth, if you show 'em.
> LD. FROTH: He, he, he, I swear that's so very pretty, I can't forbear.
> CARE: I find a Quibble bears more sway in your Lordship's Face, than a Jest. (I, iv)

Again, in a parody of the familiar railing scene, Congreve exposes Lord Froth and Brisk, along with the other coxcombs, for believing that malice is wit (III, ix, x).

Among the female coxcombs, the most fanciful and amusing Witwoud is Lady Froth, a great pretender to poetry, wit, and learning. She writes "Songs, Elegies, Satires, Encomiums, Panegyricks, Lampoons, Plays, or Heroick Poems" to give vent to her whimsies and vapours, and at the moment she is writing a heroic poem on her coachman. Lady Plyant is the "precise" woman whom we have met so often in Wycherley's plays, but she is also amusingly deficient in judgment. Being married to an uxorious fool, she prefers to take her pleasures where she can find them. Careless has laid siege to her, but finds he can get no "Answer from her, that does not begin with her Honour, or her Vertue, her Religion, or some such Cant" (III, v). When she makes advances to Mellefont, she places the onus on him and exclaims, "and then seducing me, debauching my Purity, and perverting me from the Road of Vertue, in which I have trod thus long" (II, v). But unlike Wycherley's "precise" women, she is treated with a light hand, and the struggle in her between her lust and her "preciseness" is wittily presented. "I know Love is powerful," she declares to the puzzled Mellefont, "and no Body can help his Passions: 'Tis not your Fault; nor I swear it is not mine,—How can I help it, if I have Charms: And how can you help it, if you are made a Captive? I swear it is pity it should be a Fault,—But my Honour,—well, but your Honour too—but the Sin!—well, but the Necessity—O Lord, here's some Body coming, I dare not stay" (II, v).

These passages in which the Witwouds and Witlesses are exposed are rather theatrically contrived, and lack the subtlety of such scenes in later plays. This is especially true of the parody on the railing scene, in which Lord and Lady Froth, Sir Paul Plyant, and Brisk rail senselessly at their acquaintances. But these passages are managed with such lightness of touch that we are delighted by the false wit. This quality is all the more conspicuous for the dark and somber background of evil intrigues and strong passions. As a whole, the play lacks harmony because there is too much froth in the Witwouds, too much judgment in the Truewits, and too much passion in the knaves. The Truewits are also more preyed upon than preying, and the outwitting situation gets out of their hands into those of Maskwell and Lady Touchwood.

Congreve's next comedy, *Love for Love* (1695), has something of the youthful spontaneity and high spirits that marked *The Old Batchelor*, plus a strong naturalistic flavor reminiscent of Wycherley. Palmer is of the opinion that this play is less admirable than *The Double-Dealer* because here "Congreve turned aside from the natural development of his style."[53] Such a judgment is warranted only if we assume, with the "manners" critics, that Congreve was at his best in a comedy of elegant manners, and that he was in his element in the Brisk-Lady Froth scenes. Actually, *Love for Love* is superior to *The Double-Dealer*, not only as a play, but as wit comedy. The structure is more unified, with an outwitting situation involving a pair of Truewits, their parents, and foolish rivals. The witty and naturalistic temper of the play is also more consistently maintained; and though the wit passages may be less airy and fanciful, they are more striking. Congreve no doubt recognized the difference in spirit between the two comedies, for he remarked in the prologue to *Love for Love*:

> We hope there's something that may please each Taste,
> And tho' of Homely Fare we make the Feast,
> Yet you will find Variety at least.

The homely fare is provided principally in minor figures like Ben, Miss Prue, Sir Sampson, and Foresight, who are all deficient in wit. Of these, the most amusing are Ben and Sir Sampson, with their rough, boisterous wit. Ben is a sea-wit and possesses some perspicacity, though "he wants a little polishing." He has an occasional distinction of speech, as when he tells his father, "A Man that is marry'd, d'ye see, is no more like another Man, than a Gally-Slave is like one of of us free Sailors, he is chain'd to an Oar all his Life; and may-hap forc'd to tug a leaky Vessel into the Bargain" (III, vi). To Miss Prue he declares bluntly, "Look you Forsooth, I am as it were, bound for the Land of Matrimony . . . and if you like of it, may-hap I may steer into your Harbour. How say you, Mistress? The short of the thing is, that if you like me, and I like you, we may chance to swing in a Hammock together" (III, vii). His wit, however, is extremely crude and is deficient in decorum. Despite the theatrical effectiveness of Ben, Congreve probably did not regard him as a superior

[53] *Ibid.*, pp. 188-189.

William Congreve

artistic creation, since he observed to Dennis that people of a particular trade, such as sailors, country clowns, and gamesters, are distinguished by the cant of their vocation: "One may almost give a Receipt for the Composition of such a Character: For the Poet has nothing to do, but to collect a few proper Phrases and terms of Art, and to make the Person apply them by ridiculous Metaphors in his Conversation, with Characters of different Natures. Some late Characters of this kind have been very successful; but in my mind they may be Painted without much Art or Labour; since they require little more, than a good Memory and Superficial Observation."[54]

Ben's father Sir Sampson has the same rough, outspoken wit, except that in place of sea similitudes he often uses sexual similitudes. He also displays more ebullience of spirit, and his wit lies, for the most part, in his high-spiritedness, which spouts forth in the form of exaggerated metonymy. To Ben, he cries, "To your Element, Fish, be mute, Fish, and to Sea, to rule your Helm, Sirrah, don't direct me" (v, x). In his mouth, Jeremy, whose mother sold cucumbers, becomes "this Son of a Cucumber" (ii, vii). To this intemperance of figurative speech, he adds a salaciousness of thought that leaps forth as sexual wit, as when he cries that Ben shall be married punctually to a minute, go to bed to a minute, and keep time to the clock as "Consummatum est" rings all over the parish (iii, ix). All of this is extremely high-spirited and amusing, but it is fanciful rather than the most judicious wit.

There are three Truewits in the play, of sufficiently dissimilar nature to deserve some analysis. Valentine is characterized by a sangfroid that does not desert him, until he thinks he has lost Angelica. He professes libertinism, but in no way shows it, except in retrospect: we are told that he has wasted his money in prodigal pursuits, but in the play he is completely faithful to the woman he loves. Congreve described him in the *Amendments* as a prodigal, but as honest, generous,

---

[54] Congreve, *Mourning Bride*, etc., p. 7.

[178]

William Congreve

and sincere, and denied Collier's accusation that he is a profane
or obscene young man. "In short," Congreve wrote, "the
Character is a mix'd Character; his Faults are fewer than his
good Qualities"[55]—and that is pretty much what one should
expect in a Truewit. Actually Valentine is a rather reformed
libertine, and he reveals a fundamentally sound (and even
moral) character. There is more than mere levity in his crying, "I am Truth," in his pretended madness; and he seems
concerned over the prevalence of dishonesty and insincerity
when he says, "But I'll tell you one thing; it's a Question that
would puzzle an Arithmetician, if you should ask him,
whether the Bible saves more Souls in *Westminster-Abby*, or
damns more in *Westminster-Hall*" (IV, vi). Or again, when
he remarks: "Oh, Prayers will be said in empty Churches, at
the usual Hours. Yet you will see such zealous Faces behind
Counters, as if Religion were to be sold in every Shop" (IV,
xv). Though these are witty hits at insincerity, they do not
entirely obscure a fundamentally sober strain in Valentine.

He is also more introspective and thoughtful than most
Truewits, and in this, he seems to reflect something of the
author's temper. When the play opens, he has just been reading Epictetus, as though he had every intention of becoming
a stoic. He has a mind sensitive to the undercurrents of human
existence. "I know no more why I came [into this world],"
he tells his father, "than you do why you call'd me" (II, vii).
Yet he does not remain thoughtful very long, for his mind
simply skirts such ideas without dwelling on them; a moment
later, when his father has gone, he is as lighthearted and as
unconcerned as ever. What makes Valentine a more subtle
and attractive figure than most Truewits is the suggestion of
this latent reflectiveness, of a mind sensitive enough to have
some apprehension of the undercurrents of human existence.
In one of the most poetic passages in the play, he says to

[55] Congreve, *Amendments of Mr. Collier's False and Imperfect Citations*,
London, 1698, pp. 98-99, numbered 88-89.

William Congreve

Angelica: "You're a Woman,—One to whom Heav'n gave Beauty, when it grafted Roses on a Briar. You are the Reflection of Heav'n in a Pond, and he that leaps at you is sunk. You are all white, a Sheet of lovely spotless Paper, when you first are born; but you are to be scrawl'd and blotted by every Goose's Quill. I know you; for I lov'd a Woman, and lov'd her so long, that I found out a strange thing: I found out what a Woman was good for" (iv, xvi). For one moment, Valentine puts his finger on the inscrutable and eternally feminine quality in the woman he loves. But almost immediately, his wit reasserts itself; and he tells us what a woman is good for: to keep a secret, because, though she should tell, no one would believe her. He is fundamentally a Truewit, since he remains witty in his attitude toward life, despite occasional moments of seriousness.

Like Valentine, Angelica is the most complex female Truewit depicted so far by Congreve. But her picture is not finely shaded, especially in the first part of the play, and at times she is portrayed as a free-speaking young woman, rather boisterous in her wit and frankly sexual in her allusions. She teases her uncle Foresight by maliciously suggesting that his wife is unfaithful: "if you won't lend me your Coach," she exclaims, "I'll take a Hackney, or a Chair, and leave you to erect a Scheme, and find who's in Conjunction with your Wife. . . . Uncle, I'm afraid you are not Lord of the Ascendant, ha, ha, ha" (ii, iii). When Sir Sampson, whom she is leading on, says, "Odsbud, let us find Children, and I'll find an Estate!" she cries gayly, "Will you? Well, do you find the Estate, and leave t'other to me" (v, ii).

But in her encounters with Valentine, she displays greater fineness and more subtlety of wit, and, in fact, proves superior to her lover. She has malice enough to resent being tricked into a confession of love; and she plays with Valentine, wittily pretending that he is really mad:

William Congreve

VAL: You are not leaving me in this Uncertainty?

ANG: Wou'd any thing, but a Madman, complain of Uncertainty? Uncertainty and Expectation are the Joys of Life. Security is an insipid thing, and the overtaking and possessing of a Wish, discovers the Folly of the Chase. Never let us know one another better; for the Pleasure of a Masquerade is done, when we come to shew our Faces; but I'll tell you two things before I leave you; I am not the Fool you take me for; and you are mad, and don't know it. (IV, xx)

With the same maliciously whimsical wit she rebukes Tattle when he makes love to her, saying he is saner than Valentine: "O fie for shame, hold your Tongue, A passionate Lover, and five Senses in perfection! when you are as mad as *Valentine*, I'll believe you love me, and the maddest shall take me" (IV, xvi). In her repartee with Valentine, there are some beautiful "turns," a characteristic mark of Congreve's mature wit. When Valentine confesses to her that he simulated madness so that he might preserve his inheritance, we have this exchange:

ANG: How! I thought your Love of me had caus'd this Transport in your Soul; which, it seems, you only counterfeited, for mercenary Ends, and sordid Interest.

VAL: Nay, now you do me Wrong; for if any Interest was consider'd it was yours; since I thought I wanted more than Love, to make me worthy of you.

ANG: Then you thought me mercenary. (IV, xviii)

Such wit is more than mere badinage or a firing off of epigrams; it represents the skilled fencing of Truewits aroused enough to show pique but sufficiently observant of decorum not to give way to passionate speech.

At the end, Angelica capitulates in a "proviso" scene, but one which is too full of sense and sensibility to be witty. "I have done dissembling now, *Valentine*," she says, "and if that Coldness which I have always worn before you, should turn to an extream Fondness, you must not suspect it." But when Scandal expresses wonder at having found a woman for once rewarding a lover's merit, she retorts with her usual sharpness: " 'Tis an unreasonable Accusation, that you lay upon our Sex: You tax us with Injustice, only to cover your own want of Merit. . . . The Miracle to Day is, that we find A Lover true: Not that a Woman's Kind" (v, xii). To the very end, Angelica remains rather sharp-tongued and malicious, but this is tempered by sincere affection, frankness, and a whimsical wit. If she is not as fine-grained and elegant as Mrs. Millamant, she has more verve and earthiness.

Among the other characters whom we have not accounted for, Scandal is the only Truewit, but he is not a particularly original or fresh creation. He is "a Libertine in Speech, as well as Practice"; a plain dealer who paints a caustic picture of the celebrated beauty and the professed beau, and gives vent to cynical witticisms like the following: "That Women are like Tricks by slight of Hand, / Which, to admire, we should not understand" (iv, xxi), and "He alone won't betray in whom none will Confide; / And the Nymph may be Chaste that has never been try'd" (iii, iii). At the same time, he proves a faithful friend to the penniless Valentine; and when he hears that Angelica is to marry Sir Sampson, he is so upset that he cries, "Death and Hell! Where's *Valentine?*" (v, ix). This mixture of libertinism, cynical wit, plain dealing, and fidelity is one that we have met before in figures like Careless and Freeman.

Among the coxcombs, Tattle is not only the most amusing figure, as a fool who fabricates "secrets" he cannot keep, but is also one of Congreve's finest Witwouds. He is a fluttery creature of delicate texture, and he possesses considerable fanciful wit, if not much judgment. There is some wit in his remark to Prue, who wishes to marry him: "Ay, but your Father will tell you that Dreams come by Contraries, Child— O fie; what, we must not love one another now—Pshaw, that would be a foolish thing indeed—Fie, fie, you're a Woman now, and must think of a new Man every Morning, and forget him every Night—No, no, to marry is to be a Child again, and play with the same Rattle always: O fie, marrying is a paw thing" (v, iv). But his fanciful wit is marred by affectation, and there is enough of the buffoon in him so that he enjoys raising a laugh, even at his own expense, as when he tells the absurd story of how he was revenged on a parson by initiating his daughter into "the Science" (iii, iii).

With the exception of one or two figures like Tattle and Mrs. Frail, *Love for Love* is, on the whole, rather homely fare. Even Truewits like Angelica and Valentine share the physical ebullience of spirit which pervades the play. There is more outright sexual wit in this play than in any other of Congreve's comedies, as, for example, when Tattle tries to seduce Miss Prue:

> Miss: Ah, but I'll hold the Door with both Hands, and be angry;—and you shall push me down before you come in.
> Tatt: No, I'll come in first, and push you down afterwards.
> (ii, xi)

The same laxity of speech marks the scenes in which Angelica, Sir Sampson, and Ben appear. But despite such homely fare, the play shows greater subtlety than the first two comedies in the apprehension of life: Valentine, in particular, is a little bemused at times by the human pageant, and though he is as playful in temper as any Truewit, he is more reflective. Angelica, too, has a great deal of perspicacity and feeling, which outweigh the frankness of her speech. The grosser wit of Sir Sampson and Ben may make the stronger impression, but it is the fine wit of Valentine and Angelica that gives real substance to the comedy. These two Truewits possess considerable verve in their playful attitude toward life, but, at times, they grow thoughtful.

Congreve's last play, *The Way of the World* (1700), had far less success than the earlier comedies; and he perhaps foresaw this, for he declared in the dedication that the play was not prepared for the general taste then prevalent, which

was for farce and show. He explained that instead of the gross
fools currently represented on the stage, he would present
some characters who should appear ridiculous because of their
false wit. The result is a comedy of wit, embodying the
familiar ingredients of Witwouds who are exposed for their
defective wit, Truewits who outwit others and engage in wit
combats, and rivals who are outwitted. Yet this did not produce a warm response in the audience.

The ill-success of the play cannot be attributed to a radical
change in popular taste since the performance of his last
comedy. Congreve himself complained that the critics were
not perceptive, and that they missed the distinction between
the character of Truewit and Witwoud, which, rather than
"manners," is the theme of the play. Some modern critics
explain the ill-success by stating that the plot is not strong
and that the chief excellence of the play is stylistic.[56] But it is
not certain that they have put their finger on the chief weaknesses of the play. The plot of *The Way of the World* is
actually superior to that of *Love in a Wood* or *The Old
Batchelor*, which both met with greater success. In fact, the
situation in the play is the familiar one of Truewits outwitting
rivals and guardians, exposing Witwouds, and at the same
time conducting a wit combat between themselves.

More probably the play did not appeal to popular taste because it lacks the strong naturalism and the easily appre-
hended comic wit of *Love for Love*, and because it shows
deficiencies as a comedy of wit. Mrs. Millamant hit the weak
point of Mirabell, and also of the play, I think, when she
cried, "Sententious Mirabell!" For, indeed, the play is too
full of serious reflections and learned allusions, unrelieved by
naturalistic touches and by skeptical and sexual wit. Mirabell,
for example, caps a couplet of Suckling's that Mrs. Millamant
has just spoken; Lady Wishfort, who has Quarles, Prynne,
Bunyan, and Collier in her closet, speaks familiarly of a

[56] Cf. Palmer, *Comedy of Manners*, p. 189.

character in *Don Quixote*; and even the boorish Sir Wilfull lards his speech with a reference to Pylades and Orestes. Finally, there is the intrusion of sense and sensibility to such a degree that it mars the play as wit comedy.

The Way of the World has always been a problem for the "manners" critics: it is considered the best comedy of manners—and yet it is admittedly not very successful on the stage (though the perfect comedy of manners will always be unsuccessful theatrically because its chief merits must be stylistic). The relative ineffectiveness of the play can be explained more plausibly, I think, on the grounds given above: it is not as good a comedy of wit as *The Man of Mode* or *Love for Love*. Despite a pair of elegant Truewits and a fine Witwoud, it lacks not only a strong naturalistic substratum but skeptical and sexual wit, comic wit that is easily grasped, and a consistent attitude toward life.

The character of Mirabell is perhaps the best illustration of this deficiency: he is the Restoration rake in the process of being transformed into a Wit of the age of sense and sensibility. His predominant characteristic as a Truewit is his judgment rather than fancy, and he is more addicted to *sententiae* than to similitudes. When Mirabell is metaphorical, his observation is just but not striking, as in his remark on Lady Wishfort: "An old Woman's Appetite is deprav'd like that of a Girl—'Tis the Green-Sickness of a second Child; and like the faint Offer of a latter Spring, serves but to usher in the Fall; and withers in an affected Bloom" (II, iii). He is capable of finely balanced phrases, but his remarks are characterized by subtlety of thought and elegance of expression rather than by striking figures of speech. The repartee of Mirabell and Fainall, in which the latter tries to sound out Mirabell's feelings toward Marwood, is characteristic of his elegant speech:

FAIN: You are a gallant Man, *Mirabell*; and tho' you may have Cruelty enough, not to satisfie a Lady's longing; you have too much Generosity, not to be tender of her Honour. Yet

you speak with an Indifference which seems to be affected;
and confesses you are conscious of a Negligence.

MIRA: You pursue the Argument with a Distrust that seems to
be unaffected, and confesses you are conscious of a Concern
for which the Lady is more indebted to you, than is your
Wife. (I, i)

The reply is a beautiful "turn," and shows great judgment,
but it lacks the force and concreteness that similitudes alone
can give. How different this is from the blunt retort of
Horner to Pinchwife, or Dorimant's rough raillery. Mirabell
is no longer the plain-dealing Truewit; instead he is ironical,
and launches insinuations on the sea of conversation. He has
become introspective and detached, and he is too elegant to
engage in too direct repartee.

As a man of sound sense, Mirabell also displays a modesty
of behavior that one does not find in Truewits like Bellmour
or Dorimant. He believes that good nature and true wit go
together, and he rebukes Petulant for his senseless ribaldry
in the presence of women:

MIRA: But hast not thou then Sense enough to know that thou
ought'st to be most asham'd thy self, when thou has put
another out of Countenance.

PET: Not I, by this Hand—I always take Blushing either for
a Sign of Guilt, or ill Breeding.

MIRA: I confess you ought to think so. You are in the right,
that you may plead the Error of your Judgment in defence
of your Practice.
Where Modesty's ill Manners, 'tis but fit
That Impudence and Malice pass for Wit. (I, ix)

This is a reflection of Congreve's own sensible and affectionate nature, and it shows how far the Truewit has been
transformed from the malicious and naturalistic Dorimant
and Horner. Mirabell also knows his own weaknesses too
well to be carefree and gay. Like Valentine, he exclaims, "A
Fellow that lives in a Windmill, has not a more whimsical
Dwelling than the Heart of a Man that is lodg'd in a

Woman." But where Valentine dismisses the thought with a witticism, Mirabell, more sadly and sententiously, observes, "To know this, and yet continue to be in Love, is to be made wise from the Dictates of Reason, and yet persevere to play the Fool by the force of Instinct" (II, vi).

Mirabell is also a Truewit with some principles. He is libertine enough to lie with more than one woman, but he is sensible enough to be discriminating. Despite the advantages to be gained, he refuses to satisfy Marwood's passion—perhaps because he loves Mrs. Millamant; and though he made love once to Lady Wishfort in an effort to win Mrs. Millamant, he would not stoop to debauch the old lady. Mrs. Fainall, we gather, was an attachment of the past, before he fell in love; and since she was a widow at the time, and hence, according to the naturalistic conception of widows, very inflammable, he could hardly be blamed for satisfying her sexual appetite as well as his own. When the play opens, Mirabell has apparently broken off all relations with her, and he is pursuing matrimony with a serious purpose. In the "proviso" scene he stipulates that his son must not suffer from any fanatical wish on his wife's part to be fashionable. "I denounce against all strait Lacing," he tells Mrs. Millamant, "squeezing for a Shape, 'till you mould my Boy's Head like a Sugar-loaf; and instead of a Man-Child, make me Father to a Crooked-billet" (IV, v). Mirabell is probably the first Truewit so sensible as to begin worrying about his offspring at the time he proposes to his mistress. He is prudent enough, too, to make some concessions to reputation (II, iii), and he is the one who expresses the ostensible moral of the play, "That Marriage Frauds too oft are paid in kind" (v, xiv). "Sententious Mirabell," as Mrs. Millamant so aptly calls him, is not so attractive a figure as Valentine, for the playful attitude of the Truewit is sobering into a concern with the sound conduct of life. If there is a flaw in Mirabell, it is not his supposed cynicism, but his sobriety.

William Congreve

Mrs. Millamant, like Mirabell, shows the influence of the coming age in her increased sensibility. It is quite false to her nature to characterize her as "the most witty and fearless of Dianas" whose courtship is unmarked "by one moment of real hesitation or by the disclosure of one palpitation of the heart."[57] If there is a serious criticism of her as a Truewit, it is that she has too many palpitations of the heart. She has something of the seriousness and sensibility of Araminta, plus a little of the charming affectation of Belinda. But she is much more fanciful and whimsical in her wit, with a lightness of touch uniquely hers, and a sensibility extremely refined.

It is her whimsical wit that makes her seem so airy, and one suspects that this is the becoming affectation of which Mirabell is enamoured. She declares that she is pestered with letters—"O ay, Letters—I had Letters—I am persecuted with Letters—I hate Letters—No Body knows how to write Letters; and yet one has 'em, one does not know why—They serve one to pin up one's Hair" (ii, iv). Then she plays with the conceit that only letters in verse are good—for mere prose will not curl her hair. How charming is this mixture of whimsical petulance and feminine illogic, of fancy flitting playfully from inconsequential thought to inconsequential thought.

But this is mere affectation on her part, intended for public consumption, to conceal her deep affection for Mirabell. She adopts the same whimsical tone toward him because she does not want to make a public confession of her love, and she is a little pained that he is not perspicacious enough to penetrate her playful disguise:

> MILLA: *Mirabell*, Did you take Exceptions last Night? O ay, and went away—Now I think on't I'm angry—No, now I think on't I'm pleas'd—For I believe I gave you some Pain.
> MIRA: Does that please you?
> MILLA: Infinitely; I love to give Pain.

[57] Thorndike, *English Comedy*, p. 324.

[188]

William Congreve

MIRA: You wou'd affect a Cruelty which is not in your Nature; your true Vanity is in the Power of pleasing.

MILLA: O I ask your Pardon for that—Ones Cruelty is ones Power, and when one parts with ones Cruelty, one parts with ones Power; and when one has parted with that, I fancy one's old and ugly. (II, iv)

Mrs. Millamant has a great deal of judgment, though she prefers not to display it as Mirabell does, and she even tolerates Petulant and Witwoud, as Marwood suspects, so that she may disguise her affair with Mirabell (III, x). When he blindly accuses her of lacking judgment in conversing with such fools, she answers with the mixture of sense and whimsicality that is characteristic of her wit:

MILLA: I please my self—Besides, sometimes to converse with Fools is for my Health.

MIRA: Your Health! Is there a worse Disease than the Conversations of Fools?

MILLA: Yes, the Vapours; Fools are Physick for it, next to *Assa-foetida*. (II, v)

Her whimsical wit is a shield which she holds up against the world, against Marwood and Lady Wishfort, and even against Mirabell.

Mrs. Millamant is a highly cultivated woman, so sensitive and fastidious that she wishes to avoid the grossness of wrangling and raillery. She has an aversion to illiterate men; and at times there is almost a touch of pedantry in her speech, as when she says: "There is not so impudent a Thing in Nature, as the sawcy Look of an assured Man, confident of Success. The Pedantick Arrogance of a very Husband, has not so Pragmatical an Air" (IV, v). One of the most amusing scenes in the play is her encounter with the boorish Sir Wilfull when she is reciting to herself some verses of Suckling, of whom she is very fond:

MILLA: Natural, easie *Suckling*!

SIR WIL: Anan? *Suckling?* No such Suckling neither, Cousin,
nor Stripling: I thank Heav'n I'm no Minor.
MILLA: Ah Rustick, ruder than *Gothick*. (IV, iv)

The airy disdain of her retort brushes lightly against him
like the wings of a butterfly against an ass: she is too refined
and subtle for a grosser stroke in a situation so absurd.

Mrs. Millamant is not without malice, however, though
this side of her nature is usually well concealed beneath her
affected whimsicality. She is not above teasing Mirabell when
he is too serious, and there is some malice in her remark to
Mrs. Fainall: "Dear *Fainall*, entertain Sir *Wilfull*—Thou
hast Philosophy to undergo a Fool, thou are marry'd and
hast Patience" (IV, ii). When charged by the madly jealous
Marwood with having Mirabell as a lover, Mrs. Millamant
does not spare her rival. She exclaims at the constancy of
Mirabell, and swears that if she thought she had power over
him, she would command him to show more gallantry: " 'Tis
hardly well bred to be so particular on one Hand, and so
insensible on the other. But I despair to prevail, and so let
him follow his own Way. Ha, ha, ha. Pardon me, dear
Creature, I must laugh, ha, ha, ha; tho' I grant you 'tis a
little barbarous, ha, ha, ha" (III, xi). When Marwood becomes violent in her language, Mrs. Millamant does not retort directly, but carries out her revenge in a manner more
becoming a Truewit by having a malicious song sung before
Marwood:

> 'Tis not to wound a wanton Boy
> Or am'rous Youth, that gives the Joy;
> But 'tis the Glory to have pierc'd a Swain,
> For whom inferior Beauties sigh'd in vain. (III, xii)

To such subtle raillery there is no reply, and Mrs. Millamant
has the advantage over Marwood because of her superior wit.

Mrs. Millamant is better, however, when her real feelings
come to the surface, and reveal her in her true nature, as a
woman of sincerity and deep feeling, but, at the same time,

William Congreve

a Truewit with judgment and an awareness of decorum. This side of her is best demonstrated in the famous "proviso" scene in which she capitulates to Mirabell. In this courtship scene, she tells Mirabell that she will not have any of "that nauseous Cant" of affection, such as "Wife, Spouse, my Dear, Joy, Jewel, Love, Sweet-heart, and the rest," which passes for legal currency between husbands and wives in public; she would rather be distant before others, and love each other sincerely in private (IV, v). As a Truewit, she loves good taste, restraint, and sincerity above false show and cant. She is also independent enough to demand freedom to live a life of her own, instead of having her whole nature circumscribed in the title of a wife.

Till the very end she retains mastery of herself and her emotion; and because she is afraid of losing her self-control she hides under a cloak of whimsicality:

> MILLA: Well then—I'll take my Death I'm in a horrid Fright
> — . . . I shall never say it—Well—I think—I'll endure
> you.
> MRS. FAIN: Fy, fy, have him, have him, and tell him so in plain
> Terms: For I am sure you have a Mind to him.
> MILLA: Are you? I think I have—and the horrid Man looks as
> if he thought so too—Well, you ridiculous thing you, I'll
> have you—I won't be kiss'd, nor I won't be thank'd—Here
> kiss my Hand tho'—So, hold your Tongue now, don't say
> a Word. (IV, v)

She is a Truewit till the last, but when Mirabell departs, she breaks down and confesses to her friend:

> MILLA: Well, if *Mirabell* should not make a good Husband, I
> am a lost thing;—for I find I love him violently.
> MRS. FAIN: So it seems; for you mind not what's said to you.
> (IV, vii)

In addition to her judgment and sense, Mrs. Millamant has a real capacity for deep feeling, and her love for Mirabell is all the more impressive because she has such mastery over it.

She remains a Truewit throughout the play, but the warring elements of deep feeling and of an unusually clear and perspicacious mind threaten at times to destroy her equanimity. She is a more subtle and profounder creation than any other female Truewit in wit comedy, but her capacity for deep feeling and her sensitive nature come close to transforming her into a woman of sensibility.

In contrast to the two Truewits, Fainall and Marwood are distinctly unattractive figures, with some resemblance to Maskwell and Lady Touchwood. Fainall has the marks of a Wit: he is a true libertine; he has perspicacity, considerable judgment, and a ready tongue; and in the naturalistic atmosphere of *The Man of Mode*, he would have been quite at home beside Dorimant. But in the increasingly moral atmosphere of Congreve's play, he is condemned as a complete egoist intent only on his own pleasures. Mirabell describes him thus: "I knew *Fainall* to be a Man lavish of his Morals, an interested and professing Friend, a false and a designing Lover; yet one whose Wit and outward fair Behavior, have gain'd a Reputation with the Town, enough to make that Woman stand excus'd, who has suffer'd her self to be won by his Addresses" (ii, iii). Fainall possesses the graces of the Truewit, but he is condemned by Mirabell because he is naturalistic in his principles. It is important to note, too, that it is Fainall, and not Mirabell, who exemplifies the title of the play; for it is he, and not Mirabell, who accepts infidelity in matrimony and friendship as "all in the Way of the *World*" (iii, xviii). He is sometimes entertaining in his wit, as in the fanciful sophistry of his exchange with Marwood: "Marriage is honourable, as you say; and if so, wherefore should Cuckoldom be a Discredit, being deriv'd from so honourable a Root?" (iii, xviii). He has the marks of a Truewit, especially in his distinction of speech; but he is outwitted by his cleverer adversaries, as is Marwood, who plays the scorned woman with some violence.

William Congreve

The play has a fine gallery of Witwouds and Witlesses, for Congreve's main purpose in writing was to bring out the contrast between these creatures and the Truewits. Among the coxcombs, Witwoud is easily the most amusing, though he is the cause for the familiar charge that Congreve made his coxcombs too witty. But, as Congreve observed to Dennis, witty remarks are expected from a witty man, "and even a *Fool* may be permitted to stumble on 'em by chance."[58] The best criticism of Witwoud is to be found in the comments of Mirabell:

> FAIN: he has something of good Nature, and does not always want Wit.
> MIRA: Not always; but as often as his Memory fails him, and his common Place of Comparisons. He is a Fool with a good Memory, and some few Scraps of other Folks Wit. He is one whose Conversation can never be approv'd, yet it is now and then to be endur'd. (I, v)

No doubt Witwoud sometimes says amusing things, but they are forced pell-mell on whatever company may be present. His lack of decorum (true wit) is quite evident on his first appearance:

> MILLA: Dear Mr. *Witwoud*, Truce with your Similitudes: For I am as Sick of 'em—
> WIT: As a Physician of a good Air—I cannot help it, Madam, tho' 'tis against my self.
> MILLA: Yet again! *Mincing*, stand between me and his Wit.
> WIT: Do, Mrs. *Mincing*, like a Skreen before a great Fire. I confess I do blaze to Day, I am too bright. (II, iv)

He is at best a buffoon who will raise a laugh at any price, even at his own expense, because he is deficient in judgment; and in this role he is simply a refinement on similar characters by Etherege and Wycherley.

Sir Wilfull as the boorish Witless is again not new; but unlike most fools, he has a redeeming feature in his good

---

[58] Congreve, *Mourning Bride*, etc., p. 2.

nature. Petulant is also an old character, patterned in part after Captain Bluffe: he is irascible, affects brevity, and breathes fire. "If Throats are to be cut," he mutters, "let Swords clash; snug's the Word, I shrug and am silent" (I, ix). He is rebuked, too, by Mirabell for uttering senseless ribaldry before ladies, like the boor that he is. The crude, witless raillery of Sir Wilfull and Petulant is exposed amusingly in an encounter between the two:

> PET: Sir, I presume upon the Information of your Boots.
> SIR WIL: Why, 'tis like you may, Sir: If you are not satis-
> fy'd with the Information of my Boots, Sir, if you will step
> to the Stable, you may enquire further of my Horse, Sir.
> PET: Your Horse, Sir! Your Horse is an Ass, Sir! (III, xv)

Among these ridiculous figures, the most striking creation is Lady Wishfort, and she has been highly praised by some modern critics. But I imagine that Congreve himself did not regard her too highly, because she is not sufficiently natural, and the ingredients of her character are too apparent. Like Sir Sampson, she is addicted to extreme forms of metonymy and exaggerated similitudes. To Peg, she cries, "Paint, Paint, Paint, dost thou understand that, Changeling, dangling thy Hands like Bobbins before thee? Why dost thou not stir, Puppet? thou wooden Thing upon Wires" (III, i). She uses hyperbole in the manner of Belinda, but without her charm: "Let me see the Glass—Cracks, say'st thou? Why I am arrantly flea'd—I look like an old peel'd Wall. Thou must repair me, *Foible*, before Sir *Rowland* comes" (III, v). This violence of language springs from the intemperance of her nature, and the result is a sort of bastard wit compounded of striking figures and absurd ideas. To this she adds a novel malapropism, as in her remarks to Sir Rowland, whom she wishes to marry: "But as I am a Person, Sir *Rowland*, you must not attribute my yielding to any sinister Appetite, or Indigestion of Widowhood; nor impute my Complacency to any Lethargy of Continence—I hope you do not think me prone to any Iteration of Nuptials" (iv, xii). In this character, she is better and wittier than Mrs. Malaprop, because her mistakes are not nonsensical but have an ingredient of sense in them.

One important fact about this comedy which we must note especially is that Congreve returns to the moralistic temper of *The Double-Dealer*, though not in so extreme a manner. Those who censure this play as an example of cynicism and moral indifference, as Palmer does when he speaks of the "dead level of conscience,"[59] misunderstand the play completely. It is generally assumed that the title of the play indicates a cynical acceptance by Congreve of the treachery, marital infidelity, and moral indifference that are "the way of the world." Actually, Congreve repudiates the way of the world, for he censures Fainall, Marwood, Petulant, and Witwoud, who conform to the world as it is. On the other hand, the two Truewits in the play, Mirabell and Mrs. Millamant, refuse to conform to the pattern of a world which is conventional and cynical in its human relations, which places fortune before love in matrimony, regards adultery as an accepted fact, substitutes a public display of affection for real love, and acclaims Witwoud as much as the Truewit. Fainall, both an adulterous husband and a cynical wit, is outwitted and defeated by Truewits who are not only more clever than he but more honest. In this last play, Congreve is obviously turning away from the naturalistic philosophy of wit comedy, and is making concessions to morality, good sense, and sensibility. Mrs. Millamant is the perfect female Truewit, but she has developed a heart; and Mirabell is still a striking and elegant Wit, but he begins to grow sententious and sober.

Congreve comes a generation after Etherege and Wycherley, and it would indeed be surprising if he continued to write the same type of play as they, with the same philosophical

[59] Palmer, *Comedy of Manners*, p. 192.

assumptions. *The Old Batchelor* and *Love for Love* still have the playful and libertine temper of true wit comedies; but in *The Double-Dealer* morality begins to rear its head, and in *The Way of the World* there is a shade too much of sense and sensibility. The increasing subordination of philosophical naturalism reflects the changing intellectual climate, as does the new stress on judgment and good nature over fancy and malice in wit.

It is not a far step from Congreve to Addison. But Congreve remained essentially a child of the seventeenth century, and was always a Truewit, as man and artist, though he moved among the Wits of the age of reason rather than among the rakes of Charles' court. He was, as Pope observed to Tonson, *"ultimus Romanorum."*[60] It is clear, from an examination of Congreve's life and work, that he was an intelligent, cultivated, and sensible Truewit, far different from the "manners" conception of him as a cynical stylist and "a professional funny man." The most fitting tribute to him are the words inscribed on a tablet by his dear friend Sir Richard Temple:

INGENIO,

ACRI, FACETO, EXPOLITO,

MORIBUSQUE

URBANIS, CANDIDIS, FACILLIMIS,

GULIELMI CONGREVE. [61]

[60] Spence, *Anecdotes*, p. 35.
[61] *Memoirs of the Celebrated Persons Composing the Kit-Cat Club*, London, 1821, p. 219.

VIII

CONCLUSION

THE STUDY OF CONGREVE brings to an end the analysis of wit comedy, for by 1700, when *The Way of the World* was produced, the type of play it exemplified was passing out of favor. In 1696, Cibber had written his *Love's Last Shift*, which, despite its witty elements, was symptomatic of the new morality creeping into comedy; in 1698, Collier had published his *Short View*; and even earlier, moralistic critics like Blackmore had censured the theatre for being profane and immoral. These writings all reflect the changing intellectual temper of the times—the increasing emphasis on judgment over fancy, and on morality over libertinism. This change I have pointed out to some extent in the successive comedies of Congreve.

The study of Etherege, Wycherley, and Congreve against their intellectual background shows how much they were influenced by the naturalistic, skeptical, and libertine temper of the times, and how their plays reflect the *Zeitgeist*. It is evident that these dramatists were concerned with much more than "manners," or with wit as a purely social-literary phenomenon. The study also shows that they were not superficial and corrupt, as they are often said to be. Etherege was by no means the social butterfly of popular belief whose life and art are summed up in the frivolous Sir Fopling Flutter. Wycherley was not the fierce, puritanic satirist who lashed out at humanity out of a warped misanthropy. And Congreve was not the cynical stylist he is reputed to be. All of these men were Truewits, and their plays are artistic expressions of their naturalistic and witty attitude toward life.

[197]

Conclusion

The significance of wit comedy, and the seriousness of its content, has not received much recognition, however; and this is due, in large part, to the prevalence of the "manners" interpretation. We have at least got beyond the moralistic censure of the older critics. Few readers would now agree with Archer that the criticism of life contained in the plays "is stupid, nauseous and abominable beyond anything else that can be found in the world's dramatic literature,"[1] or with Beljame that these plays represent "a perverted and deliberate search for the smutty and the bawdy; with a cold-blooded, intentional study of the lewd and licentious, with a refinement of unwholesome thinking on the part of debauchees who have drunk of life too deeply."[2] But most readers are content with the "manners" view that Restoration comedy is artificial (because it is concerned, not with the moral issues of real life, but with "manners"), that it is amoral (because it is purely intellectual in treatment and appeal), and that it is significant, aesthetically (because of the beautiful style) and historically (because of its photographic realism). If Restoration comedy is considered critical in spirit, it is generally regarded as offering only a superficial criticism of social foibles. "Criticism there was to be sure," writes a modern critic, "but of trivialities only."[3]

At first glance the "manners" interpretation seems perfectly adequate. Yet its seeming adequacy really masks the superficiality of the approach. The apologists for Restoration comedy have vindicated the plays by denying their vitality: they have repudiated the moralistic censure by affirming that the plays have nothing at all to do with life, and that they are simply beautiful reflections of a corrupt society, to be admired for their workmanship, just as an ugly toad may be admired

[1] Archer, *The Old Drama and the New*, p. 173.
[2] Alexandre Beljame, *Men of Letters and the English Public in the Eighteenth Century 1660-1744, Dryden, Addison, Pope*, tr. E. O. Lorimer, London, 1948, p. 50.
[3] James Feibleman, *In Praise of Comedy*, New York, 1939, p. 58.

Conclusion

when immortalized in jade. The "manners" critics point to the sheer beauty of the style, and insist that this, plus the social satire on current manners, and possibly the historical veracity of the picture painted, is all that matters. Since the naturalistic element and the sexual, skeptical, and cynical wit cannot be explained in terms of "manners," these are minimized, and not much is said about the significance of the witty hits at the clergy, at matrimony, and at the unnatural. If there has been any uneasiness about the seeming superficiality of Restoration comedy, the "manners" critics have held up Wycherley as a fierce satirist who grappled seriously with life, and gave to this comedy the significant content which appears to be missing in the work of Etherege and Congreve. Paradoxically, then, the most significant exponent of "manners" comedy is the one writer who does not conform to the type.

There is, it seems to me, a more adequate interpretation of Restoration comedy; and in this study I have suggested that the work of Etherege, Wycherley, and Congreve can be better explained in terms of naturalism and wit than in terms of "manners." Whereas the conception of "manners" at best leads us to the outskirts of Restoration comedy, naturalism and wit take us to its very center. The analysis of the major comic dramatists from this point of view has shown, I think, how rich and significant Restoration comedy is, and how much has been neglected by the "manners" critics. The approach suggested here also has a distinct advantage in being critically more thorough: unlike the "manners" interpretation, it takes into account the serious content of the plays, and unlike much moralistic criticism, it gives due attention to the treatment. In addition, the effect of the plays is considered. All of these aspects are, in fact, suggested in the description of Restoration comedy as naturalistic, witty, and hedonic.

To say that the plays are naturalistic is to suggest the content, and, to some extent, the treatment also. Basic to the plays is the substratum of philosophical naturalism, ex-

Conclusion

pounded with so much ardor in the seventeenth century by Hobbes. In the comedies, this is not so much a clearly formulated philosophical position as a pervasive temper—rationalistic, empirical, and libertine. The aristocratic Wits at Whitehall, being intelligent and cultivated, were most susceptible to the influence of "the new philosophy," and men like Etherege, Wycherley, and Sedley regarded with suspicion "the old philosophy" which denied the natural man and condemned man's pursuit of pleasure. They committed themselves, though not always consistently, to a point of view that accepted the naturalness, and hence the rightness, of man's egoistic, hedonic, and malicious character. In accordance with this bias, Etherege and Wycherley, and to a lesser extent Congreve, depicted the characters in their plays as egoistic and libertine creatures interested in pleasure, both intellectual and sensual. This naturalistic content, and the realistic technique that is its concomitant, gives to wit comedy its vigor and earthiness.

Furthermore, having rejected a dogmatism incompatible with reason, the Wits adopted a skeptical attitude toward life; and since they could credit the testimony of their reason and senses, though not of faith, they exposed conventions and practices that seemed irrational and unnatural. Consequently, they indulged in witty criticism of conventional morality, arranged marriages, cant about honor, the pious pretenses of the clergy, and the folly of pretenders who went against nature. This insistence on naturalness, sincerity, and sound sense, and the exposure of all that goes contrary to these, is quite compatible with modern notions of morality. A closer examination of these criteria in wit comedy would do much to dispel such views as are expressed by Schelling, that "judged by any standards applicable to actual life this entire Restoration comedy is hopelessly immoral and corrupt."[4] Or Nettleton's opinion that a serious "weakness in Restoration comedy was

---

[4] Schelling, *English Drama*, p. 268.

Conclusion

its lack of a sense of ethical values."[5] This failure to appreciate the sanity of the criticism in wit comedy is due, in large part, to the fact that the Wits, who lived in an age fundamentally religious, found it expedient to express their criticism covertly in the form of witty attacks. Since many readers confound wit with levity, the sober intention masked in witty guise is often overlooked.

This brings us to the problem of wit in Restoration comedy. I have already suggested that wit is to be equated with the playful attitude of the dramatists, and I have suggested, too, that it is the form in which the naturalistic criticism appears. Perhaps this somewhat confusing term is best explained if we turn to the seventeenth century conceptions of wit. Of the several notions, the conception of wit as fancy is the most familiar, and hence the most frequently discussed today; and our study has shown how the dramatists' interest in fancy fostered the extreme use of similitudes, the indulgence in sophistical and paradoxical wit, and the search for novelty of utterance for skeptical and sexual ideas.

More important in the seventeenth century is the identification of wit with judgment, a notion frequently neglected by modern critics because of its vagueness and unfamiliarity. To men like Congreve and Dryden, wit, in this sense, suggested such ideals as restraint, sound sense, and elegance, but above all, it stood for decorum, perhaps the most comprehensive aesthetic ideal in the period. Decorum was, in part, a naturalistic ideal in life and in literature: in writing, it represented propriety (natural thoughts naturally expressed); in life, decorum meant being true to one's nature, whether acting like a Truewit or an old man. In Restoration comedy, wit in this broad sense represents a very significant element. It is the chief criterion for the distinction between true wit and false wit; it is an important basis for the depiction of Truewit,

[5] George H. Nettleton and Arthur E. Case, eds., *British Dramatists from Dryden to Sheridan*, Boston and New York, 1939, p. 152.

Conclusion

Witwoud, and Witless; and it is the ideal by which the characters live. In its broadest sense, wit represented what was most admirable in life and in art; and in this ideal (with all that it suggests of intellectual distinction, originality, elegance, taste, and naturalness), men like Etherege, Wycherley, and Congreve found a satisfactory substitute for the conventional standards of art and ethics that their skeptical temper rejected.

Being naturalistic in their bias and witty in their attitude, these dramatists were also interested in pleasure and beauty. Above all, they were concerned with pleasure—to be derived principally from the free play of the mind and the beauty of ideas elegantly expressed. Consequently, their work will give us the most satisfaction if we approach them sympathetically, and if we likewise seek these pleasures rather than concern ourselves with "manners" or morals. In reading the comedies, we can derive pleasure from the vicarious indulgence of our sexual, malicious, and skeptical tendencies, in a purgative sense; and we can find satisfaction, too, in the beauty of the style—the fine "turns," the novel similitudes, and the striking repartee.

But the greatest pleasure comes from our association with Truewits who are graceful and elegant and, at the same time, sensible and natural in their attitude toward life. In reading wit comedy, we are transported to a world that is harmonious, free, and complete—and hence meaningful—where the mind can frolic gracefully in the free play of the intelligence. It is a world where the intelligence (wit) is valued above faith and deep emotion, and no ideals are accepted without a rational and natural basis. There is some loss, to be sure, in the exclusion of the supernatural, the mysterious, and all the dark shades that flee the light of the intellect. But there is compensation in the virtues of sound sense, intellectual discrimination, truth to nature, and sincerity. It is not a world where "energy is directed toward conforming life within the limits

Conclusion

of a narrow ideal,"[6] nor is there a slavish submission to "manners." Rather it is a place marked by intellectual freedom and the absence of sham; there is nothing counterfeit here, whether it be in men, ideals, or practices. It is a witty world and hence it is a free world. As Jean Paul observed, "Freiheit giebt Witz, und Witz giebt Freiheit."[7] But it is freedom coupled with beauty, and in the comedies of Etherege, Wycherley, and Congreve, the Truewit's philosophy is successfully wedded to beauty through the ministry of wit.

[6] D. Crane Taylor, *William Congreve*, London, 1931, p. 4.
[7] Quoted by Kuno Fischer, *Ueber den Witz*, in *Kleine Schriften von Kuno Fischer*, Heidelberg, 1896, I, 72.

BIBLIOGRAPHY

I. ANTHOLOGIES OF DRAMATIC CRITICISM AND
RESTORATION LITERATURE

Adams, Henry Hitch and Baxter Hathaway, eds. *Dramatic Essays of the Neoclassic Age*. New York, Columbia University Press, 1950.

Durham, Willard H., ed. *Critical Essays of the Eighteenth Century, 1700-1725*. New Haven, Yale University Press, 1915.

Gayley, Charles Mills and Alwin Thaler, eds. *Representative English Comedies*, Vol. IV (Dryden and His Contemporaries: Cowley to Farquhar). New York, Macmillan, 1936.

Gilbert, Allan H., ed. *Literary Criticism: Plato to Dryden*. New York, American Book Co., 1940.

Lieder, Paul R. and Robert Withington, eds. *The Art of Literary Criticism*. New York, D. Appleton-Century Co., 1941.

MacMillan, Dougald and Howard Mumford Jones, eds. *Plays of the Restoration and Eighteenth Century*. New York, Henry Holt, 1931.

Moore, Cecil A., ed. *Restoration Literature: Poetry and Prose 1660-1700*. New York, F. S. Crofts, 1947.

————*Twelve Famous Plays of the Restoration and Eighteenth Century*. New York, The Modern Library, 1933.

Moses, Montrose, J., ed. *British Plays from the Restoration to 1820*, 2 vols. Boston, Little, Brown, and Co., 1929.

Nettleton, George H. and Arthur E. Case, eds. *British Dramatists from Dryden to Sheridan*. Boston and New York, Houghton Mifflin Co., 1939.

Smith, James Harry and Edd Winfield Parks, eds. *The Great Critics*. New York, W. W. Norton and Co., rev. ed. 1939.

Spingarn, Joel E., ed. *Critical Essays of the Seventeenth Century*, 3 vols. Oxford, Clarendon Press, 1908.

Summers, Montague, ed. *Restoration Comedies*. London, Jonathan Cape, 1921.

Wiley, Autrey Nell, ed. *Rare Prologues and Epilogues 1642-1700*. London, George Allen and Unwin, 1940.

[204]

Bibliography

II. RESTORATION AND EIGHTEENTH CENTURY WORKS

Abercromby, David, *A Discourse of Wit*. London, 1686.

Addison, Joseph. *The Spectator*, 8 vols. Boston, 1856.

An Answer to the Character of an Exchange-wench; or a Vindication of an Exchange-woman. London, 1675.

The Ape-Gentle-woman, or the Character of an Exchange-wench. London, 1675.

Aubignac, Abbot of (Monsieur Hedelin). *The Whole Art of the Stage*. London, 1684.

Aubrey, John. *Brief Lives, chiefly of Contemporaries, set down by John Aubrey, between the Years 1669 & 1696*, ed. Andrew Clark, 2 vols. Oxford, Clarendon Press, 1898.

The Augustan Reprint Society. *Series One: Essays on Wit*. No. 1. Sir Richard Blackmore's *Essay upon Wit* (1716) and Joseph Addison's *Freeholder, No. 45* (1716), intro. by Richard C. Boys. Ann Arbor, 1946.

————*Series One: Essays on Wit*. No. 2. *Essay on Wit* (1748); Richard Flecknoe's *Of one that Zany's the good Companion* and *Of a bold abusive Wit* (second edition, 1665); Joseph Warton, *The Adventurer*, Nos. 127 and 133 (1754); *Of Wit* (*Weekly Register*, 1732); intro. to series by Edward N. Hooker. Ann Arbor, 1946.

————*Series One: Essays on Wit*. No. 3. John Gay, *The Present State of Wit* (1711), intro. by Donald F. Bond. Excerpts from *The English Theophrastus: or the Manners of the Age* (1702), intro. by W. Earl Britton. Ann Arbor, 1947.

————*Series One: Essays on Wit*. No. 4. [Corbyn Morris], *An Essay towards Fixing the True Standard of Wit, Humour, Raillery, Satire, and Ridicule* (1744), intro. by James L. Clifford. Ann Arbor, 1947.

Aulnoy, Baronne Marie Catherine D'. *Memoirs of the Court of England in 1675*. London and New York, John Lane, 1913.

Behn, Mrs. Aphra. *Plays, Histories, and Novels*, 6 vols. London, 1871.

Berkeley, George-Monck. *Literary Relics*. London, 1789.

Betterton, Thomas. *The History of the English Stage, including the Lives, Characters and Amours of the Most Eminent Actors and Actresses*. Boston, 1814.

Bibliography

Blackmore, Sir Richard. *A Collection of Poems on Several Subjects.* London, 1718.

———*Essays upon Several Subjects.* London, 1716.

Blount, Sir Thomas Pope. *Essays on Several Subjects.* London, 1691.

Brown, Thomas. *The Works of Mr. Thomas Brown, in Prose and Verse; Serious, Moral, and Comical.* London. Vols. I & II, 1707. Vol. III, 1708. Vol. IV, 1711.

Buckingham, Duke of. *The Works of His Grace, George Villiers, Late Duke of Buckingham,* 2 vols. London, 1715.

Bulstrode, Sir Richard. *Memoirs and Reflections upon the Reign and Government of King Charles the Ist and K. Charles the IId.* London, 1721.

Burnaby, William. *The Dramatic Works,* ed. F. E. Budd. London, The Scholartis Press, 1931.

Burnett, Gilbert. *Bishop Burnet's History of His Own Times,* 4 vols. London, 1818.

———*Some Passages of the Life and Death of the Right Honourable John Earl of Rochester.* London, 1680.

Butler, Samuel. *The Genuine Remains in Verse and Prose of Mr. Samuel Butler,* 2 vols. London, 1756.

Bysshe, Edward. *The Art of English Poetry.* London, 1702.

[Casa, Giovanni della]. *The Refin'd Courtier.* London, 1663.

The Character of a Town-Gallant; Exposing the Extravagant Fopperies of some vain Self-conceited Pretenders to Gentility and good Breeding. London, 1675.

The Character of a Town Misse. London, 1675.

Charleton, Walter. *Natural History of the Passions.* London, 1674.

Cibber, Colley. *Colley Cibber's Apology for His Life.* London and New York, Everyman's Library, 1914.

———*The Dramatic Works,* 5 vols. London, 1777.

Cibber, Theophilus. *The Lives and Characters of the Most Eminent Actors and Actresses of Great Britain and Ireland, from Shakespear to the Present Time.* London, 1753.

———*The Lives of the Poets of Great Britain and Ireland to the Time of Dean Swift,* 5 vols. London, 1753.

Clarendon, Edward Hyde. *A Brief View and Survey of the Dangerous and Pernicious Errors to Church and State, in Mr. Hobbes's Book, Entitled Leviathan.* 1676.

[206]

Bibliography

————*Essays Moral and Entertaining on the Various Faculties and Passions of the Human Mind*, 2 vols. London, 1815.

————*The Life of Edward Earl of Clarendon*, 3 vols. Oxford, 1759.

Collier, Jeremy. *A Defence of the Short View.* London, 1699.

Congreve, William. *Amendments of Mr. Collier's False and Imperfect Citations.* London, 1698.

————*Comedies by William Congreve*, ed. Bonamy Dobrée. Oxford University Press, 1944.

————*The Comedies of William Congreve*, ed. Joseph Wood Krutch. New York, Macmillan, 1927.

————*The Comedies of William Congreve*, intro. by Norman Marshall. London, John Lehmann, 1948.

————*The Mourning Bride, Poems, & Miscellanies*, ed. Bonamy Dobrée. Oxford University Press, 1928.

————*William Congreve*, intro. by William Archer. New York, American Book Co., 1912.

Cotton, Charles. *Poems of Charles Cotton 1630-1687*, ed. John Beresford. London, R. Cobden-Sanderson, 1923.

Cowley, Abraham. *The English Writings of Abraham Cowley*, ed. A. R. Waller, 2 vols. Cambridge, 1905-1906.

Crowne, John. *The Dramatic Works*, 4 vols. Edinburgh, 1873-1874.

Davenant, Sir William. *Gondibert: An Heroick Poem.* London, 1651.

Defoe, Daniel. *Writings*, 2 vols. London, 1705.

Dennis, John. *The Critical Works.* ed. Edward Niles Hooker, 2 vols. Baltimore, Johns Hopkins Press, 1939, 1943.

————*A Defence of Sir 'Fopling Flutter.'* London, 1722.

————*Miscellanies in Verse and Prose.* London, 1693.

————*Original Letters, Familiar, Moral and Critical.* London, 1721.

————*The Select Works of Mr. John Dennis*, 2 vols. London, 1718.

Downes, Rev. John. *Roscius Anglicanus, or, an Historical Review of the Stage.* London, 1789.

Dryden, John. *The Letters of John Dryden*, ed. Charles E. Ward. Durham, N.C., Duke University Press, 1942.

————*Miscellany Poems*, 6 vols. London, 1716.

————*The Works of John Dryden*, ed. Sir Walter Scott and George Saintsbury, 18 vols. Edinburgh, 1882-1893.

Bibliography

D'Urfey, Thomas. *The Comical History of Don Quixote*, Parts I, II, III. London, 1729.

Eachard, John. *The Grounds and Occasions of the Contempt of the Clergy and Religion Enquired into In a Letter written to R. L.* London, 1670.

——*Mr. Hobbs's State of Nature Considered; In a Dialogue between Philautus and Timothy.* London, 1672.

Etherege, Sir George. *The Dramatic Works of Sir George Etherege*, ed. H. F. Brett-Smith, 2 vols. Oxford, Basil Blackwell, 1927.

——*The Letterbook of Sir George Etherege*, ed. Sybil Rosenfeld. Oxford University Press, 1928.

——*The Works of Sir George Etheredge: Plays and Poems*, ed. A. Wilson Verity. London, 1888.

Evelyn, John. *The Diary of John Evelyn*, 3 vols. London, Macmillan, 1906.

——*The Miscellaneous Writings of John Evelyn.* London, 1825.

Farquhar, George. *The Complete Works of George Farquhar*, ed. Charles Stonehill, 2 vols. Bloomsbury, Nonesuch Press, 1930.

Fenton, Elijah. *Poems on Several Occasions.* London, 1717.

Forneron, Henri. *Louise de Keroualle, Duchess of Portsmouth, 1649-1734.* London, 1887.

Gay, John. *The Poetical Works of John Gay*, ed. G. C. Faber. Oxford University Press, 1926.

Gildon, Charles. *The Lives and Characters of the English Dramatick Poets. First begun by Mr. Langbain.* London, 1699.

——*Memoirs of the Life of William Wycherley, Esq; with a Character of his Writings by the Right Honourable George, Lord Lansdowne. To which are added, Some Familiar Letters, Written by Mr. Wycherley.* London, 1718.

——, ed. *Miscellany Poems upon Several Occasions.* London, 1692.

——*The Post-Boy Robb'd of his Mail: or, The Pacquet Broke Open.* London, 1706.

Glanvill, Joseph. *Essays on Several Important Subjects in Philosophy and Religion.* London, 1676.

——*Scepsis Scientifica: Or, Confest Ignorance, the Way of Science; In An Essay of The Vanity of Dogmatizing, and Confident Opinion.* London, 1665.

Bibliography

Gracián y Morales, Baltasar. *Agudeza y Arte de Ingenio*. Buenos Aires, 1942.

──────*The Art of Worldly Wisdom*, tr. Joseph Jacobs. London, 1892.

Halifax, Marquess of. *The Complete Works of George Savile, First Marquess of Halifax*, ed. Walter Raleigh. Oxford, Clarendon Press, 1912.

Hamilton, Count Anthony. *Memoirs of Count Gramont*, ed. Allan Fea. London, Bickers and Son, 1906.

Hatton. *Correspondence of the Family of Hatton*, ed. Edward M. Thompson, 2 vols. Printed for the Camden Society, 1878.

[Head, Richard]. *Proteus Redivivus: or the Art of Wheedling, or Insinuation*. London, 1675.

Hobbes, Thomas. *The English Works of Thomas Hobbes*, 11 vols. London, 1839.

Hopkins, Charles. *Boadicea Queen of Britain A Tragedy*. London, 1697.

──────*Epistolary Poems*. London, 1694.

Howard, Sir Robert. *Plays*. London, 1700.

Huarte, Juan. *Examen de Ingenios: or, the Tryal of Wits*, tr. by Mr. Bellamy. London, 1698.

Jacob, Giles. *An Historical Account of the Lives and Writings of Our most Considerable English Poets*. London, 1720.

──────*The Poetical Register: or, The Lives and Characters of the English Dramatick Poets*. London, 1719.

Lacy, John. *The Dramatic Works*. Edinburgh and London, 1875.

Langbaine, Gerard. *An Account of the English Dramatick Poets*. Oxford, 1691.

Lansdowne, Lord. "A Letter with a Character of Mr. *Wycherly*," in *The Genuine Works in Verse and Prose of the Right Honourable George Granville, Lord Lansdowne*, Vol. 1. London, 1732.

La Rochefoucauld, François. *Moral Maxims and Reflections*. London, Methuen, 1912.

A Letter to Mr. Congreve on His Pretended Amendments. London, 1698.

Locke, John. *An Essay Concerning Human Understanding*, ed. Alexander C. Fraser, 2 vols. Oxford, Clarendon Press, 1894.

The Management of the Tongue (Done out of French). London, 1706.

Bibliography

Marvell, Andrew. *The Complete Works in Verse and Prose*, 4 vols. 1872.

Molière. *Oeuvres de Molière*. 2 vols. Paris, n.d.

Moyle, Walter. *The Whole Works of Walter Moyle*. London, 1727.

Mulgrave. *The Works of the Most Noble John Sheffield, Late Duke of Buckingham*. London, 1721.

Oldys, John. "Sir George Etherege," in *Biographia Britannica* (Vol. iii). London, 1747-1766.

Otway, Thomas. *The Complete Works of Thomas Otway*, ed. Montague Summers, 3 vols. Bloomsbury, Nonesuch Press, 1926.

Pack, Richardson. *The Whole Works of Major Richardson Pack*. London, 1729.

Pepys, Samuel. *The Diary of Samuel Pepys*, ed. Henry B. Wheatley, 2 vols. New York, Random House, 1946.

Perceau, Louis, ed. *Theophile de Viau et Les Libertins* (*Le Cabinet Secret du Parnasse*). Paris, 1935.

The Person of Quality's Answer to Mr. Collier's Letter, Being a Disswasive from the Play-House. London, 1704.

Phillips, Edward. *Theatrum Poetarum*. London, 1675.

The Polite Gentleman; or Reflections Upon the several Kinds of Wit (*Done out of French*). London, 1700.

Pope, Alexander. *Mr. Pope's Literary Correspondence for Thirty Years; from 1704 to 1734*, 5 vols. London, 1735.

Raillerie a la Mode Consider'd: or the Supercilious Detractor. London, 1673.

Rochester, Earl of. *Collected Works of John Wilmot Earl of Rochester*, ed. John Hayward. London, Nonesuch Press, 1926.

——*Familiar Letters: Written by the Right Honourable John Late Earl of Rochester . . . with Letters written by . . . Mr. Thomas Otway, and Mrs. K. Philips, etc.* London, 1697.

——*The Rochester-Savile Letters, 1671-1680*, ed. John Harold Wilson. Columbus, Ohio State University Press, 1941.

——*A Satire Against Mankind and Other Poems*, ed. Harry Levin. Norfolk, Conn., New Directions, 1942.

St. Evremond. *The Works of Monsieur de St. Evremond*, 3 vols. London, 1728.

Bibliography

A Search after Wit; or, A Visitation of the Authors. London, 1691.

Sedley, Sir Charles. *The Poetical and Dramatic Works*, ed. V. De Sola Pinto, 2 vols. London, Constable and Co., 1928.

Selden, John. *Table-Talk*. London, Arber Reprints, 1868.

Shadwell, Thomas. *The Complete Works of Thomas Shadwell*, ed. Montague Summers, 5 vols. London, Fortune Press, 1927.

Shaftesbury, Earl of. *Characteristicks of Men, Manners, Opinions, Times*, 3 vols. London, 1737.

Spence, Rev. Joseph. *Anecdotes, Observations, and Characters, of Books and Men*. London, 1858.

Spinoza, Baruch de. *The Philosophy of Spinoza*. New York, The Modern Library, 1927.

Sprat, Thomas. *The History of the Royal Society of London, for the improving of Natural Knowledge*. London, 1722.

The Stage Acquitted. London, 1699.

Steele, Richard. *The Correspondence of Richard Steele*, ed. Rae Blanchard. Oxford, Clarendon Press, 1941.

————*The Lucubrations of Isaac Bickerstaff Esq.* [*The Tatler*], 4 vols. London, 1713.

Swift, Jonathan. *The Correspondence of Jonathan Swift*, ed. F. Elrington Ball, 6 vols. London, G. Bell and Sons, 1910-1914.

————*Journal to Stella*, ed. Harold Williams, 2 vols. Oxford, Clarendon Press, 1948.

Temple, Sir William. *The Works of Sir William Temple*, 2 vols. London, 1720.

Thomson, James. *The Poetical Works of James Thomson*, 2 vols. London, 1860.

The Town-Misses Declaration and Apology; or, An Answer to the Character of a Town-Misse. London, 1675.

Tuke, Sir Samuel. *The Adventures of Five Hours*, ed. A. E. H. Swaen. Amsterdam, 1927.

Vanbrugh, Sir John. *The Complete Works of Sir John Vanbrugh*, ed. Bonamy Dobrée, 4 vols. Bloomsbury, Nonesuch Press, 1927.

————*Sir John Vanbrugh*, ed. W. C. Ward, 2 vols. London, 1893.

A Vindication of the Stage, with the Usefulness and Advantage of Dramatick Representation, in Answer to Mr. Collier's Late

Bibliography

Book, Entituled, A View of the Prophaness and Immorality, etc. London, 1698.

Wells, Staring B., ed. *A Comparison between the Two Stages.* Princeton University Press, 1942.

Wilson, Charles. *Memoirs of the Life, Writings, and Amours of William Congreve.* London, 1730.

Wilson, John. *The Dramatic Works.* Edinburgh and London, 1874.

Winstanley, William. *The Lives of the most Famous English Poets.* London, 1687.

Wood, Anthony à. *The Life and Times of Anthony à Wood,* ed. Llewelyn Powys. London, Wishart and Co., 1932.

The Works of the British Poets, Vol. VI (Dryden, Rochester, Roscommon, Otway, *et al.*). London, 1795.

Wright, J. *Historia Histrionica: An Historical Account of the English Stage.* London, 1699. (In Dodsley, R., *A Select Collection of Old Plays*).

Wright, James. "Of the Modern Comedies," in *Country Conversations.* London, 1694.

Wycherley, William. *The Complete Works of William Wycherley,* ed. Montague Summers, 4 vols. Soho, Nonesuch Press, 1924.

———*The Posthumous Works of William Wycherley Esq.; in Prose and Verse. To which are Prefixed, Some Memoirs of Mr. Wycherley's Life By Major Pack.* London, 1728.

———*William Wycherley,* ed. W. C. Ward. London, 1893.

III. GENERAL WORKS

Alleman, Gellert Spencer. *Matrimonial Law and the Materials of Restoration Comedy.* Wallingford, Pa., 1942.

Allen, Robert J. "The Kit-Cat Club and the Theatre." *Review of English Studies,* VII, 56-61 (1931).

Archer, William. *The Old Drama and the New.* New York, Dodd, Mead and Co., 1929.

Aristotle. *The Nicomachean Ethics.* New York, Carlton House, n.d.

———*The Rhetoric of Aristotle,* tr. Lane Cooper. New York, D. Appleton and Co., 1932.

Avery, Emmett L. *Congreve's Plays on the Eighteenth-Century Stage.* New York, Modern Language Association, 1951.

Bibliography

Bastiaenen, Johannes Adam. *The Moral Tone of Jacobean and Caroline Drama.* Amsterdam, 1930.

Beljame, Alexandre. *Men of Letters and the English Public in the Eighteenth Century 1660-1744, Dryden, Addison, Pope,* tr. E. O. Lorimer. London, Kegan Paul, Trench, Trubner and Co., 1948.

Bergson, Henri. *Laughter,* tr. Cloudesley Brereton and Fred Rothwell. New York, Macmillan, 1913.

Bernbaum, Ernest. *The Drama of Sensibility.* Boston, Ginn and Co., 1915.

Bond, Donald Frederic. " 'Distrust' of Imagination in English Neo-Classicism." *Philological Quarterly,* xiv, #1, 54-69 (Jan., 1935).

————"The Neo-Classical Psychology of the Imagination." *A Journal of English Literary History,* iv, 245-264 (1937).

Boswell, Eleanore. *The Restoration Court Stage (1660-1702).* Cambridge, Harvard University Press, 1932.

Bredvold, Louis I. *The Intellectual Milieu of John Dryden.* Ann Arbor, University of Michigan Press, 1934.

Bryant, Arthur. *The England of Charles II.* London and New York, Longmans, Green and Co., 1934.

————*King Charles II.* London and New York, Longmans, Green and Co., 1934.

Bundy, Murray Wright. " 'Invention' and 'Imagination' in the Renaissance." *The Journal of English and Germanic Philology,* xxix, 535-545 (1930).

————*The Theory of Imagination in Classical and Mediaeval Thought.* University of Illinois Studies in Language and Literature, xii, Urbana, Illinois, 1927.

Catlin, George E. G. *Thomas Hobbes as Philosopher, Publicist and Man of Letters: An Introduction.* Oxford University Press, 1922.

Chancellor, E. Beresford. *The Lives of the Rakes* (Vol. i, *Old Rowley*; Vol. ii, *The Restoration Rakes*). London, Philip Allan and Co., 1924.

Clark, G. N. *The Later Stuarts 1660-1714.* Oxford, Clarendon Press, rev. ed. 1940.

Coffin, Charles Monroe. *John Donne and the New Philosophy.* New York, Columbia University Press, 1937.

Connely, Willard. *Brawny Wycherley.* New York and London, Charles Scribner's Sons, 1930.

Bibliography

Cooper, Lane. *An Aristotelian Theory of Comedy*. New York, Harcourt, Brace and Co., 1922.

Crane, William G. *Wit and Rhetoric in the Renaissance*. New York, Columbia University Press, 1937.

Crawford, Bartholow V. "High Comedy in Terms of Restoration Practice." *Philological Quarterly*, VIII, 339-347 (Oct., 1929).

Cunningham, Peter. *The Story of Nell Gwyn, and the Sayings of Charles the Second*. London, 1852.

Dewey, John. *Art as Experience*. New York, Minton, Balch and Co., 1934.

Dobrée, Bonamy. *Essays in Biography 1680-1726*. Oxford University Press, 1925.

————*Restoration Comedy 1660-1720*. Oxford, Clarendon Press, 1924.

————*Rochester: A Conversation between Sir George Etherege and Mr. Fitzjames*. London, Hogarth Press, 1926.

————*William Congreve: A Conversation Between Swift and Gay*. Seattle, University of Washington Book Store, 1929.

Doran, Dr. *"Their Majesties' Servants": Annals of the English Stage, from Thomas Betterton to Edmund Kean*. New York, 1865.

Dowlin, Cornell March. *Sir William Davenant's 'Gondibert,' Its Preface, and Hobbes's Answer*. Philadelphia, University of Pennsylvania, 1934.

Draper, John W. "Theory of the Comic in Eighteenth-Century England." *The Journal of English and Germanic Philology*, XXXVII, 207-223 (1938).

Eastman, Max. *Enjoyment of Laughter*. New York, Simon and Schuster, 1936.

————*The Sense of Humor*. New York, Charles Scribner's Sons, 1922.

Edman, Irwin. *Arts and the Man*. New York, W. W. Norton and Co., 1939.

Ellehauge, Martin. *English Restoration Drama*. Copenhagen, 1933.

Elwin, Malcolm. *The Playgoer's Handbook to Restoration Drama*. London, Jonathan Cape, 1928.

Empson, William. "Wit in the Essay on Criticism." *Hudson Review*, II, #4, 559-577 (Winter, 1950).

Bibliography

Feibleman, James. *In Praise of Comedy*. New York, Macmillan, 1939.

Fischer, Kuno. *Ueber den Witz*, in *Kleine Schriften von Kuno Fischer*, Vol. I. Heidelberg, 1896.

Foster, Dorothy. "Sir George Etherege." *Review of English Studies*, VIII, 458-459 (1932).

Freud, Sigmund. *Wit and Its Relation to the Unconscious*, in *The Basic Writings of Sigmund Freud*, tr. A. A. Brill. New York, Modern Library, 1938.

Gosse, Edmund. *Life of William Congreve*. London, 1888.

——"Sir George Etheredge," in *Seventeenth Century Studies*. New York, Dodd, Mead and Co., 1897.

Grant, Mary A. *The Ancient Rhetorical Theories of the Laughable*. University of Wisconsin Studies in Language and Literature, XXI, Madison, 1924.

Granville-Barker, Harley. "Wycherley and Dryden," in *On Dramatic Method*. London, Sidgwick and Jackson, 1931.

Greig, J. Y. T. *The Psychology of Laughter and Comedy*. New York, Dodd, Mead and Co., 1923.

Hazlitt, William. *Lectures on the English Comic Writers*, in *The Collected Works of William Hazlitt*, ed. A. R. Waller and Arnold Glover, Vol. VIII. London, J. M. Dent and Co., 1903.

Heldt, W. "A Chronological and Critical Review of the Appreciation and Condemnation of the Comic Dramatists of the Restoration and Orange Periods." *Neophilologus*, VIII, 39-59, 109-128, 197-204 (Oct., 1922; Jan. and April, 1923).

Heltzel, Virgil B. "Chesterfield and the Anti-Laughter Tradition." *Modern Philology*, XXVI, 73-90 (Aug., 1928).

Hodges, John C. *William Congreve the Man*. New York, Modern Language Association, 1941.

Hotson, Leslie. *The Commonwealth and Restoration Stage*. Cambridge, Harvard University Press, 1928.

Houghton, Walter E., Jr. "Lamb's Criticism of Restoration Comedy." *A Journal of English Literary History*, X, 61-72 (March, 1943).

Hughes, Leo. "Attitudes of Some Restoration Dramatists toward Farce." *Philological Quarterly*, XIX, 268-287 (July, 1940).

Hunt, Leigh. "Biographical and Critical Notices," in *Dramatic Works of Wycherley, Congreve, Vanbrugh, and Farquhar*. London, 1875.

Bibliography

Jones, Richard F. "Science and Criticism in the Neo-Classical Age of English Literature." *Journal of the History of Ideas*, I, 381-412 (1940).

Kallen, Horace M. *Art and Freedom*, 2 vols. New York, Duell, Sloan and Pearce, 1942.

Krapp, Robert M. "Class Analysis of a Literary Controversy." *Science and Society*, X, #1, 80-92 (Winter, 1946).

Krikorian, Yervant H., ed. *Naturalism and the Human Spirit*. New York, Columbia University Press, 1944.

Krutch, Joseph Wood. *Comedy and Conscience after the Restoration*. New York, Columbia University Press, 1924.

Lamb, Charles. "On the Artificial Comedy of the Last Century," in *The Works in Prose and Verse of Charles and Mary Lamb*, ed. Thomas Hutchinson, Vol. I. Oxford University Press, 1908.

Lipps, Theodor. *Komik und Humor, Eine Psychologisch-Äesthetische Untersuchung*. Hamburg and Leipzig, 1898.

Livet, Charles-Louis. *Précieux et Précieuses*. Paris, 1859.

Lovejoy, Arthur O. " 'Nature' As Aesthetic Norm." *Modern Language Notes*, XLII, 444-450 (Nov., 1927).

Lynch, Kathleen M. *A Congreve Gallery*. Cambridge, Harvard University Press, 1951.

——"Congreve's Irish Friend, Joseph Keally." PMLA, LIII, 1076-1087 (Dec., 1938).

——"D'Urfe's L'Astree and the 'Proviso' Scenes in Dryden's Comedy." *Philological Quarterly*, IV, 302-308 (1925).

——*The Social Mode of Restoration Comedy*. University of Michigan Publications, III, New York, Macmillan, 1926.

Macaulay, Thomas Babington. "Leigh Hunt: Comic Dramatists of the Restoration," in *Critical, Historical, and Miscellaneous Essays*, Vol. IV. New York, 1877.

McCamic, Frances Smith (Mrs. Wesley Rayner Tinker, Jr.). *Sir George Etherege*. Cedar Rapids, The Torch Press, 1931.

Mathewson, Louise. "Bergson's Theory of the Comic in the Light of English Comedy." *University of Nebraska Studies in Language, Literature, and Criticism*, V, Lincoln, 1920.

Meindl, Vincenz. *Sir George Etheredge*. Vienna, 1901.

Memoirs of the Celebrated Persons Composing the Kit-Cat Club. London, 1821.

Meredith, George. *An Essay on Comedy and the Uses of the*

Bibliography

Comic Spirit, ed. Lane Cooper. New York, Charles Scribner's Sons, 1918.

Mignon, Elizabeth L. *Crabbed Age and Youth: The Old Men and Women in the Restoration Comedy of Manners*. Durham, Duke University Press, 1947.

Miles, Dudley Howe. *The Influence of Molière on Restoration Comedy*. New York, Columbia University Press, 1910.

———"Morals of the Restoration." *Sewanee Review*, XXIV, 105-114 (Jan., 1916).

Montgomery, Guy. "The Challenge of Restoration Comedy," *Essays in Criticism*. University of California Publications in English, I, Berkeley, University of California Press, 1929.

Nettleton, George Henry. *English Drama of the Restoration and Eighteenth Century*. New York, Macmillan, 1914.

Nicoll, Allardyce. *A History of Restoration Drama*. London, Cambridge University Press, 1923.

———*The Theory of Drama*. New York, Thomas Y. Crowell, 1931.

Noyes, Robert Gale. *Ben Jonson on the English Stage 1660-1776*. Cambridge, Harvard University Press, 1935.

Palmer, John. *Comedy*. New York, George H. Doran Co., 1914.

———*The Comedy of Manners*. London, G. Bell and Sons, 1913.

Pepper, Stephen C. *The Basis of Criticism in the Arts*. Cambridge, Harvard University Press, 1946.

Perromat, Charles. *William Wycherley Sa Vie—Son Oeuvre*. Paris, 1921.

Perry, Henry Ten Eyck. *The Comic Spirit in Restoration Drama*. New Haven, Yale University Press, 1925.

———*Masters of Dramatic Comedy and Their Social Themes*. Cambridge, Harvard University Press, 1939.

Pinto, Vivian De Sola. *Sir Charles Sedley*. London, Constable and Co., 1927.

Pratt, James Bissett. *Naturalism*. New Haven, Yale University Press, 1939.

Praz, Mario. *Studies in Seventeenth-Century Imagery*, Vol. I. London, The Warburg Institute, 1939.

Prinz, Johannes. *John Wilmot Earl of Rochester*. Leipzig, 1927.

Protopopesco, Dragosh. *Un Classique Moderne William Congreve Sa Vie, Son Oeuvre*. Paris, 1924.

Quintilian. *The Institutio Oratoria*, tr. H. E. Butler, 4 vols. Lon-

Bibliography

don, W. Heinemann; New York, G. P. Putnam's Sons; 1921-1922.

Rapp, Albert. *The Origins of Wit and Humor*. New York, Dutton, 1951.

Rose Anthony, Sister. *The Jeremy Collier Stage Controversy 1698-1726*. Milwaukee, Marquette University Press, 1937.

Rosenfeld, Sybil. "Sir George Etherege in Ratisbon." *Review of English Studies*, x, 177-189 (1934).

Santayana, George. *The Sense of Beauty*. New York, Charles Scribner's Sons, 1896.

Sawyer, Newell W. *The Comedy of Manners from Sheridan to Maugham*. Philadelphia, University of Pennsylvania Press, 1931.

Schelling, Felix E. *English Drama*. London, S. M. Dent and Sons; New York, E. P. Dutton; 1914.

Smith, Dane Farnsworth. *Plays about the Theatre in England from 'The Rehearsal' in 1671 to the Licensing Act in 1737*. Oxford University Press, 1948.

Smith, R. Jack. "Shadwell's Impact upon John Dryden." *The Review of English Studies*, xx, #77, 29-44 (Jan., 1944).

Snider, Rose. "Satire in the Comedies of Congreve, Sheridan, Wilde, and Coward." University of Maine Studies, *The Maine Bulletin*, xl, #1 (Aug., 1937).

Stephen, Leslie. *Hobbes*. London, Macmillan, 1928.

Stoll, E. E. "Literature and Life Again." pmla, xlvii, 283-302 (March, 1932).

———"The 'Real Society' in Restoration Comedy: Hymeneal Pretenses." *Modern Language Notes*, lviii, 175-181 (March, 1943).

Strachey, Giles Lytton. "Congreve, Collier, Macaulay, and Mr. Summers," in *Portraits in Miniature*. New York, Harcourt, 1931.

Sully, James. *An Essay on Laughter*. London, Longmans, Green and Co., 1907.

Summers, Montague. *The Playhouse of Pepys*. London, Kegan Paul, Trench, Trubner and Co., 1935.

———*The Restoration Theatre*. London, Kegan Paul, Trench, Trubner and Co., 1934.

Taylor, A. E. *Thomas Hobbes*. London, Constable and Co., 1908.

Bibliography

Taylor, D. Crane. *William Congreve.* Oxford University Press, 1931.

Theophrastus. *The Characters of Theophrastus,* tr. and ed. J. M. Edmonds. London, Wm. Heinemann; New York, G. P. Putnam's Sons; 1929.

Thomas, J. A. "Some Contemporary Critics of Thomas Hobbes." *Economica,* IX, 185-191 (1929).

Thompson, Elbert N. S. *The Controversy between the Puritans and the Stage.* New York, Henry Holt and Co., 1903.

Thorndike, Ashley H. *English Comedy.* New York, Macmillan, 1929.

Thorpe, Clarence DeWitt. "Addison and Some of His Predecessors on 'Novelty.'" PMLA, LII, 1114-1129 (1937).

———*The Aesthetic Theory of Thomas Hobbes.* Ann Arbor, University of Michigan Press, 1940.

Trowbridge, Hoyt. "Dryden's 'Essay on the Dramatic Poetry of the Last Age.'" *Philological Quarterly,* XXII, 240-250 (July, 1943).

Tuve, Rosemond. *Elizabethan and Metaphysical Imagery.* Chicago, University of Chicago Press, 1947.

Ustick, W. Lee and Hoyt H. Hudson. "Wit, 'Mixt Wit,' and the Bee in Amber." *The Huntington Library Bulletin,* VIII. Cambridge, Harvard University Press, 1935.

Vincent, Howard P. "The Death of William Wycherley." *Harvard Studies and Notes in Philology and Literature,* XV, 219-242 (1933).

Vivas, Eliseo. "A Definition of the Esthetic Experience." *The Journal of Philosophy,* XXXIV, 628-634 (1937).

Whistler, Laurence. *Sir John Vanbrugh Architect & Dramatist 1664-1726.* New York, Macmillan, 1939.

Wilcox, John. *The Relation of Molière to Restoration Comedy.* New York, Columbia University Press, 1938.

Williamson, George. "The Rhetorical Pattern of Neo-Classical Wit." *Modern Philology,* XXXIII, 55-81 (Aug., 1935).

Wilson, John Harold. *The Court Wits of the Restoration.* Princeton University Press, 1948.

———*The Influence of Beaumont and Fletcher on Restoration Drama.* Columbus, Ohio State University Press, 1928.

Wolf, A. *A History of Science, Technology, and Philosophy in the 16th and 17th Centuries.* London, George Allen and Unwin, 1935.

[219]

INDEX

Index

Index

Index

80; views on women and matrimony, 82-83, 124, 143; as a diplomat, 83; views on writing, 84-86; his achievements, 115-116; naturalistic views, 200

The Comical Revenge, or Love in a Tub, 87-96, 115; Aurelia, 95, 102, 130; Beaufort, 89, 95, 113; Betty, 88; Bruce, 130; Sir Nicholas Cully, 37, 86, 87, 89, 93-95, 115; Dufoy, 88, 91, 93, 94, 95, 115; Sir Frederick Frollick, 88-92, 93, 94, 95, 115, 149; Grace, 89, 94, 95; Graciana, 95, 102, 113; Jenny, 90; Lucy, 89; Palmer, 87, 89; Widow Rich, 88, 89, 90-92, 93, 95, 110, 115; Wheadle, 87, 89, 93-94, 95, 115

The Letterbook, 26, 75-86 *passim*

"The Libertine," 78-79

The Man of Mode, or Sir Fopling Flutter, 68, 104-116, 185, 192; Belinda, 107, 113; Old Bellair, 113; Young Bellair, 109, 110, 111, 113, 114; Dorimant, 26, 49, 50, 66, 76, 77, 86, 88, 89, 93, 105-109, 110, 111, 112, 113, 115, 116, 154, 155, 157, 166, 186, 192; Emilia, 113, 114; Sir Fopling Flutter, 37, 68, 69, 86, 105, 107, 109, 114-115, 136, 175, 197; Harriet, 8, 26, 66, 76, 77, 93, 101, 107-108, 109, 110-113, 115, 116, 154, 155, 157; Loveit, 86, 107, 108-109, 113, 170; Medley, 105, 109-110, 113, 115; Pert, 108; Lady Townley, 68; Lady Woodvill, 107, 111, 113

She Would if She Could, 96-104, 115, 165; Ariana, 101-104, 110; Lady Cockwood, 86, 96-98, 99, 102, 104, 115, 128, 129, 132, 142; Sir Oliver Cockwood, 98-99, 100, 101, 102; Courtall, 50, 97, 98, 99-101, 102, 103, 104, 106, 115, 129, 166; Freeman, 99-101, 103, 106, 115; Gatty, 101-104,

110; Sir Joslin Jolly, 98-99, 101, 102; Rake-hell, 98; Sentry, 97

Sir Martin Mar-all (by Dryden), prologue, 85-86

"To a lady, asking him how long he would love her," 82

Evelyn, John, against raillery, 25-26; atheism in theater, 46; on epicureanism, 49; on *The Comical Revenge*, 87

Faber, G. C., 160

Fainall (*The Way of the World*), 66, 185-186, 192, 193, 195

Fainall, Mrs. (*The Way of the World*), 190, 191

false wit, *see* wit; *see also* Witwoud

fancy, *see* wit

Farquhar, George, *double-entendre*, 35; hedonic aesthetics, 51
    The Constant Couple, 35
    The Inconstant, 19
    Love and a Bottle, 36, 46-47
    Sir Harry Wildair, prologue, 51

Farrell, James, 54, 60

Fashion, Sir Novelty, 37

Faulkner, William, 60

Fea, Allan, 22

Feibleman, James, 198

Fenton, Elijah, 126

Fidelia (*The Plain Dealer*), 148

Fidget, Lady (*The Country Wife*), 126, 139, 141, 142-143, 154

Fidget, Mrs. Dainty (*The Country Wife*), 143

Fidget, Sir Jasper (*The Country Wife*), 139, 141, 142, 145

Fischer, Kuno, 203

Fitzjames, James, 81

Flecknoe, Richard, 13, 23

Fletcher, John, 36

Flippant, Lady (*Love in a Wood*), 128-129, 133, 154

Flirt (*The Gentleman Dancing-Master*), 137, 138

Flutter, Sir Fopling (*The Man of Mode*), 37, 68, 69, 86, 105, 107, 109, 114-115, 136, 175, 197

Index

Index

Index

Index

Index

Index

Index